THE CHALLENGES OF EDUCATIONAL CHANGE

DANIEL L. DUKE

University of Virginia

PEARSON

Boston ■ New York ■ San Francisco
Mexico City ■ Montreal ■ Toronto ■ London ■ Madrid ■ Munich ■ Paris
Hong Kong ■ Singapore ■ Tokyo ■ Cape Town ■ Sydney

Series Editor: *Arnis E. Burvikovs*
Editorial Assistant: *Christine Lyons*
Marketing Manager: *Tara Whorf*
Production Administrator: *Anna Socrates*
Editorial-Production Service: *Omegatype Typography, Inc.*
Manufacturing Buyer: *Andrew Turso*
Composition and Prepress Buyer: *Linda Cox*
Cover Administrator: *Kristina Mose-Libon*
Electronic Composition: *Omegatype Typography, Inc.*

Between the time Website information is gathered and then published, it is not unusual for some sites to have closed. Also, the transcription of URLs can result in typographical errors. The publisher would appreciate notification where these errors occur so that they may be corrected in subsequent editions.

Library of Congress Cataloging-in-Publication Data

Duke, Daniel Linden.
    The challenges of educational change / Daniel L. Duke.
      p. cm.
    Includes bibliographical references (p.) and index.
    ISBN 0-205-36020-3
    1. Educational change.   2. School management and organization.   3. Change.
  I. Title.

LB2805.D86   2004
371.2—dc21

2002038644

Printed in the United States of America

10 9 8 7 6 5 4 3 2 1   08 07 06 05 04 03

For Cheryl and Devan—who continually change my life for the better, in the process proving that old dogs can learn anything except how to hit a 2-iron.

BRIEF CONTENTS

CONTENTS

CHAPTER NINE

Explaining Educational Change   235

PREFACE

Though it opens a book, the preface frequently is the last piece to be written. This preface was written two years after I began the book. Because the book's subject was change, I couldn't help wondering whether I was the same person I had been in the fall of 2000 when writing commenced. So much has happened in the interim—the loss of loved ones, the birth of grandchildren, the globalization of terrorism, the evaporation of retirement savings, the inexorable erosion of health, the deepening of relationships. I still do the same things I did two years ago—awake early, write, teach, advise students, play golf, entertain—but I don't necessarily do them the same way.

Many of the changes we experience are not of our choosing. They happen, and we are left to adjust and endure. In other cases, we openly seek change—altering our eating habits, lowering our handicaps, acquiring greater proficiency with a computer, and so on. We need not be reminded that the achievement of these desired changes is extremely difficult. Multiply this difficulty by one hundred teachers and two thousand students and the task of changing an entire school seems truly daunting. Yet schools do manage to grow and improve.

This book examines what is known about educational change, especially change related to teaching and learning. It addresses two basic challenges—how to understand educational change and how to achieve it. The latter, I argue, is unlikely without the former.

The Challenges of Educational Change could not have been written without the wise counsel of many individuals who daily demonstrate that genuine improvement is more than a mirage on the educational landscape. I am particularly indebted to the following individuals: Bill Brenner, Kevin Castner, Tom DeBolt, Jane Freeman, John Kidd, Bob Moje, Jean Murray, Sharron Nelson, N. Andrew Overstreet, Ann Randall, Jean-Ives Rochon, and Marie Slobojan. Thanks also are due the students in my courses on educational change, and to Sandy West—who was steadfast in her commitment to typing the manuscript. I also thank the reviewers of this book: Naftaly S. Glasman, University of California, Santa Barbara; Larry Hughes, University of Houston; Tony Rigazio-DiGilio, Central Connecticut State University; and Whitney Sherman, Georgia State University. Finally, a debt of gratitude is due Allyn and Bacon's Arnis Burvikovs, Christine Lyons, and Anna Socrates for supporting this project.

Daniel L. Duke

INTRODUCTION

In the annals of schoolwide educational change, it is hard to find a better example than Littleton High School in Littleton, Colorado. In the late 1980s, the superintendent and school board of the affluent Denver suburb committed to restructuring their high schools in order to prepare graduates for a world they considered to be rapidly changing. Littleton High School assumed the vanguard position in this initiative.

After consulting local business leaders and other community members and reviewing research on the latest educational practices, educators at Littleton High School drafted a comprehensive plan, Direction 2000, to transform their school into a twenty-first-century learning environment. Aware of the uneven track record of educational change, they heeded advice regarding how to go about the change process. Ample time was set aside to develop and implement Direction 2000. The school district set up its own foundation to raise funds beyond what the tax base could provide. These funds were used to support, among other activities, an extensive staff development program. A public relations firm was hired to get the message of Direction 2000 out to the community. A number of "coffees" were held in parents' homes so details regarding the new initiative could be explained.

Direction 2000 incorporated many of the most highly touted ideas and practices related to educational excellence and school restructuring. The heart of the initiative was a set of performance-based graduation requirements clustered into nineteen "performance areas." Many of these, such as ethics, communications, and personal growth, cut across traditional disciplines. The performance areas served as the basis for thirty-six "demonstrations," each with its own standards and scoring procedures, that students had to complete successfully in order to graduate. No longer would graduation be based solely on the number of Carnegie units students earned by getting passing grades in courses. Littleton's educational leadership felt confident that students who mastered the performance areas would be well prepared to tackle the challenges of an increasingly technology-based global economy.

To support the innovative performance expectations and assessments, Littleton High School introduced a new advising system. Each student was assigned a faculty advisor to guide him or her during all four years of high school. To cultivate student responsibility, as well as meet the standard for personal growth, every student was expected to maintain a portfolio of demonstrations and work samples. Advisors periodically reviewed portfolios to determine whether students were making adequate progress toward graduation.

Anticipating that the kinds of changes being sought would require widespread teacher support, school district officials initiated school-based management. Faculty members at Littleton High School consequently became active participants in developing the new performance standards, interdisciplinary curriculums, and school policies required to implement Direction 2000. So promising was Littleton's initiative that the Association for Supervision and Curriculum Development produced a video on high school restructuring based exclusively on Littleton High School's Direction 2000 program.

Those, including this author, who admired Direction 2000 from a distance and attempted to follow its progress were shocked to read an extensive report entitled "Requiem for a Reform" (Bradley, 1994) in the June 1, 1994, issue of *Education Week.* The article recounted the development of opposition to reforms at Littleton High School and the district's other two high schools. What originated as parental concern over changes in graduation requirements quickly grew into a full-scale "back to basics" movement that eventually led to the election of three new school board members and the resignation of Littleton's superintendent. Much of the Direction 2000 program at Littleton High School, including the performance-based graduation requirements, fell victim to the anti-reformers. By a 3 to 2 vote, the new school board decided that Littleton High School would return to its 1984 graduation requirements, based solely on passing courses and accumulating Carnegie units.

Littleton's experience stunned educational reformers across the country. The school district seemed to have taken to heart so much of the prevailing wisdom regarding educational change. Members of the community were involved in planning from the outset. Parents were kept apprised of developments every step of the way. Teachers participated in the adoption and implementation of changes and received extensive training related to curriculum development and performance-based assessment. The school district facilitated the change process by securing ample resources to support reform and avoiding impossible deadlines. The reform process was allowed to evolve over nearly eight years. During this time district and high school leadership remained stable. Perhaps most important, Littleton's reforms were motivated by a sincere desire to prepare young people for the rapidly changing world around them.

Anyone committed to constructive educational change cannot help but look at Littleton and ask, "What went wrong?" How could such a placid and well-to-do Rocky Mountain community become so divided over the education of its young people? How could so seemingly sensible a set of reforms and so well thought out a change process come to such a sad end?

Opinion varies concerning the reasons for Littleton's troubles. What is clear, however, is that the demise of Direction 2000 cannot be traced to conservative religious groups. While these organizations campaigned against many educational reforms elsewhere in the United States during the nineties, they did not target Littleton's restructuring program (Bradley, 1994, p. 22). One of the three new board members believed that the school district ran into problems because it had lost touch with the sentiments of parents, many of whom feared their children would not be able to graduate. A new mail-in ballot system also made it easier for disgruntled voters to support the back-to-basics slate of candidates.

Closer examination of faculty feelings revealed that some teachers were not sorry to see the new graduation requirements go. These teachers, along with many parents, questioned the nonacademic performance requirements, such as those related to ethics and personal growth. Other questions were raised concerning the adequacy of teacher training in the development and evaluation of performance-based demonstrations. Student reaction to the reforms also reflected divided opinion. When the first groups of students confronted the prospect of not graduating because of low performance on demonstrations, their support, along with that of their parents, evaporated.

Reflecting on Littleton's experience, Self (1994) identified three problems with the change process. First, Littleton High School tried "to do too much too fast." While observers might praise Direction 2000 for stretching implementation of the new graduation requirements over four years, one grade level at a time, this phase-in period involved no pilot testing and experimentation. In other words, no time was set aside to "iron out the kinks." In addition, the justification for the entire initiative was by no means clear to everyone. Parents and students continued to wonder why a school system already characterized by academic excellence needed such drastic changes.

A second problem derived from the first. Insufficient time was available for teachers to become proficient at designing good performance assessments and adept at evaluating student demonstrations. Self (1994) contended that this lack of sufficient preparation contributed to high failure rates on the initial demonstrations in certain areas such as math skills. Seeing that a relatively small percentage of students had passed these early performance-based assessments, students and parents understandably became alarmed.

The third problem involved the sheer number of new performance requirements. Besides taking courses and fulfilling course requirements, students had to complete 36 demonstrations over four years. The additional time and energy demanded of students and teachers seemed overwhelming.

Self (1994) went on to identify other problems that may have adversely affected implementation of the Direction 2000 program. He speculated that support might have been greater if the first demonstrations had covered less controversial topics than "community involvement" and "ethics." Launching Direction 2000 with ninth graders, in hindsight, also seemed unwise. Had Littleton initiated the program with incoming kindergartners, thereby giving students and parents ample time to adjust to the new graduation requirements, things might have worked out differently. Another, more subtle problem, concerned the fact that students continued to take discipline-based courses while preparing for interdisciplinary demonstrations. Self suggested that this dual system of expectations created a degree of complexity for which many students were unprepared.

A veteran school board member expressed a different view of the demise of Direction 2000. "The major issue for us, underneath all this stuff, is that there are major philosophical differences in the community . . . and we don't know how to address them and talk about them with each other" (Bradley, 1994, p. 24). The exclamation point for this board member's observation was provided by a headline in the November 15, 1995, edition of *Education Week:* "'Back to Basics' Slate in Littleton Trounced by 2-to-1 Margin."

Two years after the election of the three new board members responsible for reversing Littleton's restructuring program, a trio of moderate candidates routed back-to-basics advocates (Gamble, 1995). The latter group had vowed to accelerate Littleton's return to "traditional schooling." Did their defeat signal a shift in popular opinion regarding Direction 2000 or simply a rejection of extremist views and the politicization of public schooling? Had the election of the back-to-basics candidates in 1993 been a fluke? Could Littleton High School have averted problems by requiring fewer demonstrations, sticking to academic performance areas, and beginning the phase-in process with kindergartners instead of ninth graders? Questions such as these make the study of educational change both fascinating and challenging.

LEARNING FROM LITTLETON

The story of Littleton High School's efforts to restructure illustrates the drama and complexity of educational change and, in so doing, helps to explain the title of this book. Educational change entails many challenges. Some involve achieving educational change; others concern understanding educational change. Achieving educational change calls for action. Images arise of visionary and dedicated teachers, principals, superintendents, parents, and policy makers working above and beyond the call of duty to improve learning for young people. Understanding educational change calls for analysis and reflection. We think of researchers and evaluators collecting and interpreting data, testing theories, and patiently trying to account for successful and unsuccessful reforms.

The Challenges of Educational Change represents an effort to address in one volume what it takes to understand educational change *and* to achieve educational change. Indeed, it is the central thesis of this book that the latter is unlikely without the former. There are many excellent books on educational change, but they tend to focus either on achieving educational change or on understanding educational change. The first group cater primarily to practitioners and policy makers, while the second tend to be written by researchers for researchers. It is my sincere hope that all those interested in educational change, whether for practical or academic purposes, will find value in the contents of this book.

A PERSONAL NOTE

I came of age in the 1960s, a time that forever will be linked in the popular imagination with change. During college I regarded continuity as a curse and change as a virtue. While I still see value in change, I have learned that some change can lead to conditions that are worse than those for which improvements were sought. I also realize that continuity and change often make very compatible bedfellows.

During more than three decades in education, I have been involved in starting new schools, launching school improvement initiatives, evaluating the impact of educational innovations, and studying the factors that contribute to successful and failed change. I have examined change from the perspective of individuals, groups, organizations, and systems. It was only when I was invited to design a new course on educational change for graduate students, however, that I became aware of how much, and how little, is known about change. Designing a new course is one of the best ways I know to grapple with issues of what is known, what is worth knowing, and what needs to be investigated further.

The Challenges of Educational Change is a direct result of my search for an appropriate text for "Implementing Organizational and Instructional Change." At the end of each semester, I have spent part of the last day of class asking students what they would like to see in a text for the course. Although different individuals have expressed different preferences, a predictable pattern of overall interests has emerged over the years.

By far, the topic of greatest interest to students is individual change. They intuitively grasp what most change researchers empirically discover—there can be no meaningful change in groups, organizations, and systems unless individuals change. Graduate school is an ideal setting in which to reflect on individual change because so many graduate students themselves are experiencing important changes on both a personal and a professional level.

Another "must" for any text on change, at least according to my students, are actual examples of educational change. Students value that which is real, regardless of whether the account records successful change or failed change. Students also acknowledge that the closer the examples correspond to their own experiences and circumstances, the more beneficial they are.

Models of the change process are a popular request. Although most students understand that change is more often iterative and circuitous than linear, they find it helpful to concentrate on one phase of the change process at a time. Many agree that, before taking a course on educational change, they concentrated only on the implementation of change. By examining different models of the change process, they acquired an appreciation of what happens prior to implementation—determining when change is called for, investigating different ways to address the need for change, overcoming resistance to change, and adopting a specific change program or agenda.

A significant percentage of students, to my surprise, expressed a desire for information on theories of change. Some indicated that the theories we discussed in class helped them to understand the conditions under which educational change was most and least likely. Others noted that theories were useful for isolating key variables in the change process and predicting the consequences of change initiatives.

A final topic that many students wanted to see addressed was the evaluation of educational change. They wondered about the appropriate criteria for judging whether or not change had been successful and what methods for collecting evaluative data were most useful. They also requested information concerning how evaluation data actually can be used to improve education.

I am grateful to my students for their suggestions, and I trust that *The Challenges of Educational Change* is a worthy reflection of their interests and concerns.

The two primary goals of this book, as indicated earlier, are to assist those who aspire (1) to achieve educational change and (2) to understand educational change. Furthermore, it is my hope that these aspirants are one and the same. The cause of constructive change cannot be well served when understanding is divorced from action.

Readers of this book should be better able to answer a variety of puzzling questions regarding educational change, including the following:

- What is educational change?
- What constitutes evidence of educational change?
- What assumptions have guided educational change efforts?
- What are the first steps in the educational change process?
- How can educators determine that a need for change exists?
- How can educators match specific changes with specific needs?
- What are the possible goals of educational change?
- To what extent must schools and those who work in them change in order to achieve the goals of educational change?
- Under what conditions are schools and school systems most likely to change?
- Under what conditions are teachers and school administrators most likely to change?
- Is it necessary for beliefs to change before behavior changes?
- What resources are needed to support educational change?
- By what criteria can educational change be evaluated?
- Do theories exist that help to explain educational change?
- Is it possible to predict when an effort to change will succeed?
- What is involved in leading educational change?

ORGANIZATION OF THE BOOK

The organization of topics in this book did not "spring full blown" from my forehead. Perhaps it is only fitting that the sequencing of content in a book on educational change should have changed many times during the course of planning this volume. Realizing that my goal was to investigate the practical as well as the academic aspects of change, I agonized over how best to begin. As any reader knows, how a book opens often determines how its contents will be comprehended. In some cases, readers may venture no further than the first pages of a book because they fail to find the discussion compelling.

Should I begin *The Challenges of Educational Change* with the elements of the change process, an approach that would allow me to raise a variety of practical questions and review engaging examples of actual change efforts? Such a plan would make sense in terms of capturing the attention of readers, especially those who are practitioners, but it also would mean that certain basic issues regarding the nature of change in general, and educational change in particular, would come later in the book, perhaps too late to be of benefit. I decided, albeit reluctantly, to begin with a reflective section on the nature of change and a brief survey of recent educational change. Readers who stick with the discussion in the first two chapters hopefully will be rewarded with a solid grasp of the change process that, in turn, will enable them to gain more from the main body of the book, which covers the essential elements of educational change. The concluding section of the book returns to the reflective mode, examining different ways of making sense of the change process.

"Thinking about Change," the first section of this book, addresses a variety of questions about the nature of change and the pleasures and perils of studying it. Chapter 1, "Change as a Focus for Thought and Action," acknowledges that the concept of change can mean many different things to different people, and different things to the same people under different circumstances. The chapter explores various conceptions of change, examines ways that change has been studied and differentiated, and reviews several models of the change process. Chapter 2, "A Chronicle of Recent Educational Change," places educational change in temporal perspective by tracing major trends in educational reform over the past half century. Important impetuses to, and goals of, reform are identified and discussed.

Part II, "Preparing for Educational Change," shifts focus to the specific activities involved in undertaking educational change, particularly those that occur prior to implementation. Chapter 3 deals with the discovery phase of the change process, when reasons why change is necessary are identified and justified. The design phase serves as the central concern of Chapter 4. This is the point when alternative ways to address the need for change are explored. As the chapter reveals, educational change may require alterations in the purposes of schooling, the organization of schools, professional practice, and even the attitudes and beliefs of educators. The final element of preparing for educational change involves the development of a plan for implementing change—the focus of Chapter 5. Among the issues taken up in this chapter are different planning strategies, assessing an organization's capacity for change, and sources of difficulty during the development phase.

Once a plan exists, attention turns to achieving educational change. Part III deals with two key aspects of this part of the change process. The actual implementation of educational change is examined in Chapter 6. Various hurdles on the road from implementation to integration of change are identified, along with ways to surmount them. Chapter 7 is devoted to the challenges associated with leading educational change. Particular attention is given to countering resistance, reducing uncertainty, inspiring commitment, and sustaining momentum for change.

Part IV, "Understanding Educational Change," returns to a reflective mode in order to investigate different ways of making sense of the change process. Evaluation, the subject of Chapter 8, represents an important way of understanding educational change. Different approaches to and methods for evaluating reforms are presented and discussed. The book concludes with an examination of theories, models, and narratives that help to account for educational change. "Explaining Educational Change," Chapter 9, reviews the current state of knowledge regarding the causes and consequences of educational change.

To enhance the experience of reading *The Challenges of Educational Change,* several forms of highlighting are employed. Examples of particular kinds of educational change are provided in the form of periodic "case studies of educational change." Particularly recalcitrant aspects of the change process are noted in the text as "challenges of change." Vital concepts for understanding educational change show up in the form of "key terms," and unresolved issues related to educational reform are spotlighted as "change controversies."

I hope this book will demonstrate to advocates of educational change, as well as those who have grown skeptical of the promise of reform, that constructive change is possible when action and understanding are combined. It would be false advertising to suggest that *The Challenges of Educational Change* provides a set of recipes for effecting successful change. The book's purpose is closer to a travel guide than a cookbook. In the pages that follow, readers will traverse the territory of educational change, visiting important landmarks and learning about the location of detours and potholes. Reading the book will not ensure that the destination of successful educational change is reached, but it should make the journey less arduous.

REFERENCES

Bradley, Ann. "Requiem for a Reform." *Education Week* (June 1, 1994), p. 21–24.

Gamble, Cheryl. " 'Back to Basics' Slate in Littleton Trounced by 2-to-1 Margin." *Education Week* (November 15, 1995), p. 12.

Self, Elliott. "Learning from Littleton, Colorado." *Education Week* (September 14, 1994), pp. 36–37.

PART I

THINKING ABOUT CHANGE

How are we to make sense of the phenomenon called "change"? Is it a product or a process, a cause or a consequence? Is change, by nature, good, bad, or value free? Is real change rare or ubiquitous? The answer, only partly in jest, is "Yes."

Michael Fullan (1991, p. 30), a leading student of change, puts the matter straightforwardly when he asks, "What does change really mean?" Fullan probably would derive little clarity from Charles Handy's (1990, p. 7) ruminations on the nature of change:

> Where the same word is used to describe the trivial (a *change* of clothes) and the profound (a *change* of life), how can we easily distinguish whether it is heralding something important or not? When the same word can mean "progress" and "inconsistency," how should we know which is which? We might well ask whether the English language was devised to confuse the foreigner, or ourselves?

Part I tries to clear up some of the confusion with regard to change in general and educational change in particular. Thinking about change compels us to regard it as both a focus of inquiry and of action. As beings endowed with the capacities of self-improvement and reflection, we try to achieve constructive change and to understand why our efforts do not always turn out as we expected.

The first chapter in Part I examines many of the connotations of change. Chapter 1 also identifies key dimensions of change and compares different models of the change process.

Chapter 2 narrows the aperture to consider the phenomenon of educational change—the central concern of this book. An overview of the recent history of educational change provides a temporal context in which to think about the topic. This overview offers a basis for assessing the extent to which teaching, learning, school organization, and the goals of schooling have changed over the past half century. The chapter closes with an analysis of various impetuses to educational change.

QUESTIONS TO CONSIDER BEFORE READING PART I

1. What does the word *change* mean to you? Do the meaning and significance of the word change, depending on the situation?

2. Take five minutes and list as many changes as you can think of. Review the list. Is it possible to group certain changes together? What distinct types of change can you derive from your list?
3. Complex concepts like change often can be understood better by recognizing various dimensions. Can you think of several dimensions of change? (Hint: One possible dimension of change is the size or extent of change.)
4. Earlier you identified different types of change. Is there any reason to believe that educational change is different from other types of change? Why or why not?
5. Choose several examples of change with which you are reasonably familiar. Can you identify the steps involved in accomplishing each example of change? Are the steps in the process of change similar or different in each example?
6. Compare schools today with the schools that you attended. In what ways are they similar and different? How would you characterize the extent of educational change since you were a student?
7. Educational change can be traced to a variety of causes and conditions. In your judgment, what have been the most important causes and conditions leading to educational change over the past fifty years?
8. Considerable debate is heard regarding the consequences of educational change. One person's step forward is another's step back. What do you believe has been the most constructive educational change in the last half century? Why?

REFERENCES

Fullan, Michael G. *The New Meaning of Educational Change,* 2nd edition. New York: Teachers College Press, 1991.

Handy, Charles. *The Age of Unreason.* Boston: Harvard Business School Press, 1990.

■ ■ ■ ■ ■

CHAPTER 1

CHANGE AS A FOCUS FOR THOUGHT AND ACTION

MAJOR IDEAS

- A variety of meanings are associated with the concept of change.
- The concept of change is, itself, subject to change.
- Change can be intentional or inadvertent.
- To understand change requires awareness of its different dimensions.
- Change is a focus for inquiry for many academic disciplines.
- Different models of the change process have been developed to enhance an understanding of change.
- Educational change is distinct from, but related to, other types of change.

Recall your childhood. Now consider the world in which you currently live. Has anything changed since you were young? If so, how would you characterize these changes?

If you are like many people, you can easily identify a variety of changes that have occurred since you were a child. You may feel, for example, that the world is less safe and secure than it used to be. Is it possible, however, that your perception of the world, rather than the world itself, has changed? It is not uncommon for young children who grow up in stable, middle class families to feel relatively safe and secure. As they grow up, they become more aware of the dangers that might have always been around, particularly for those less fortunate.

Before we delve into the subject of educational change, it is necessary to think about change itself. Trying to understand the idea of change is analogous to hitting a moving target from a moving vehicle while we are bouncing on a trampoline. As we attempt to understand change, the world around us is changing. Simultaneously, we, too, are changing. We acquire new information. We have new experiences. We age. If this were not enough, the idea of change itself is subject to change. Change, like other ideas, is a social construction. What change meant to our forefathers is not necessarily what it means today. In studying and writing about change, I have confirmed the very topic that I am addressing. The more that I think about change, the more my views change!

The primary goal of Chapter 1 is to examine the idea of change and clarify what it is and what it is not. The chapter opens with an analysis of change and the various ways it has been differentiated. Differentiation suggests complexity. So, too, does multidimensionality. The chapter investigates some of the key dimensions of change, dimensions that need to be studied and analyzed in an effort to determine what, where, and when change has occurred.

The chapter next examines different models of the change process. A conception of the change process that draws on common aspects of these models is put forward in order to facilitate the organization of the main body of the book. The concluding section distinguishes educational change from other types of change.

THE FIRST CHALLENGE

Leaders face the challenges of initiating, implementing, and sustaining change. The rest of us grapple with our own challenges—What changes are being proposed by leaders? Why are they necessary? Should we embrace or resist the changes? Will we be required to change in order to accommodate the proposed change? Students of change face additional challenges as they search for ways to describe, explain, and predict change. In all of these instances, the first challenge of change is understanding what change is and what it is not. It goes without saying that we are less likely to achieve change, cope with change, and fathom the mysteries of change if we do not have a clear idea of the nature of change.

CHALLENGE OF CHANGE

What Is the Nature of Change?

One reason confusion cloaks change is the ambiguous nature of the term. Change may refer to the process by which change is initiated as well as the object of the change process—namely, the change itself. The object of change can vary from an individual to an entire society, from a particular piece of equipment to a huge corporation. Products can change, but so, too, can processes. Even the process of change is subject to change.

As I was beginning this book, the terrorist attacks of September 11, 2001, plunged the United States into a nightmare of suffering and anxiety. Journalists proclaimed that the nation would be forever changed by this tragedy. The point is that change can occur without warning. We are blindsided by acts of humans and nature. Change, of course, also can result from acts purposely intended to alter business as usual. In these instances, despite our most careful planning, we cannot be certain that the changes we intend will turn out to be the changes we achieve.

Another source of confusion concerns the fact that change may represent both cause and effect, or to use the language of researchers, independent and dependent variables. In other words, a change, such as a downturn in the economy, can trigger other changes, such as social upheaval and destabilization of political institutions. It is not always easy to determine which change constitutes the cause and which the effect. In fact, in some instances cause and effect interact in ways that make it virtually impossible to distinguish between the two. Which came first—altered academic expectations or student achievement decline? A case, in fact, can be made for each.

Depending on a person's beliefs, change generally may be regarded as desirable or undesirable. Conservatism frequently is associated with suspicion regarding change, while liberalism for many people connotes a readiness to embrace new ideas and reform. Students of change, meanwhile, often prefer to treat change as a neutral phenomenon awaiting the attribution of value by those affected by it.

With regard to change, one thing seems clear. Change is definitely not continuity. Yet even in this regard caution must be exercised. Watzlawick, Weakland, and Fisch (1974, p. 1) note that "persistence and change need to be considered together, in spite of their apparently opposite nature." Successful change, it turns out, often depends on a reasonable degree of stability.

Saul Alinsky (1972, p. 21), the community organizer, offered a very simple definition of change—"Change means movement." He went on to observe that movement implies friction. Anyone who has experienced profound change can testify to its disruptive impact. In many cases, however, we are unaware that sweeping change is taking place until well after the fact. Alinsky's definition of change also begs the question of whether "movement" is forward or backward.

This brief discussion of the nature of change suggests that some effort to clarify what is meant by the term must precede any systematic effort to understand educational change. Is change process or product, intended or inadvertent, good or bad?

Change Is Complex

Academics are known for taking ideas and dividing them into subcategories with nuanced meanings. Sometimes these exercises serve more to obfuscate than clarify. In other cases, they are helpful because the ideas have grown too complex. In other words, an idea can acquire so many meanings that it is no longer clear what we mean when we apply it. In an effort to lend greater precision to references to the idea, scholars employ modifiers, usually in the form of adjectives, to differentiate the multiple meanings of the idea. The idea of change has undergone and continues to undergo such a process of differentiation.

Politicians, pundits, and professors, for example, often distinguish between evolutionary and revolutionary change. The former typically is characterized by relatively small increments of change which, over long periods of time, can add up to a substantial alteration in the status quo. Revolutionary change, on the other hand, is rapid and typically very disruptive. Particularly tumultuous can be the overthrowing of a belief system. In the aptly titled *Reality Isn't What It Used to Be,* Anderson (1990, p. 27) observed:

> The collapse of a belief system can be like the end of the world. It can bring down not only the powerful, but whole systems of social roles and the concepts of personal identity that go with them. Even those who are most oppressed by a belief system often fear the loss of it. People can literally cease to know who they are.

Advocates of revolutionary political change claim that incremental change, or reform, fosters the impression of change while permitting those in power to retain control. Alinsky (1972, p. 3) maintained that:

> The significant changes in history have been made by revolutions. There are people who say that it is not revolution, but evolution, that brings about change—but evolution is simply the term used by non-participants to denote a particular sequence of revolutions as they synthesized into a specific major social change.

It is not our purpose here to contest or verify Alinsky's observation. What it indicates, though, is that certain efforts to differentiate change pertain to the *process* by which change is achieved. Another process-centered distinction involves planned versus unplanned change (Bennis, 1969). Unlike change which results from spur-of-the-moment reaction and opportunism, planned change entails methodical preparation, the careful identification of intentions, and the mobilization of support and resources.

The quest to clarify the concept of change goes beyond the change process to the nature of the change itself, or what Hargreaves (1994, p. 6) refers to as the "substance of change." Aristotle, one of the first students of change, identified four types of change (Barnes, 2000, pp. 75–76): change in (1) substance, (2) quality, (3) quantity, and (4) place. A change in substance involves coming into existence or ceasing to exist. Qualitative change, or *alteration,* occurs when some aspect of the nature of something changes. Quantitative change, on the other hand, represents an increase or decrease in the amount of something. Change in respect to place constitutes *motion.*

The ordering or sequencing of change also may serve as a basis for differentiation. We refer to the ultimate change that we desire to achieve as the *primary* change. In order to realize the primary change, however, *prerequisite* changes may be necessary. Policy makers, for example, may want to improve their nation's competitive advantage in a global economy. In order to achieve this primary change, it may be important to increase the technological literacy of the workforce.

A popular distinction among contemporary students of change is first-order versus second-order change. First-order change "occurs within a given system which itself remains unchanged," whereas second-order change represents a change in the system itself (Watzlawick, Weakland, and Fisch, 1974, p. 10). A system can be an individual, an organization, or an ideology. Episodic dieting by someone whose compulsiveness and self-image remain unaltered constitutes first-order change. Only when the individual understands and alters the beliefs that cause him or her continually to abandon efforts to lose weight can second-order change be said to have taken place.

Sometimes distinctions in the nature of change take the form of explicit value judgments. Historians, philosophers, and social critics frequently debate, for example, whether the cumulative effect of technological and cultural change constitutes progress or decline (Barzun, 2000; Herman, 1997). Rather than objective statements on the condition of humankind, terms like *progress* and *decline* represent social constructions that reveal the beliefs and values of particular groups at particular points in time. As Herman (1997, p. 13) notes in *The Idea of Decline in Western History,* "Virtually every culture past or present has believed that men and women are not up to the standards of their parents and forebears."

The desire to differentiate between cause and effect also can lead to distinctions related to the idea of change. Chambers (1997, p. 194), for example, observes that confusion often results when writers fail to distinguish between *innovation* and *change.* Innovation, in one scheme, is considered to be a cause, whereas *change* refers to the impact of the innovation. Others (Hall and Hord, 2001) find it more difficult to separate impetus and impact.

The notion of impact, or the consequences of change, suggests another possibility for differentiation. Kottler (2001, pp. 41–42), for instance, observes that some change is short-lived, while other change is lasting. Specifically addressing change in individuals, he identifies four characteristics of lasting change:

1. The change is internalized, becoming a part of the individual's make-up.
2. The change is substantial, resulting in shifts in perception and behavior.
3. The change affects all facets of the individual's life.
4. The change remains stable over time until it is no longer of benefit.

Short-lived change may not necessarily be bad. In *The Temporary Society* Bennis and Slater (1969) point out that Western culture tends to equate success with longevity. They go on, though, to make a brief for that which is temporary. In a study of alternative schools (Duke, 1978), the argument was made that the brief lifespan of many alternative schools should not automatically be regarded as an indication of failure. For the students involved in the initial creation of an alternative school, the experience often was extremely valuable and even life-altering. If the school subsequently closed, it did not render it any less important for the founding group.

The preceding discussion indicates the complexity of change as a focus for inquiry as well as action. Change can refer to the antecedents of change, the consequences of change, or that which is changed. It can be gradual or rapid, temporary or lasting, superficial or profound, planned or unplanned. There are dangers, of course, in such dichotomies. Ultimately, the complexity of change may be better captured by regarding it as continuous rather than orthogonal.

For present purposes, certain distinctions are more important than others. When the word **change** is used, it will refer to a difference, a departure from the status quo. Change that results from intentional efforts to alter existing conditions or circumstances will be the primary focus of attention. Some scholars (Hall and Hord, 2001) prefer to use the term *innovation* when discussing change, but this reference can be misleading. A change may not necessarily be innovative. Consider, for example, changes that involve returning to prior practices or conditions. Furthermore, innovation seems more appropriate for changes involving new programs and practices than changes in people. When *change* is used in this book, it can refer to alterations in the beliefs and behaviors of individuals and groups, as well as new programs, policies, processes, and structures.

The process by which a change is accomplished is referred to as the **change process.** Because the central concern of this book is intentional change, rather than change that is accidental or unexpected, the change process typically is characterized by premeditation and planning.

When a change is implemented, an impact of some kind can be expected. While some refer to this impact as *the* change, we shall regard the results of intentional change efforts as the **effects of change.** The effects of change may be expected or unexpected, temporary or lasting, desirable or undesirable. Effects are always subject to reinterpretation as time passes and subsequent events unfold. It is important to note that effects of change presume that change of some kind actually occurs.

These key terms can be illustrated by considering the aftermath of the Brown decision in 1954. The Supreme Court ordered the elimination of the dual system of schools found throughout the South and other parts of the United States. The desegregation of public schools was the intended change. School systems, either voluntarily or under court order, initiated *change processes* for planning and implementing desegregation. These processes often involved committees of educators and other citizens, staff training, and reassignment of personnel. Some of these elements of the change process also constituted changes in their own right when they remained in effect after schools were desegregated. The *effects* of desegregation efforts varied over time and from school system to school system. In the short run, there was some disruption and even violence, but white and black students began to share the same facilities and classes. Over time, many school systems experienced "white flight," and individual schools became almost as racially isolated as they had been before the Brown decision. Other schools demonstrated convincingly that students of different races could learn together productively and peacefully.

Key Terms

Change   A difference or departure from the status quo.

Change process   The process by which an individual, group, or organization attempts to achieve change.

Effects of change   The impact or consequences of achieved change.

Change Is Multidimensional

By now it should be apparent that thinking about change is more complicated than deciding that something is no longer working well and must be fixed. Deciding to change involves a variety of considerations. One way that researchers try to capture the complicated nature of a concept like change is by identifying its various *dimensions.* By regarding change as multidimensional, they acknowledge the fact that it cannot be understood fully by investigating only one aspect. Six dimensions of change are especially important to understand: purpose, unit, nature, magnitude, extent, and duration.

Purpose of Change.   Intentional change, by definition, is designed for some purpose or purposes. The general purpose of virtually all intentional change is to improve conditions. It is difficult to imagine purposeful change intended to leave conditions the same or worse than they were previously.

The terms *first-order* and *second-order change* capture a fundamental distinction in the possible purposes of intentional change (Watzlawick, Weakland, and Fisch, 1974). Change can be intended to improve the existing system or to change the system. Improving the existing system, the focus of first-order change, may entail two types of alterations: (1) changes designed to return the system to a prior, desired state and (2) changes intended to improve performance or conditions without altering the basic nature of the system. Second-order change, on the other hand, involves altering such foundational aspects of the system as its goals, underlying assumptions, and relationship patterns (Barott and Raybould, 1998, p. 35).

The purpose of intentional change can be differentiated in another way. Some change efforts are designed to address specific problems, for example, inefficiency, ineffectiveness, retrenchment, or unmet needs. Other change efforts are intended to respond to opportunities. While eliminating or reducing a problem is the focus of the former, creating something new is the object of the latter. Issues related to the purpose of intentional change, including determining whether a need for change exists in the first place, are considerations of the Discovery Phase of the change process. These matters will be addressed in Chapter 3.

Unit of Change.   In *Implementing Change,* Hall and Hord (2001, pp. 14–15) propose twelve principles related to educational change. Change Principle 9 holds that "the school is the primary unit for change." The authors explain, "The school's staff and leaders will make or break any change effort, regardless of whether the change is initiated from the inside or outside" (p. 14).

Unit of change refers to the primary focus, or the location, of change efforts. For present purposes, the most elemental focus of change is the individual. A reform initiative designed to convince skeptical teachers that all students are capable of mastering difficult content exemplifies this basic unit of change. Other possible units of change include groups or teams, departments, organizations (for example, a school), systems of organizations (for example, a school district), and communities.

Because change efforts sometimes involve different "units," it may not be easy in all cases to identify the primary unit of change. In such cases, it is helpful to refer to the purpose of the intended change. In the previous example, the unit of change would shift from individual teachers to the school as a whole if the ultimate purpose of convincing teachers that all students are capable of mastering difficult content was to enable the school to achieve mandated passing rates on standardized tests, thereby preserving the school's accredited status.

Nature of Change.   To observe that a particular team or department is targeted for change is to locate the change, but not to offer any details about the kind of change involved. Daft (1983, pp. 266–267) identifies four general kinds of change:

1. *Technology changes.* Changes in the production process
2. *Product changes.* Changes in outputs, including goods and services
3. *Administrative changes.* Changes in supervision and management
4. *People changes.* Changes in the attitudes, skills, expectations, and behavior of individuals

Using Daft's scheme, it is possible to imagine an initiative aimed at changing what an organization produces. To accomplish such change may require people changes in all departments. The new skills needed to change production, however, may vary from one department to another.

The two lists below contain terms that have been used in recent years to capture the general nature of change in educational and other organizations. Change, for the sake of simplicity, may involve people and things. The latter can include processes as well as products. The terms associated with changing people and things, however, are too vague to provide a clear idea of exactly what is being changed. Additional language is needed to convey the *nature* of intended change.

CHANGING PEOPLE	CHANGING THINGS
Behavior modification	Organization design
In-service training	Organization development
Learning	Reculturing
On-the-job training	Re-engineering
Professional development	Re-inventing
Staff development	Restructuring

When it comes to changing people, Zaltman and Duncan (1977, p. 26) specify three objects of change efforts: attitudes, behavior, or both. Some also might add values and beliefs to this list. Mechanisms for accomplishing changes in individuals range from self-initiated learning to externally arranged behavior modification programs. Organizations rely on various processes to alter the performance of employees. These include inservice or on-the-job training, professional development, and staff development.

Zaltman and Duncan (1977, p. 26) go on to note that changing human beings often necessitates changing the contexts in which they function as well as direct efforts to change their attitudes and behavior. Entire fields, such as organization design and organization development, have emerged as a result of interest in the relationship between context and competence. Legions of consultants graduate annually from business schools, prepared to assist firms in modifying work environments so that productivity can be improved.

Galbraith (1977, p. 5), an expert in organization design, characterized the process as one involving "choices of goals and purposes, choices of different organizing modes, choices of processes for integrating individuals into the organization, and finally a choice as to whether goals, organizations, individuals, or some combination of them should be changed in order to adapt to changes in the environment." Bolman and Deal (1997, p. 320) note that three powerful levers for organizational change are restructuring, recruiting, and retraining. The first focuses on modifying the context in which people work, while the second and third levers entail hiring new employees and increasing the knowledge and skills of existing staff members.

What is entailed in restructuring? Daft (1983, p. 202) identifies four key components of organization structure:

1. The allocation of tasks and responsibilities to individuals and departments
2. Formal reporting relationships, including the number of levels in the hierarchy and the span of control of managers and supervisors
3. The grouping together of individuals into departments and the grouping of departments into the total organization
4. Systems to ensure effective communication, coordination, and integration of efforts in both vertical and horizontal directions

Changing organization structure, according to this model, may involve altering the roles of employees, the relationships between employees, the units into which the organization is subdivided, and the formal mechanisms designed to facilitate interaction between individuals and units. Additional elements of structure include the rules, regulations, and policies that constrain the conduct of organization members. To ensure that members follow these guidelines, organizations employ a variety of control mechanisms, including evaluation, supervision, incentives, and sanctions.

Because the nature of intended changes can become very complicated, some observers prefer to think of a streamlined three-part framework. Change, at least as it relates to organizations, entails adjustments to inputs, throughputs, and outputs. *Outputs* refers to the expected outcomes achieved by the organization. Both products and services can be outcomes. To achieve outcomes, organizations secure resources or inputs. Resources range from employees and the skills they possess to capital and raw materials. What is done with these resources to achieve desired outcomes is the domain of *throughputs*. Faced with declining productivity or other challenges, an organization may decide to change inputs, throughputs, outputs, or all three.

The nature of change can be distinguished in another way. It is one thing to create a new organization and quite another to improve an existing organization. Both, of course, are major undertakings, but each entails unique challenges. Sarason (1971, pp. 212–213) conveys an appreciation of the differences when he notes the problems faced by educators who tried to emulate John Dewey's famous model of progressive education. Dewey had the luxury of creating a new school at the University of Chicago to embody the learning principles he advocated. Those who admired Dewey's Laboratory School, however, typically faced the necessity of transforming an existing school with existing programs and policies and a staff accustomed to conventional pedagogy. The nature of change, therefore, may be characterized by creation or revision. A more detailed discussion of the nature of educational change can be found in Chapter 4.

Magnitude of Change.   An organization that attempts to change its inputs, throughputs, and outputs is tackling a very ambitious initiative. *Magnitude* refers to the scope of intended change. Terms such as *comprehensive, systemic,* and *large-scale* are often used to characterize big change efforts. In the arena of educational change, such efforts are represented by the Chicago School Reform Act of 1985, Great Britain's Education Reform Act of 1988, and the Kentucky Educational Reform Act of 1990. Each of these acts called for new governance and accountability measures, school restructuring, and the retraining of professional staff.

Chambers (1997, pp. 192–193) observes that the preferences of change experts differ on the matter of magnitude. Small-scale change is more likely to be accomplished, but less likely to produce significant differences in performance and outcomes. Large-scale change is riskier, but more likely to achieve impressive outcomes if it succeeds. Chambers concludes that any decision on the magnitude of intended change must be contingent on a clear understanding of context and conditions.

Extent of Change.   An intended change may not be implemented overnight. In fact, Sarason (1971, pp. 219–220) notes that some adopted changes are never implemented at all. Because of the complicated nature of a proposed change, its magnitude, and the possibility of active resistance to it, full implementation may require a lengthy period of time. One need only examine the history of school integration or special education legislation to realize that the distance between the drawing board and substantive change may be measured in years. It therefore is important to understand the extent to which an intended change actually has been achieved.

Hall and Hord (2001, p. 88) have contributed greatly to our thinking about the extent of change through their development of the "Levels of Use of the Innovation" instrument. Persons trained to use this instrument can determine how individuals are responding to a particular change that requires them to adopt new behaviors or practices. Levels of Use of the Innovation is based on eight classifications, ranging from nonuse of an innovation to *renewal,* where the user goes beyond the innovation to seek better alternatives. Table 1.1 provides a brief description of each level.

Hall and Hord's classification system can assist change agents in preparing for differential responses to change. In situations where a number of individuals are involved in implementing an innovation, it is possible to find some individuals at each level. While certain persons, for example, may be seeking more information about the innovation, others will have implemented it as expected. Still others may have begun to modify the innovation in order to increase outcomes.

Another way to think about the extent of change is in terms of deviation from that which was initially intended. Chapter 8, which focuses on the evaluation of

TABLE 1.1   Levels of Use of the Innovation

	LEVEL	DESCRIPTION
Users	VI	*Renewal* State in which the user re-evaluates the quality of use of the innovation, seeks major modifications of or alternatives to present innovation to achieve increased impact on clients, examines new developments in the field, and explores new goals for self and the system.
	V	*Integration* State in which the user is combining own efforts to use the innovation with related activities of colleagues to achieve a collective impact on clients within their common sphere of influence.
	IVB	*Refinement* State in which the user varies the use of the innovation to increase the impact on clients within immediate sphere of influence. Variations are based on knowledge of both short- and long-term consequences for clients.
	IVA	*Routine* Use of the innovation is stabilized. Few if any changes are being made in ongoing use. Little preparation or thought is being given to improving innovation use or its consequences.
	III	*Mechanical use* State in which the user focuses most effort on the short-term, day-to-day use of the innovation with little time for reflection. Changes in use are made more to meet user needs than client needs. The user is primarily engaged in a stepwise attempt to master the tasks required to use the innovation, often resulting in disjointed and superficial use.
Nonusers	II	*Preparation* State in which the user is preparing for first use of the innovation.
	I	*Orientation* State in which the user has recently acquired or is acquiring information about the innovation and/or has recently explored or is exploring its value orientation and its demands upon user and user system.
	0	*Nonuse* State in which the user has little or no knowledge of the innovation, no involvement with the innovation, and is doing nothing toward becoming involved.

Source: From *Implementing Change: Patterns, Principles, and Potholes* by G. E. Hall and S. M. Hord. Boston: Allyn and Bacon, 2001.

change, discusses *intrinsic evaluation.* This type of evaluation investigates discrepancies between the original planned change and the actual change that eventually is implemented. In some cases, there are legitimate reasons why an intended change needs to be modified; in other cases, failure to implement that which is intended can be traced to human error and incompetence. In either case, it is important for change agents to know the extent to which intended changes have been achieved.

Duration of Change.   How long a particular change remains in effect may also be of interest, especially to historians and others who study change. Because many cultures place a premium on longevity, long-lived changes often are regarded as greater successes than fleeting ones. The latter frequently are derided as fads. It should be noted, though, that some changes are not intended to last a long time. Faced with a crisis, a government may suspend normal operations and declare martial law. The expectation is that emergency measures will be withdrawn when the crisis passes. Problems may arise when expectations regarding the duration of change vary between those responsible for the change and those subject to it.

Different ways to think about the relationship between time and change are captured in a classification system for use with clients in short-term therapy (Kottler, 2001, p. 45). Clients can be characterized by three kinds of change:

1. Interrupted change is a brief burst of progress followed by a return to previous patterns.
2. Minimal change is a modest gain that happens after initial resistance.
3. Consistent change is stable, progressive, and permanent.

With some minor adjustments, this scheme could be applied to changes involving organizations. A point of possible controversy, however, might concern the rationale for considering any change—organizational or individual—to be permanent. Some research on innovation suggests that change actually may be cyclical, with a cycle lasting between ten and fifteen years (Chambers, 1997, p. 191). The cycle commences with some source of "dysfunctional stress," which leads, in turn, to the adoption of a relatively large-scale change. Changing circumstances cause the large-scale change to be amended, refined, and resuscitated over time. Eventually, these modifications are unable to provide the corrective action needed, and a new large-scale change is required. The cycle begins anew.

While other dimensions of change doubtless can be identified and discussed, the dimensions of purpose, unit, nature, magnitude, extent, and duration probably are sufficient to convey a reasonable appreciation for the complexity of change.

CLARIFYING THE CHANGE PROCESS

The preceding discussion conveyed the complex nature of change. The process by which change is achieved, or at least attempted, is no less complicated. To help people better understand the change process, experts have developed various kinds of models. Some models are prescriptive and provide individuals with formulas for how change should be accomplished. Models may capture the steps involved in changing people or organizations. Certain models focus on particular aspects of the change process, such as problem solving, decision making, creating, innovating, and disseminating innovations.

Efforts to model the change process are not the exclusive province of contemporary scholars. Ancient Greek philosophers, especially Plato and Aristotle, were intrigued by change and sought to understand those ideals that were immutable and the forces that moved humans toward "the good." Hegel offered his famous dialectical model with its thesis, antithesis, and synthesis to capture the interactive nature of the change process. Karl Marx drew on Hegel's work to fashion a comprehensive philosophy of history. Chapter 9 contains a more detailed discussion of the use of models to explain, as well as describe, change and the change process.

Models of the change process frequently overlap in significant ways, suggesting that particular elements of the process may be universal. Because experts sometimes use different terminology, however, areas of overlap are not always obvious. Models offer students of change a number of benefits. Not only do they render the complex more understandable, but they can provide "insights that explain various phenomena that we see occurring in day-to-day practice" (Chambers, 1997, p. 192). Models also can present problems, in that they oversimplify and foster the impression that the change process is entirely predictable. Perhaps it is best to regard models of the change process as a starting place, a first step to understanding a phenomenon that ultimately is highly variable and often confusing.

To appreciate what models can and cannot provide, let us consider several. For present purposes, the primary focus will be models of *organizational* change, innovation, and change leadership. Models of *individual* change, such as those tracking stages of human development and therapeutic models identifying the steps involved in altering dysfunctional behavior, can be of great value to those interested in educational change, but space does not allow an in-depth discussion at this point. Challenges related to individual change are addressed later, especially in Chapter 5.

Rogers' Diffusion Model

One of the most frequently cited models concerns the innovation-development process. Rogers (1995, p. 132) sees this process as consisting of "all the decisions and activities, and their impacts, that occur from recognition of a need or a problem, through research, development, and commercialization of an innovation, through diffusion and adoption of the innovation by users, to its consequences." Figure 1.1 provides an overview of Rogers' model.

According to Rogers' model, the process of innovation commences when a problem or need is identified. Problems and needs may be based on an examination of current conditions, laboratory work, or the anticipation of future developments. Once a problem or need has been isolated, researchers begin to investigate its nature and how it can be addressed. This phase may involve considerable experimentation and invention. Development begins when attention shifts from understanding the problem or need to "putting a new idea [to address a problem or need] in a form that is expected to meet the needs of an audience of potential adopters" (Rogers, 1995, p. 137). The result of the development phase is an innovation. Commercialization entails the production, marketing, and distribution of the innovation. Developers hope that their efforts to spread the word about the innovation (diffusion) will result in its adoption by enough users to make continued production economically viable. This desired outcome, of course, depends on the consequences of adopting the innovation.

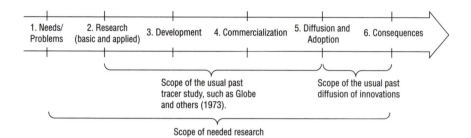

FIGURE 1.1 Six Main Phases in Rogers' Innovation-Development Process. This shows the limited scope of past tracer studies and of past diffusion studies. These six phases are somewhat arbitrary in that they do not always occur in exactly the order shown here, and certain of the phases may be skipped in the case of certain innovations.

Reprinted with the permission of The Free Press, a division of Simon and Schuster Adult Publishing Group, from *Diffusion of Innovations*, Fourth Edition by Everett M. Rogers. Copyright © by Everett M. Rogers. Copyright © 1962, 1971, 1983 by The Free Press.

There are several interesting aspects of Rogers' innovation-development model. First, it is based on a mixture of decisions, activities, and consequences. In other words, it is a process model that consists of more than just processes. Second, the model originally was applied to the development and diffusion of new products, particularly those created in corporate and government research and development centers. Rogers (1995, p. 143) acknowledged, however, that innovations do not necessarily result from research and development: "They may instead arise from practice as certain practitioners seek new solutions to their needs/problems." Schon (1983, pp. 50–54) referred to this on-the-spot innovation as knowing-in-action. The possibility of practitioner-generated innovation becomes especially important when we turn to the case of educational change.

Kanter's Innovation Model

Kanter (1988, p. 172) contends that the structural and social conditions for innovation "can be understood best if the innovation process is divided into its major tasks." Toward this end, she offers what might be regarded as a streamlined version of Rogers' diffusion model. The four central tasks of innovation include the following:

1. *Idea generation.* "The activation of some person or persons to sense or seize a new opportunity" (p. 173).
2. *Coalition building.* The acquisition of power "by selling the [innovation] project to potential allies" (p. 184).
3. *Idea realization.* "Assembling a working team to 'complete' the idea by turning it into a concrete and tangible object . . . that can be transferred to others" (p. 190).

4. *Transfer.* Diffusion of the innovation "to those who will exploit the innovation or embed it in ongoing organizational practice" (p. 198).

While both Rogers's and Kanter's models draw heavily on change research, they are more prescriptive than descriptive in nature and purpose. Neither expert claims that all innovation neatly follows the steps in their model. They do suggest, however, that effective innovation is likely to involve the elements or tasks they have identified.

Havelock's Linkage Model

One of the first experts to focus on understanding the process of educational change was Ronald G. Havelock of the University of Michigan's Center for Research on Utilization of Scientific Knowledge. Havelock's linkage model of the change process is based on a systems perspective (Havelock, 1973). To understand educational change, he maintained, we must study two systems: the user system and the resource system. The user system is guided by the need to solve a problem, while the resource system represents the source of information to guide the user in his efforts to solve the problem. The crucial factor in this model is the transfer of information from the resource system to the user system, or what Havelock characterized as the *linkage.* Neale, Bailey, and Ross (1981, p. 110) contend that understanding the knowledge transfer process requires knowing "*who* transfers *what* knowledge *how* (by what channel or medium) to *whom* for *what purpose.*"

Havelock's primary audience consisted of change agents, individuals who regarded it as their responsibility to facilitate the change process in educational settings. This point becomes clear when we examine his model of the six stages of the change process (Havelock, 1973). The very first stage involves building a constructive relationship between the change agents and their clients. Havelock offers his model as a preferred sequence of steps rather than a descriptive map tracing the actual course of educational change. The stages include the following:

1. *Building a relationship.* Change agents focus on initiating constructive relations with their clients.
2. *Diagnosis.* Change agents assist clients in identifying problems and opportunities that might necessitate change.
3. *Acquiring relevant resources.* Resources are obtained to support various aspects of the change process, including implementation and evaluation.
4. *Choosing the solution.* Research-based ideas for addressing problems or responding to opportunities are identified, and a decision is made to adopt a particular idea.
5. *Gaining acceptance.* Change agents work with those expected to adopt a change to develop support for the initiative.
6. *Stabilizing the innovation and generalizing self-renewal.* Efforts are made to ensure continuing support for the initiative and see that the change is integrated into the structure of the organization.

Rand Model

Between 1973 and 1978 the Rand Corporation, with support from the United States Office of Education, conducted one of the first large-scale studies of educational change (Berman and McLaughlin, 1978). Four major federal initiatives aimed at changing educational practice were investigated. They included the Elementary and Secondary Education Act, Title III (Innovative Projects); the Elementary and Secondary Education Act, Title VIII (Bilingual Projects); the Vocational Education Act, Part D (Exemplary Programs); and the Right-to-Read Program. While the primary purpose of the study was to determine factors that promoted or inhibited educational change, the researchers hypothesized a parsimonious model of the change process to guide their data collection and analysis. According to Berman and McLaughlin (1978), the change process in schools involves three stages:

1. *Initiation.* During this stage, support for the change must be generated.
2. *Implementation.* The change is actually carried out, a process that may result in alterations to both the new program or practice and the organization affected by the change.
3. *Incorporation.* The change is completed, resulting in the new program or practice becoming a permanent part of the organization.

What becomes apparent when the Rand model is compared with the Havelock model is the former's lack of focus on the initial steps toward change. Neale, Bailey, and Ross (1982, p. 135) note that the Rand researchers actually were critical of Havelock's model and its "preoccupation" with "what happens *before* decisions to change existing practices." Berman and McLaughlin (1978) maintained that the chief obstacles to educational change arose *after* the adoption stage (Havelock devoted only one of his six stages to the postadoption period of the change process).

ACOT Model

Another model of the educational change process, this one involving five stages, grew out of a study of the introduction of computers into classrooms (Dwyer, Ringstaff, and Sandholtz, 1991). After observing teachers who volunteered to participate in the Apple Classrooms of Tomorrow (ACOT) project, researchers concluded that desired changes in instruction and learning had evolved in a gradual fashion. As they put it, "text-based curriculum delivered in a lecture-recitation-seatwork mode is first strengthened through the use of technology and then gradually replaced by far more dynamic learning experiences for students" (Dwyer, Ringstaff, and Sandholtz, 1991, p. 47). The ACOT model of the instructional change process includes the following five stages:

1. *Entry.* Teachers continue to use familiar techniques while computers are installed in their classrooms. Teachers begin to receive instruction in the use of computers.
2. *Adoption.* Teachers begin to feel more comfortable with computers. Their concerns shift from connecting the computers to how computers can be used for instructional purposes.

3. *Adaptation.* Teachers integrate the computers into traditional classroom practice; although lecture, recitation, and seatwork remain the main forms of activity.
4. *Appropriation.* As some teachers begin to master the new technology, they solve their own problems and discover novel uses for the computers.
5. *Invention.* Teachers begin to think differently about teaching and learning.

This five-stage model is reminiscent in some ways of Hall and Hord's Levels of Use framework. It focuses on how individual teachers respond to a particular innovation—classroom computers. Models of the change process therefore can be used to capture how individuals as well as organizations undertake change. As we see in the next section, a third focus of models of the change process involves the change or innovation itself.

Chambers's Model

Drawing on two actual cases of change—the adoption of a new Malaysian school curriculum and a revised Australian credit law, Chambers (1997) proposes a four-step descriptive model of the life cycle of an innovation. Step 1 is represented by a large-scale innovation. Invariably, according to Chambers, a major initiative encounters many problems during implementation. In order to deal with these problems, which can include nostalgia regarding old ways, "small amending innovations" are required. The purpose of these alterations is to correct problems "which for various reasons had not been identified prior to the implementation of the large-scale innovation or which are caused directly by its implementation" (Chambers, 1997, p. 189).

Eventually, the large-scale innovation, assisted by amending innovations, settles into place and begins working smoothly. As time passes, however, minor adjustments, or "small refining innovations," are required to improve the functioning of the large-scale innovation.

Conditions within the wider system of which the innovation is but a small part continue to change. Eventually, despite various small refining innovations, the large-scale innovation ceases to meet the demands created by changing conditions in the macrosystem. Effectiveness flags, and a new large-scale innovation is necessitated. At this point the innovation cycle has come full circle, a period that may take ten to fifteen years (Chambers, 1997, p. 191).

Kotter's Eight-Stage Process

Another focus for models of the change process is leadership for change. One of the best known of these models is the Eight-Stage Process of Creating Major Change by John Kotter (1996). Offered as a prescription for successful change, the model begins with establishing a sense of urgency and concludes with integrating changes into the culture of the organization. The eight stages are listed below:

1. Establishing a sense of urgency
2. Creating the guiding coalition

3. Developing a vision and strategy
4. Communicating the change vision
5. Empowering broad-based action
6. Generating short-term wins
7. Consolidating gains and producing more change
8. Anchoring new approaches in the culture

Kotter's model commences with the identification of a need for change that is sufficiently compelling to generate a genuine sense of urgency. Such a need may result from a crisis, potential crisis, or careful analysis of the market. Armed with a compelling need, a leader next must form a group with enough influence and power to push forward a proposed change. The third stage entails the formulation of a vision and a strategy to direct the energies of those involved in implementing the change. A vision is of little value if only its developers know about it; so the fourth stage calls for widespread communication of the vision.

Once all the relevant actors know about and understand the vision, it is necessary for the leader and his or her team to confront sources of resistance to change. When obstacles have been removed and risk-taking encouraged, the time for full-scale implementation begins. The leader's initial goal should be to achieve some short-term wins in order to boost confidence and provide opportunities to reward performance. Stage 7 entails producing change throughout the organization in order to realize the vision. When the changes become an accepted part of an organization's culture, the change process has been completed.

Comparing Models

We have examined a variety of models of the change process. While each deals in some way with the process of change, the focus of attention varies from the individuals who are expected to change and the particular organization undergoing change to the life cycle of the change itself and the obligations associated with leading the change process. Different models sometimes employ the same terminology, but particular terms may mean different things to different experts. When Havelock (1973) refers to *adoption,* for example, he implies a relatively formal decision to proceed with a proposed change. Dwyer, Ringstaff, and Sandholtz (1991), on the other hand, use *adoption* to describe what teachers do when they begin to feel comfortable with technological change.

Although models of the change process vary in many ways, they also share common features. Table 1.2 presents the key elements of six of the previously mentioned models. Comparing the lists reveals a number of similarities.

Four phases of the change process are found in two or more of the models in Table 1.2. Sections II and III of this book provide a detailed discussion of each of the phases. These common elements will be referred to as *discovery, design, development,* and *implementation.* They are described as follows:

COMMON ELEMENTS OF THE CHANGE PROCESS

- *Discovery.* The initial phase of the change process during which a need for change is identified.
- *Design.* The phase during which a new or improved way to address the need is created or chosen.
- *Development.* The phase during which planning related to implementing change is undertaken and support is secured.
- *Implementation.* The phase when the change is introduced and adapted to a particular setting.

It is important to repeat an earlier caution. Models of the change process that specify distinct phases or stages foster the impression of linearity—a fixed sequence of events moving inexorably from inception to implementation. Most experts are quick to point out, however, that the change process typically is messier than the models suggest. Phases may be skipped or repeated. Still, where change is intended, the

TABLE 1.2   Six Models of the Change Process

ROGERS	KANTER	HAVELOCK
Needs/problems	Idea generation	Building a relationship
Research	Coalition building	Diagnosis
Development	Idea realization	Acquiring relevant resources
Commercialization	Transfer	Choosing a solution
Diffusion and adoption		Gaining acceptance
Consequences		Stabilizing the innovation and generalizing self-renewal

RAND	DWYER ET AL.	KOTTER
Initiation	Entry	Establishing a sense of urgency
Implementation	Adoption	Creating the guiding coalition
Incorporation	Adaptation	Developing a vision and strategy
	Appropriation	Communicating the change vision
	Invention	Empowering broad-based action
		Generating short-term wins
		Consolidating gains and producing more change
		Anchoring new approaches in the culture

process is rarely a completely random affair. People do think about and plan change. Though oversimplified, models of the change process can reasonably approximate reality. It is typical of the change process, therefore, that a need for change is identified (discovery), a change that addresses the need is generated (design), a process for achieving the change is determined (development), and the process is carried out to some extent (implementation).

ZEROING IN ON EDUCATIONAL CHANGE

This book is concerned primarily with educational change. The discussion so far, however, has dealt mostly with change in general. In order to proceed further, it is necessary to distinguish educational change from other forms of change.

Hardly any academic field exists that does not devote considerable attention to the study of change. Aristotle (Barnes, 2000, p. 75) contended that the essence of natural science involved understanding how things are moved and changed. Social science as well is preoccupied with change. Demographers carefully track changes in the size, make-up, and location of the population. Sociologists investigate the forces that produce and inhibit social change. Cultural change beckons to anthropologists, while individual growth and development attract the interest of psychologists. Academics of various persuasions debate whether change actually has occurred and, if so, to what extent and effect.

Students of educational change have no alternative but to draw heavily on the work of researchers from other fields. As a field of human endeavor, education is influenced by virtually every imaginable kind of change. Population shifts affect which students attend which schools. Social and cultural change influence what schools are expected to teach and their overall mission. Breakthroughs in our understanding of human growth and development guide instructional practice and the design of learning environments.

Is it fair, then, to argue that educational change is the sum total of all other change? Although it is understandable, such a position fails to recognize that most societies expect certain individuals and institutions to assume responsibility for the formal transfer of knowledge from one generation to another. Schools and teachers are affected by economic, social, and cultural change, to be sure, but economic, social, and cultural change are not educational change. That educational change is distinct from other types of change can be seen in the lag time between economic, social, and cultural change, on one hand, and change in schools, on the other.

Educational change is interesting, if not unique, in that it can serve as both an antecedent and a consequence of other types of change. A change in school policy concerning special education, for example, may constitute a response to changing demographics or a cause of demographic change.

What, then, is **educational change**? The abbreviated definition is *Any intentional change designed to improve teaching and learning*. A more complete definition goes like this: *Educational change is a change intended to alter the goals of educa-*

tion and to improve what students are expected to learn, how students are instructed and assessed, and how educational functions are organized, regulated, governed, and financed. A change in the distribution of wealth or a change in popular culture certainly can affect education in profound ways, but these changes initially are not intended to influence education. In fact, they may not be intended at all, but simply byproducts of other developments in society.

Key Term

Educational change   A change intended to alter the goals of education and/or to improve what students are expected to learn, how students are instructed and assessed, and how educational functions are organized, regulated, governed, and financed.

Some experts prefer to think of *school* change rather than educational change. Others (myself included) do not share this preference because we find the term school change too limiting. Not all intentional efforts to educate take place in organizations called schools. In addition, educational change, particularly with regard to law and policy, takes place at the level of the nation, state, region, and school system, not the individual school. Other examples of educational change may pertain to units smaller than a school—individuals, departments, grade levels, and the like.

CONCLUSION

This chapter has shown that understanding and achieving change are hardly simple and straightforward endeavors. They require a grasp of the complicated nature of change and the change process. Change—the object of the change process—can be characterized by various dimensions, including purpose, unit, nature, magnitude, extent, and duration. The change process—the process by which an individual, group, or organization attempts to achieve a change—also is complicated. Models of the change process focus on the steps individuals and organizations go through in achieving change, the life cycle of a particular innovation, the tasks associated with innovation, and the responsibilities of those leading change. Models may be descriptive or prescriptive. Key elements of the change process include the discovery of a need for change, the design of a change to address the need, the development of a plan to implement the design, and the actual implementation of the design. The chapter concludes by zeroing in on educational change as a special case of change. Educational change is defined as change intended to alter the goals of education and to improve what students are expected to learn, how students are instructed and assessed, and how educational functions are organized, regulated, governed, and financed. Although educational change is subject to the influence of other types of change, such as social and cultural change, it constitutes a distinct focus for inquiry and action. Subsequent chapters investigate what is involved in understanding and achieving educational change.

REFERENCES

Alinsky, Saul D. *Rules for Radicals.* New York: Vintage, 1972.

Anderson, Walter Truett. *Reality Isn't What It Used to Be.* San Francisco: Harper, 1990.

Barnes, Jonathan. *Aristotle: A Very Short Introduction.* Oxford: Oxford University Press, 2000.

Barott, James E. and Raybould, Rebecca. "Changing Schools into Collaborative Organizations." In Diana G. Pounder (ed.), *Restructuring Schools for Collaboration.* Albany: State University of New York Press, 1998, pp. 27–42.

Barzun, Jacques. *From Dawn to Decadence.* New York: HarperCollins, 2000.

Bennis, Warren G. "Theory and Method in Applying Behavioral Science to Planned Organizational Change." In Warren G. Bennis, Kenneth D. Benne, and Robert Chin (eds.), *The Planning of Change.* New York: Holt, Rinehart and Winston, 1969, pp. 62–78.

Bennis, Warren G. and Slater, Philip E. *The Temporary Society.* New York: Harper & Row, 1969.

Berman, Paul and McLaughlin, Milbrey W. *Federal Programs Supporting Educational Change,* Vol. VIII: Implementing and Sustaining Innovations. Santa Monica, CA: Rand, 1978.

Bolman, Lee G. and Deal, Terrence E. *Reframing Organizations,* 2nd edition. San Francisco: Jossey-Bass, 1997.

Chambers, Fred. "The Life Cycle of an Innovation: Implications for Implementation in Education." In James Lynch, Celia Modgil, and Sohan Modgil (eds.), *Education and Development: Tradition and Innovation: Volume One.* London: Cassell, 1997, pp. 187–197.

Daft, Richard L. *Organization Theory and Design.* St. Paul, MN: West Publishing Co., 1983.

Duke, Daniel L. *The Retransformation of the School.* Chicago: Nelson-Hall, 1978.

Dwyer, David C.; Ringstaff, Cathy; and Sandholtz, Judy H. "Changes in Teachers' Beliefs and Practices in Technology-Rich Classrooms," *Educational Leadership,* Vol. 49, no. 9 (May 1991), pp. 45–52.

Fullan, Michael G. *The New Meaning of Educational Change,* 2nd edition. New York: Teachers College Press, 1991.

Galbraith, Jay R. *Organization Design.* Reading, MA: Addison-Wesley, 1977.

Hall, Gene E. and Hord, Shirley M. *Implementing Change.* Boston: Allyn and Bacon, 2001.

Hargreaves, Andy. *Changing Teachers, Changing Times.* New York: Teachers College Press, 1994.

Havelock, Ronald G. *The Change Agent's Guide to Innovation in Education.* Englewood Cliffs, NJ: Educational Technology Publications, 1973.

Herman, Arthur. *The Idea of Decline in Western History.* New York: Free Press, 1997.

Kanter, Rosabeth Moss. "When a Thousand Flowers Bloom: Structural, Collective, and Social Conditions for Innovation in Organization." In Barry M. Staw and L. L. Cummings (eds.), *Research in Organizational Behavior,* Vol. 10. Greenwich, CT: JAI Press, Inc., 1988, pp. 169–211.

Kotter, John P. *Leading Change.* Boston: Harvard Business School Press, 1996.

Kottler, Jeffrey A. *Making Changes Last.* London: Brunner-Routledge, 2001.

Neale, Daniel C.; Bailey, William J.; and Ross, Billy E. *Strategies for School Improvement.* Boston: Allyn and Bacon, 1981.

Rogers, Everett M. *Diffusion of Innovations,* 4th edition. New York: Free Press, 1995.

Sarason, Seymour B. *The Culture of the School and the Problem of Change.* Boston: Allyn and Bacon, 1971.

Schon, Donald A. *The Reflective Practitioner.* New York: Basic Books, 1983.

Watzlawick, Paul; Weakland, John; and Fisch, Richard. *Change.* New York: Norton, 1974.

Zaltman, Gerald and Duncan, Robert. *Strategies for Planned Change.* New York: Wiley, 1977.

CHAPTER 2

THE PERSISTENT QUEST FOR EDUCATIONAL CHANGE

MAJOR IDEAS

- The extent to which education has changed, and to what effect, are matters of considerable debate.
- The recent history of educational reform is linked to important public ideas.
- Consensus regarding how best to translate ideas into actions has been rare.
- Impetuses to educational change have been varied and as likely to come from non-educators as educators.
- The focus of educational change has shifted over time from classrooms and programs to schools and school systems.
- Efforts by policy makers to address a particular public idea often lead to reactions reflecting other public ideas.
- Despite their criticisms of schools and educational practices, the public still believes that educators are capable of constructive reform.

Opinions vary regarding the extent of educational change in the United States. At least four basic positions can be identified. Position One holds that the only constant in education is change. Schools are subject to a continuous parade of adjustments, alterations, and modifications. Bandwagons beckon, fads come and go, and new mandates flow endlessly over local schools. This position is captured in the opening lines of Baldridge and Deal's (1983, p. 1) essay, "The Basics of Change in Educational Organizations":

> The most stable fact about organizations, including schools and colleges, is that they change. You can count on it—if you leave an organization for a few years and return, it will be different.

Keizer (2001, p. 43) puts the constancy of educational change this way:

> Whenever our society changes, or wishes to change, schools and teachers are enlisted in the cause. If we decide that cyberspace is the place to go, we start by sending the second

grade. . . . No teacher can hear the phrase "launching a new initiative" without knowing that the launching pad is going to be located on top of his desk.

Position One treats change descriptively. No value judgment is implicit in statements such as the ones above. Position Two also recognizes the ubiquitousness of educational change, but this quality is regarded as a basic flaw, a manifestation of uncertainty or even gullibility on the part of educators and those responsible for education policy. Children are portrayed as the victims of mindless reform. An influential exponent of Position Two is E. D. Hirsch, father of "cultural literacy" and "core knowledge." Reflecting on the impact of educational change in the wake of the National Commission on Excellence in Education, Hirsch (1996, pp. 2–3) wrote,

> Despite much activity, American school reform has not improved the nation's K–12 education during the decade and more since publication of *A Nation at Risk: The Imperative for Educational Reform* (1983).

Position Three argues that the most common characteristic of education, particularly public education, is the absence of change. Educators and bureaucratized schools are portrayed as highly resistant to new ideas and improved practice. Position Two and Position Three, though 180 degrees apart, share one feature—they both constitute critiques of the education establishment. Maeroff (2000, pp. 9–10) conveys the essence of Position Three:

> The world has been upended outside the schoolhouse; but, inside, education seems mostly mired in 1965. Knowledge transactions continue to consist largely of teachers who stand, front and center, talking at students. The Socratic method is as elusive as ever. In most classrooms the computer, for all its promise, tends to be little more than a cybernetic artifact that figures only tangentially in the core program.

Position Four is popular among some scholars who study educational change. Following the French idiom, they maintain that the more things change in schools, the more they remain the same (Sarason, 1971, p. 29). Thus, change is acknowledged to occur, but to little effect. Why this is so is open to argument. Sarason (p. 86) has contended, for example, that many reform initiatives fail to address the "existing regularities" in schools, thereby condemning reforms to failure and ensuring that the basic mode of educational operation continues.

It is interesting to note that one position is conspicuously absent. We rarely, if ever, hear of people praising public schools for being responsive to the need for change. While private industry is lauded for embracing continuous change (Brown and Eisenhardt, 1997), schools are attacked for similar action. They also are criticized for failing to change. Perhaps this curious mixed message—schools have problems, but they should not change—can be traced to the central role of schooling in society. In times of endemic change, schools may be looked to as an oasis of stability and continuity. At the same time, interestingly, parents invest great hope in the ability of schools to prepare their children for the very societal changes that they find so threatening. The irony of public response to educational change calls to mind the title of a Broadway play. Instead of "I Love You, You're Perfect, Now Change," however, the title for the drama of American education should be, "I'm Worried about You, You're Flawed, but Stay the Same."

Chapter 2 opens with a personal reflection on the extent to which schools have changed. I compare the high school that I attended in the early sixties to the high school from which my daughter graduated in 2001. The main body of the chapter traces a half century of efforts to reform public education. To facilitate this historical overview, several key public ideas are identified. These ideas—equality of opportunity, educational excellence, accountability, choice, school safety, professionalization—have been influential in efforts to change educational policies, programs, and practices. By chronicling some of the better-known initiatives associated with these ideas, it is possible to gain a basic understanding of the scope of educational change. The chapter concludes with some lessons regarding the nature of recent reforms and the process of educational change.

HAS SCHOOLING CHANGED?

In 1961, I entered the ninth grade at Thomas Jefferson High School in Richmond, Virginia. Four decades later my daughter graduated from Monticello High School in Charlottesville, Virginia. Approximately sixty-five miles separates the two public high schools. Would visitors to Monticello in 2001 find anything that differed substantially from what they would have encountered at Thomas Jefferson in 1961?

Thomas Jefferson enrolled more than two thousand students in 1961, though not a single student was African American. The school's first black student arrived the following year.[1] Housed in an art deco masterpiece occupying an entire city block, Thomas Jefferson was recognized as one of the finest high schools in Virginia. Teachers placed great value on educating students to be "well-rounded," an expression that encompassed academic achievement, personal integrity, involvement in extra-curricular activities, and service to the school through student government and other organizations. Faculty members would have felt uncomfortable stressing any one of these elements of well-roundedness over the others.

Students could choose to pursue one of three diploma tracks—college preparatory, business, and general. Classes were organized by ability, ranging from basic to honors and Advanced Placement. The Advanced Placement courses were the pride of the school and covered virtually every subject in which AP exams were given. No special education department existed at Thomas Jefferson in 1961. "Slow" students, if they remained in school, tended to enroll in courses leading to a general diploma. In

---

[1]Much of the account of Thomas Jefferson High School is taken from my book *The School That Refused to Die* (Albany: State University of New York Press, 1995).

1961, 4 percent of students at Thomas Jefferson took an extra year of high school in order to graduate.

To acquire a diploma, students were required to earn 23 Carnegie units, 18 of which had to be earned in grades 9 through 12. At the time, the eighth grade also was included in high school, though students attended a junior high school to earn their eighth grade credits. Specific course requirements varied according to the type of diploma. Foreign language, for example, was not required to earn a general or business diploma. Students in the college preparatory track generally took the Scholastic Aptitude Test in junior and senior year. Otherwise, students were not subject to external tests in high school.

Thomas Jefferson was led by a principal and two assistant principals. A guidance department handled college placement and career counseling. The school's most important organizational unit was the academic department, and department chairs wielded considerable influence. They participated in hiring decisions and teacher evaluation as well as curriculum development and the assignment of teaching responsibilities.

Student life mirrored adult life in its degree of structure and organization. A student-run Honor Council enforced the Honor Code and adjudicated various types of cases, including cheating and plagiarism. Students also operated the Character Committee, which assumed responsibility for promoting honesty and integrity. Student government consisted of homeroom units, which sent elected representatives to class councils, and the Student Participation Association, a schoolwide governing body. The latter was made up of a Senate and a House of Representatives, each consisting of elected representatives from each class plus the class presidents. A Club Affiliation Committee made up of the presidents of every school club and society coordinated nonathletic activities. Thomas Jefferson boasted a large Cadet Corps, literary magazine, school newspaper, and complete arts program, including dramatic productions, chorus, band, and orchestra.

The high school from which my daughter graduated in 2001 resembled Thomas Jefferson in some ways, but in other ways it was quite different. Monticello High School enrolled approximately half as many students as Thomas Jefferson, a little over one thousand. Despite the school's smaller size, the principal was assisted in his duties by an associate principal, two assistant principals, a director of guidance, and an athletic director. In addition, a school resource officer—a uniformed police officer—was on duty to deal with threats to school safety. Like Thomas Jefferson, the school was organized around academic departments, each with a department chair. The largest department, however, was the Special Education Department, a unit that did not exist in 1961. To foster a sense of community, Monticello also was organized into three "houses," each with its own area of the building and identifying features. All ninth graders were assigned to the same house, an arrangement designed to smooth the difficult transition from middle school to high school. Middle schools did not replace junior high schools until well after 1961.

While in certain ways Monticello was more highly organized than Thomas Jefferson, student life was not as structured. Absent from Monticello was the Honor Council, Character Committee, and extensive Student Participation Association. Although Monticello students, especially girls, had more athletic activities in which to engage, fewer clubs and creative opportunities in general were available. Monticello offered band and chorus, but not orchestra. No Cadet Corps was available.

Monticello High School, like other public high schools in Virginia, was subject to a new statewide accountability program which exerted a major influence on the school's academic program. The state developed Standards of Learning for most subject matter areas and required each school to align its course content with these standards. To ensure that schools did so, state tests were administered in various courses on an annual basis. As of 2004, students who did not pass a specified number of these tests would not be able to graduate. Schools failing to achieve a specified passing rate on the tests would be denied accreditation as of 2007. Parents of Monticello students received annual notification of schoolwide performance on the state tests.

Gone were the general and business diplomas. Students at Monticello could earn a regular academic diploma or an advanced diploma. Provision was made for a modified diploma for special education students unable to meet the requirements for a regular academic diploma.

Students at Monticello, as at Thomas Jefferson, were assigned to courses organized by ability. In core subjects, the options included standard, advanced, and honors levels. A number of Advanced Placement courses were available on site, though not as many as Thomas Jefferson had offered. Students who desired an Advanced Placement course that was unavailable on site were able to take it online. My daughter enrolled in an AP Biology course offered through Northwestern University, but she found the lack of labs and teacher contact dissatisfying. Monticello students also were allowed to take courses at the adjacent community college and at the University of Virginia, when accelerated work was called for. Needless to say, my daughter was exposed to far more technology than I had been. Technology, for me, was an electric typewriter and a movie projector.

The student body and faculty at Monticello were far more diverse than at Thomas Jefferson. Monticello enrolled a significant number of African American and Hispanic students as well as large numbers of special needs students and poor students. With diversity came benefits and costs. One cost was increased friction between groups of students from different backgrounds. To help deal with confrontations, Monticello initiated a Peer Mediation program and provided teachers with special training on how to defuse conflict.

Changes in state graduation requirements meant that Monticello students had less opportunity to choose elective courses than their predecessors at Thomas Jefferson. My daughter needed 24 Carnegie units to graduate, one more than I had needed, but her units could only be earned in grades 9 through 12. I was required to earn 18 units over a comparable period. Eighth grade units were not counted toward graduation in 2001, as they had been in 1961. In addition to academic requirements, all Monticello students had to complete a community service requirement. My daughter satisfied this requirement by helping to clear a network of local walking trails.

My daughter's daily schedule was quite different from the one I had followed. Thomas Jefferson operated a seven-period day, and students normally took five or six courses. When not in class, students were assigned to a study hall. My daughter's school ran a block schedule with four classes a day, each roughly double the length of my 44-minute classes. Students at Monticello did not take the same classes every day, with the exception of one class that operated on a daily basis. Most classes met every other day, allowing teachers to focus on fewer students each day and relieving students of homework assignments in all of their courses every night.

Monticello's schedule did not include homeroom period, as had mine. Teachers were expected to mentor students, however. Periodically, time was set aside so that Monticello teachers could meet with their assigned group of students. While the guidance counselors at Thomas Jefferson focused primarily on college placement and career advisement, Monticello's guidance counselors balanced these duties with supervision of various testing programs, running counseling groups for students with special concerns, and assisting with the development of plans for special education students.

Against these differences must be weighed various similarities. Most students at both schools were expected to take courses with roughly the same titles. Courses were sequenced similarly. For example, Algebra I was taken before Geometry, which in turn was taken before Algebra II. Students tended to take one course in each core area at a time, rather than taking, say, three or four science courses simultaneously. The specific content of particular courses, such as Physics or U.S. History, obviously changed over 40 years, but many of the topics that my daughter studied sounded very familiar to me. Instruction continued to emphasize teacher-led lessons supplemented by individual seatwork. My impression is that my daughter's classes involved more group work than mine did. To determine whether students had learned what they were expected to learn, teachers at both schools relied on quizzes and written tests, and courses still culminated in final examinations. Students were apprised of their standing on report cards containing letter grades.

As for student life at both schools, dating, driving, and sports absorbed considerable interest and energy. Ninth graders occupied the lowest rungs of the social ladder, and each succeeding grade brought greater prestige and influence. By senior year, students were anxious to move on to bigger and better things. My daughter's complaints about certain classmates who seemed to care little about school work and who interfered with effective learning in class echoed my own.

This brief comparison of two high schools separated by four decades suggests that those who argue that nothing ever changes in public education are wrong. Whether the preceding examples of educational change are meaningful or preferable to that which went before are normative and empirical questions. I believe that the real issue is not whether education changes. Any careful analysis of educational programs, policies, and practices over time reveals changes. The question is whether the changes have made any difference in the quality of the educational experience for young people or the well-being of our society.

Lest I be accused of too quickly rejecting Position Three—the "schools never change" argument—it should be noted that a verdict ultimately may depend on the span of time over which possible changes are tracked. If educators, for example, repeat similar changes every generation or so, then observers looking at educational change over a century or more may see recurring cycles of reform. In other words, what might appear to be an innovation when examined at one point in time may turn out to be part of a merry-go-round of predictable reforms, reactions to reforms, and efforts to compromise. Perceptions of educational change and stability obviously are related to each observer's temporal perspective.

AN OVERVIEW OF RECENT EDUCATIONAL CHANGE

Much of this book deals with specific educational changes, how they were achieved, what they accomplished, and what they tell us about educational change as a field of inquiry. Before diving into these murky waters, it is important to scan the ocean. A useful way to approach this daunting task is to focus on some of the most important "public ideas" related to education over the past half century. These ideas have provided the foundation for much reform in education.

What is a public idea? Elsewhere I have written (Duke, 2000, p. 17),

> The desires of the public frequently are captured by ideas. Ideas, of course, are always floating around, set adrift by pundits, professors, and politicians. The vast majority of these ideas soon sink from sight. A few, however, refuse to disappear. They gather density, like islands building around coral reefs. We call these ideas "public ideas," terms that capture the concerns and the mood of a large number of citizens at a given point in time.

In his polemic concerning the course of educational reform, E. D. Hirsch (1996, p. 15) prefers to indict ideas rather than those who dream them up and adopt them:

> American schools need to be transformed, and to accomplish that, many ideas (including even the pseudo-idea of "radical transformation") need to be repudiated. But to attack ideas is not to attack the human participants in what Harriett Tyson Bernstein has termed "a conspiracy of good intentions."

Much of the recent history of educational change, at least in the United States, can be traced to six key ideas—equality of educational opportunity (and the related idea of equity), educational excellence, accountability, choice, school safety (and the related term *discipline*), and professionalization. These ideas approximate ideals for many people. They animate debate, capture people's imagination, inspire collective action, and influence policy and practice.

In their brief but intriguing analysis of educational reform, Tyack and Cuban (1995, p. 40) contend that we have spent more energy talking about public ideas in education than actually doing anything about them. They do not regard this policy talk as "futile and irrational but as an inevitable result of conflicts of values and interests built into a democratic system of school governance and reflecting changing climates of public opinion" (p. 41). While some educational ideas never escape the orbit of policy talk, the six ideas discussed in this chapter clearly have prompted educators to act. Whether this action has made a lasting contribution to the quality of public schooling, of course, remains an open question.

Equality of Educational Opportunity

No public idea has influenced more educational change over the past 50 years than equality of educational opportunity and the related notion of educational equity. With its decision in May 1954 in *Brown v. Board of Education of Topeka* (Kansas), the United States Supreme Court struck down the notion that students of different races could receive an equal education in separate facilities. What began as a court decision based on racial discrimination eventually would involve all three branches of the federal government as well as state and local governments. The initial focus on African American students would widen over the ensuing decades to encompass poor students, female students, non-English-speaking students, and students with disabilities.

In the years immediately following the Brown decision, however, educational change could be measured in inches, not miles. Token desegregation took place in some schools, while entire states, like Virginia, refused to comply with the Supreme Court's mandate. No effort was made in the early years to address racially segregated schools outside of the South. Forcing the idea of equal educational opportunity off the drawing board and into the classroom took President Eisenhower's decision to send federal troops to Little Rock, Arkansas, to protect black students assigned to the previously all-white Central High School; the resolve of his successor, President John F. Kennedy, to promote the rights and welfare of African Americans; and the pressure generated by the Civil Rights Movement and leaders like Martin Luther King, Jr.

In the wake of President Kennedy's assassination, the task of achieving equal educational opportunity was left to President Lyndon Baines Johnson. His administration was responsible for two landmark pieces of legislation. The Civil Rights Act of 1964 included two provisions related directly to public education. Title IV authorized the Attorney General of the United States to initiate lawsuits to compel school districts to desegregate. Title VI called for withholding federal funds from schools with racially discriminatory programs. The following year, 1965, saw the passage of the Elementary and Secondary Education Act (ESEA), the most comprehensive education bill initiated up to that time by the federal government. Title I of the ESEA provided financial assistance to schools to help them educate disadvantaged students. The ESEA marked the broadening of the idea of equal educational opportunity to include poor students as well as African American students. Operation Head Start, a federally supported preschool program for poor children, also was initiated by the Johnson administration at this time, thereby ushering in the era of early intervention.

Efforts by federal, state, and local government to address the needs of poor and minority students over the next two decades produced many changes, some intended and others unintended. Since discrimination still characterized residential patterns in U.S. communities, school systems faced with desegregation orders were compelled to bus students out of their neighborhoods. Initially, however, black students were the ones expected to travel to previously all-white schools. As these schools enrolled more black students, many white parents withdrew their children and placed them in private schools or moved to all-white suburbs. "White flight" in some urban areas resulted in de facto segregation within a relatively short period of time. In other communities, however, schools desegregated successfully without the departure of high percentages of white students.

One popular strategy for holding white students, or in some cases attracting them back to desegregated schools, involved the creation of magnet schools. Magnet schools offered specialty programs, in areas such as performing arts and technology, to students from all over the community, not just a particular neighborhood. In some instances, admission was linked to racial quotas in order to maintain balanced enrollment. Other strategies for maintaining racial balance included controlled choice policies and voluntary metropolitan desegregation plans involving urban and suburban school systems. Educators also were compelled to take a careful look at time-honored practices, such as tracking and ability grouping, that permitted vestiges of segregation to exist within presumably desegregated schools.

In 1994, Congress reauthorized ESEA, calling the new legislation the Improving America's Schools Act. Federal funds continued to be earmarked for poor students in the form of Title I teachers, teacher training, special pullout programs, teacher aides, schoolwide instructional improvement projects, and extended learning time opportunities. By 1997, Title I of the new act was affecting 11 million students. Of this number, 28 percent were African American students and 30 percent were Hispanic students (Elementary and Secondary Education Act, Title I, 2001, p. 109).

In 1999, equality of educational opportunity became closely linked to two other public ideas—educational excellence and accountability—when Congress once again reauthorized ESEA, this time in the form of the Educational Excellence for All Children Act. The bill shifted the focus of reform for Title I students from remediation to meeting the challenging standards being adopted by virtually every state in the United States. States receiving federal assistance were expected to implement a rigorous accountability system for all schools.

Extending the Idea of Equal Opportunity

African American and poor students were not the only beneficiaries of efforts to promote equal educational opportunity. Beginning in the seventies, court decisions and legislation targeted female students, non-English-speaking students, and students with disabilities. Arguments were made that each of these groups had been unable to enjoy the full benefits of a public education.

Equal Rights for Girls.   In 1972 Congress passed Title IX of the Education Amendments Act. This landmark legislation declared that:

> No person in the United States shall, on the basis of sex, be excluded from participation in, be denied the benefits of, or be subjected to discrimination under any education

program or activity receiving federal financial assistance. (Sadker and Sadker, 1991, p. 463)

In the wake of Title IX school systems throughout the nation re-examined access to traditionally all-male courses and programs, including vocational education and athletic programs. Guidance counselors were compelled to consider how they advised young women regarding career opportunities. Discriminatory discipline practices and sex-role stereotyping came under increasing scrutiny.

Students Not Fluent in English. The needs of non-English-speaking students surfaced in the form of a 1974 court decision in the case of *Lau v. Nichols*. The San Francisco school system was sued for failure to provide equal educational opportunity to students of Chinese ancestry who did not speak English. While the U.S. Supreme Court did not prescribe what the school system should do to correct the problem, it acknowledged that the plaintiff's argument was valid and that students of Chinese ancestry had been victims of discriminatory practice.

In addressing the needs of non-English-speaking students, school systems in the post-Lau period abandoned the sink-or-swim strategy of placing non-English-speakers in regular classrooms where many failed to stay afloat. Bilingual education, with English typically taught as the second language, became one solution, though it engendered considerable controversy. While learning English, students received academic content in their native language, a method that advocates claimed would enhance student self-concept and respect for native culture. Critics argued that bilingual education constituted a form of segregation, one that did not appear to result in higher rates of achievement (Sadker and Sadker, 1991, p. 446).

Students with Disabilities. Few efforts to promote equal educational opportunity have had a more profound effect on schools and classrooms than the crusade to help students with disabilities. The centerpiece of this drive was Public Law 94-142, the Education for All Handicapped Children Act of 1975. The act guaranteed procedural due process for all children identified as having special needs based on physical, cognitive, and emotional handicaps. So-called special education for these students required that an individualized education program (IEP) be developed and drafted in the form of a written plan that addressed each student's needs. Every IEP had to include an assessment of the student's current performance and needs, short-term and long-term goals, a description of the nature and duration of instructional and non-instructional services designed to meet the goals, and provisions for monitoring student progress and evaluation.

To implement Public Law 94-142 and subsequent legislation related to special education, school systems needed to expand the ranks of special education teachers. Specialty areas such as behavior disorders and learning disabilities have grown within special education because of the extensive training required to deal with particular disabilities. In many contemporary schools, special education may be one of the largest departments. As of 2001, special education mandates affected 6.1 million students at a cost of 41.5 billion dollars annually (Bolick, 2001).

Various arrangements have been made since 1975 to ensure that special education students receive services in the "least restrictive environment." This legal requirement was instituted to prevent most special needs students from being segregated in self-contained classrooms. While many of these students have received some services in resource rooms specifically designed and staffed to accommodate their needs, they also have spent time learning in regular education classrooms. "Mainstreaming" has required extensive staff development for regular education teachers. In addition, special education teachers and teacher aides have been assigned to work in tandem with regular education teachers.

Some of the changes resulting from special education laws and policies have not been as well received as others. Teachers and administrators complain about the extensive paperwork and numerous meetings required to determine student eligibility for services, develop IEPs, and monitor and evaluate student progress. Ministering to the needs of mainstreamed special education students sometimes results in regular education students receiving less attention. Controversy has attended efforts to medicate and discipline students with particular disabilities. When special needs students have failed to receive the services that parents and advocates expected, school systems have wound up in court. Few contest the fact that ensuring equal educational opportunity for students with disabilities has greatly increased the complexity, litigiousness, and bureaucratization of public education.

In 1978 Congress appropriated funds to study the cumulative effects of federal education policies at the local level. One group of researchers focused on the impact of policies designed to promote equal educational opportunity (Knapp et al., 1991). The policies were associated with Title I of the ESEA, Public Law 94-142, the Bilingual Education Act of 1968 (Title VII of the ESEA), Title IX, and other civil rights legislation. The researchers found that "students who were intended to benefit from federal programs and mandates generally did receive special services in some degree tailored to their individual needs" (Knapp et al., p. 111). These services were provided, in most cases, by staff members who had been specially trained to address the needs of target students. Furthermore, these staff members could not or would not have been hired without the impetus of federal intervention.

Educational Excellence

Compared to equality of educational opportunity, educational excellence is a relatively imprecise idea. One problem concerns what constitutes evidence that the idea is being realized. Experts can measure whether poor or disabled students are receiving equal inputs (in terms of funding, instructional services, well-trained teachers, and the like) or achieving equal outcomes (graduation rates or performance on standardized tests, for example). But how can educational excellence be measured? Excellence, by its very nature, is open-ended. It is much easier to define and measure ignorance than excellence (Duke, 1985).

Since the early eighties, educational excellence has been associated with two basic beliefs: (1) all students need to receive rigorous academic instruction, regardless of their future plans and (2) standards in academic subjects need to be raised significantly (Toch, 1991, p. 3). Prior to this time, however, advocates of educational excellence sought somewhat different goals.

In the late fifties, concern over the Cold War and Soviet gains in science and technology prompted professors and policy makers to press for more advanced coursework in American high schools. Realizing that many students would be unable to succeed in newly created honors and Advanced Placement courses, reformers such as former Harvard president James Bryant Conant urged that small high schools consolidate, thereby creating a large enough pool of talented students to sustain ability grouping and accelerated courses (Conant, 1959). To ensure that these students were exposed to the latest research and scholarly thought, the National Science Foundation funded a variety of curriculum development projects. Classroom teachers were replaced as curriculum developers by eminent scientists. The latter regarded their job as creating "teacher-proof" curricula. By the mid-sixties, thousands of high school teachers were spending part of their summers receiving training in the "new math" and a variety of new science curricula.

In 1970 Congress mandated that "Provisions Related to Gifted and Talented Children" be added to the ESEA Amendments of 1969. Consequently, programs for gifted and talented students qualified for federal assistance under Titles III and V of ESEA. To ensure a steady flow of bright students into advanced high school programs, elementary schools developed various programs for "talented and gifted" (TAG) students. The TAG programs assumed various forms, from self-contained classes to pull-out programs. Exceptionally gifted students were encouraged to skip grades and take accelerated courses. By junior and senior year of high school, some students were able to take courses in local colleges.

Educational excellence continued to be associated with gifted education until President Reagan's Secretary of Education, Terrel H. Bell, created the National Commission on Excellence in Education in 1981. Concern had grown that the U.S. economy was being outstripped by Japan and Germany. Blame was laid at the schoolhouse doorstep. In 1983 the National Commission issued its report, *A Nation at Risk: The Imperative for Educational Reform.* The prescription for educational excellence that emerged from this report and a number of subsequent calls for reform differed in important ways from previous prescriptions. Instead of focusing on opportunities for the brightest students, the new strategy involved raising standards for *all* students. In order to implement higher standards, reformers insisted on eliminating all vestiges of progressive education, including coursework that attended more to "relevance" than rigor and instructional techniques that focused on affective more than cognitive development. What students needed, they believed, was a firm grounding in such basics as reading and mathematics, highly structured coursework, and discipline-based content.

Within a decade of the publication of *A Nation at Risk,* most states had developed or were in the process of developing new curriculum standards. Elective courses began to disappear from high school courses of study as graduation requirements in core areas were raised. States eliminated nonacademic diplomas, insisting that virtually all students were capable of achieving educational excellence. The practice of ability grouping came under attack because it denied rigorous content to some students while allowing other students to be exposed to stimulating learning opportunities. One of the few reminders of earlier notions of educational excellence were so-called Governor's Schools. These high-powered centers of learning were designed for top-performing students, drawn from across a state or region. Offering a specialized curriculum in such areas as science and technology, these schools operated as regular day schools, boarding schools, or summer schools, depending on the state.

Accountability

Two public ideas of different origin can become linked over time. Such has been the case with educational excellence and accountability. Since the mid-1990s, education policy at both the federal and the state levels has yoked together high academic standards and accountability for student outcomes. According to Goertz (2001, p. 62), basing accountability on student outcomes represented a shift away from procedural accountability where educators were only responsible for complying with rules and regulations.

Some observers credit President Richard M. Nixon with popularizing the idea of educational accountability (Lessinger, 1971, pp. 62–63):

> In his March 3rd (1970) Education Message, President Nixon stated, "From these considerations we derive another new concept: *Accountability*. School administrators and school teachers alike are responsible for their performance, and it is in their interest as well as in the interest of their pupils that they be held accountable."

Within a brief period of time following President Nixon's remarks, states and school systems were devising various schemes for ensuring educational accountability. Timpane (1978, pp. 181–182) noted that, by 1978, "every state but two [has] a state-wide assessment system in operation or in the planning phase, and many other states and school systems [have] new comprehensive planning schemes designed in one way or another to assure that local educational programs measure up to some standard of performance." Teacher evaluation, which either did not exist or consisted primarily of anecdotal comments by administrators, became formalized, systematic, and research-based. Improved student achievement presumably depended on teachers being held accountable for using proven teaching methods. Performance contracting was another accountability measure implemented during the seventies. Private corporations contracted with school systems to take over classroom instruction and *guarantee* that designated student outcomes were achieved. If achievement targets were not hit, the corporations received no funds. Although statewide assessment and more rigorous teacher evaluation were accountability strategies that have persisted, performance contracting all but disappeared for several decades when results proved disappointing and accusations were made that students were being "taught to the test."

Private enterprise again became interested in public education in the nineties. School systems that had been unsuccessful in raising student achievement contracted with private, for-profit corporations to take over not only classroom instruction, but the administration of schools. The money received by these providers was tied, in part, to student achievement as measured by standardized tests. Private providers relied on technology, highly structured instructional programs, special curriculum materials, and inexpensive teaching assistants to raise student achievement.

Contemporary notions of educational accountability are virtually synonymous with standardized testing. Almost every state in the United States has implemented a testing program based on state learning standards. Students are tested at various points along the road to graduation, and failure to pass state tests can result in retention at grade level and even denial of graduation. To keep students—and teachers—marching along, curriculum frameworks and pacing guides are used. Students who fail key tests are expected to participate in various types of assistance programs, ranging from in-school and after-school tutorials to Saturday school and summer school.

Many states have introduced sanctions for schools and school systems that fail to produce prescribed passing rates on standardized tests. Sanctions can include loss of accreditation, state takeover, and reconstitution. Some states offer rewards to schools that succeed in raising student achievement. Critics fear that equating accountability and educational excellence with performance on standardized tests will result in lower teacher morale and greater student anxiety. Proponents counter that there is nothing wrong with teachers and students being clear about what students are supposed to learn.

Few dispute the fact that statewide accountability initiatives have made an impact at the school and classroom level. In one series of studies of Virginia's accountability plan, researchers (Duke, Grogan, Tucker, and Heinecke, 2003) found that teachers have begun to discuss curriculum content and share ideas more than they did previously. Lessons in subjects for which state tests were administered were highly formatted, with each lesson tied to a state content standard. When teachers tested students in class, they used the same types of questions and prompts that students could expect to find on state tests. Administrators made certain that teachers reviewed their students' performance on state tests and analyzed patterns of missed answers. It remains to be seen whether these changes will result in costs as well as benefits. Some fear that overemphasizing performance on standardized tests may harm students who do not test well and diminish classroom creativity.

Choice

For some observers, the ultimate form of educational accountability is choice, not standardized testing. Proponents of educational choice insist that the market should determine which schools flourish and which schools flop. They contend that public schools' virtual monopoly over education is inconsistent with the freedom of choice supposedly enjoyed by members of a democratic society.

The idea of educational choice, of course, is hardly new. In the distant past, however, only the wealthiest families could afford to choose private tutors and private schools. In the sixties, middle class parents who were critical of conventional educational practice began to create alternative schools for their children (Duke, 1978). Alternative schools appeared within as well as outside of public school systems. They tended to be smaller than regular public schools and more experimental with regard to curriculum content and instructional methods. Parents typically played a major role in the operation and governance of alternative schools.

Magnet schools provided further impetus to the movement to expand educational choice. While the primary goal of many magnet schools was to ensure student diversity, magnets offered students options beyond their neighborhood or assigned public school.

Another manifestation of interest in educational choice has been political pressure for vouchers. Vouchers supposedly function like food stamps. They take the form of coupons that can be redeemed at the school of one's choice. The federal government supported a voucher experiment of sorts in the early seventies in the Alum Rock (California) School District, but interest in the idea did not garner widespread attention until it received vocal support from President Reagan (Henig, 1994, pp. 71–74). Reagan regarded vouchers as a way to support private and parochial schools as well as reflect his strong belief in free market economics. To expand his base of support, Reagan argued that vouchers would allow the poor to exercise the same degree of choice traditionally enjoyed by more affluent citizens. Critics, however, maintained that vouchers would undermine the entire public education system.

While voucher plans failed to take hold in more than a handful of localities, another form of educational choice—charter schools—fared better. Nathan (1996, p. 1) has offered the following characterization of charter schools:

> Charter schools are public schools, financed by the same per-pupil funds that traditional public schools receive. Unlike traditional public schools, however, they are held accountable for achieving educational results. In return, they receive waivers that exempt them from many of the restrictions and bureaucratic rules that shape traditional public schools.

By the beginning of the twenty-first century, thirty-four states had adopted some form of charter school legislation. Approximately 2,400 charter schools had been created, reflecting a variety of educational philosophies, curricular focuses, and instructional approaches (Viadero, 2001). Most charter schools were created as a result of teacher and parent initiative, and most tended to be relatively small.

Yet another impetus to educational choice resulted from the collaboration of the federal government and private enterprise. In the summer of 1991, Secretary of Education Lamar Alexander and CEOs from major U.S. corporations launched the New American Schools Development Corporation (NASDC). The NASDC funded the design and deployment of break-the-mold schools. In so doing, it generated a variety of comprehensive reform programs for consideration by school systems and community groups committed to systemic change. By 2001, more than 3,500 schools across the United States were using NASDC designs (Mirel, 2001, p. vi). Although the results of this novel approach have been mixed, the NASDC symbolized the belief that there was no single best way to improve the schooling of U.S. children.

The discussion so far has focused on *school* choice. It is important to note, however, that in the eighties and nineties, increasing numbers of parents opted to home-school their children rather than enroll them in any school. No single reason accounts for this movement. While many parents expressed religious justifications for educating their children at home, others noted academic reasons and concerns for their children's safety and well-being.

School Safety

There was a time when most parents could send their children to school confident that they would be protected from harm. Confidence has eroded over the past half century as an assortment of threats migrated from the streets into schools. The late fifties saw the rise of teenage gangs in urban schools.[2] During the next decade, safety threats related to student demonstrations and efforts to desegregate schools alarmed parents and educators. The seventies were characterized by concern for adolescent drug use, fighting, and vandalism. The eighties and nineties witnessed continued concern for student drug use, along with the consumption of alcoholic beverages. In addition, serious violence involving weapons entered the picture, as disgruntled young people expressed their dissatisfaction by shooting classmates and instructors. Less dramatic safety threats, including psychological abuse, hazing, and sexual harassment, also began to attract attention during this time. With each wave of new concerns came exhortations for action, new policies, and government programs. These initiatives resulted in, or were matched by, local changes in the management of schools and classrooms.

When Congress passed the Drug Abuse Education Act in 1970, it signaled the federal government's willingness to address school safety issues in a comprehensive manner. The bill called for drug awareness curricula to be developed, teachers to be trained to recognize indications of student drug use, and community drug education programs to be created. In the decades that followed, schools implemented a variety of measures to combat drug use and related problems. Besides offering instruction on the dangers of drug and alcohol use, educators promulgated policies that dealt harshly with students caught possessing or distributing controlled substances in school. Special drug abuse counseling was provided, and some schools began to administer random drug tests.

Concern for weapons, gangs, and violence on campus sparked other initiatives. The right of school officials to search students and student lockers was upheld by the courts. Educators began to receive sophisticated training in how to handle dangerous situations. Many school systems created security offices to coordinate safety efforts. In other instances, school systems developed relationships with local police departments so that uniformed police officers could be assigned to schools. *Zero tolerance* policies required school officials to expel students caught with drugs and weapons or involved in serious acts of violence. School districts were required by state authori-

[2]For a concise history of school safety concerns, see Daniel L. Duke, *Creating Safe Schools for All Children* (Boston: Allyn & Bacon, 2002), pp. 3–26.

ties to develop an official code of student conduct specifying rules and consequences for those who disobeyed the rules. Students faced with suspension or expulsion had to be accorded due process.

To reduce threats to student safety, schools and school systems have explored a variety of new programs and practices. Diversity training and multicultural education have been provided for students and staff members in an effort to foster greater understanding between different groups. Peer mediation, peer counseling, anger management, and conflict resolution programs have been created. Students who pose a threat to classmates have been assigned to self-contained classes and alternative schools. In-school suspension programs have been developed. Behavior modification programs and special incentives have been implemented in order to deal with disruptive students.

So central had become concern for school safety by the nineties that one of the seven national education goals was devoted to it. Goal 7 stated, "By the year 2000, every school in the United States will be free of drugs, violence, and the unauthorized presence of firearms and alcohol and will offer a disciplined environment conducive to learning" (Duke, 2002, p. 12). Congress supported this goal by passing the Safe and Drug-Free Schools and Communities Act (1994), which provided technical assistance to schools for the development and implementation of school safety plans. No greater evidence of the need for such plans could be found than the tragic killings at Columbine High School on April 20, 1999. Today every public school is expected to have contingency plans for dealing with various emergency situations. Staff members must be familiar with these plans and trained to do all they can to reduce the likelihood of harm to innocent students.

Although concern over school safety is nearly universal, opinions vary regarding the most appropriate strategies and policies for achieving it. Some people emphasize more rules and harsher punishments, whereas others maintain that the first line of defense should be opportunities for students to engage in interesting learning activities. Still others stress the need for smaller schools and classes where teachers can establish closer and more caring relationships with students. Parent and community involvement are regarded by many observers as crucial elements of any effective school safety effort. One element that has been common to virtually all safety initiatives is teacher training and staff development. It is hard to imagine improvements in school safety without educators who understand the origins of safety problems and how to handle them when they arise.

Professionalization

All of the preceding public ideas have depended, to some extent, on the existence of competent professional educators. The professional status of teachers, however, has been an area of contention. Arguments can and have been made that teachers do not enjoy the same autonomy, rigorous training, prestige, and influence of other professions. As a consequence, pressure has built over the past fifty years, both within and outside the field of education, to professionalize teaching.

The vanguard of the movement to professionalize teaching has been occupied by teacher organizations, especially the National Education Association (NEA) and the American Federation of Teachers (AFT). Although these powerful groups have differed on some issues, such as whether teachers should go on strike, they agree that teachers should be well trained and involved in making important decisions related to curriculum, instruction, evaluation, and school operations. Both organizations now support collective bargaining as a means for teachers to exercise influence over salary, benefits, and working conditions.

Although many states still do not recognize the right of teachers to collectively bargain, the ascendancy of teacher organizations has meant that the voice of class-room teachers cannot be ignored by those seeking to change schools. Various forms of shared decision making have emerged over the past fifty years, ensuring teacher involvement in school improvement efforts. The importance of teacher leadership has been acknowledged by educational administrators and students of educational change (Walling, 1994). Despite these gains, some observers feel that the journey to full professionalization has only begun. Darling-Hammond (2000, p. 359) has offered the following observation:

> The nation has paid little attention to developing its human resources for education. Recruitment is ad hoc; much of teacher preparation is insufficiently aligned with the needs of contemporary classrooms and diverse learners' selection and hiring are too often disconnected either to specific school system goals or to a clear vision of quality teaching; mentoring and professional development are frequently scattershot, and opportunities for teacher learning are likely to be the first programs eliminated when districts cut their budgets.

It would be a mistake, however, to conclude that scant progress has been made in recent years. Teachers and those who prepare them today are able to draw on a rich body of research regarding instructional effectiveness. Many states have raised the standards for teacher licensing to reflect this scholarship. In pursuit of full professional status for teaching, the NEA and AFT have pressed for state professional standards boards controlled by educators. While this goal has yet to be fully achieved, a National Board for Professional Teaching Standards (NBPTS) has been created. The NBPTS is headed by a board, the majority of whom are classroom teachers. It administers certification examinations in educational specializations. Achieving board certification is considered one of the highest honors a teacher can receive.

Opinions vary regarding the impact of efforts to professionalize teaching on schools and classrooms. Where collective bargaining is permitted, teachers often play a more active role in determining such matters as how they will be evaluated, length of the school day, and maximum class size. Even without collective bargaining, teachers typically are represented when decisions are made regarding the adoption of new programs and practices. Teacher organizations provide local educators with a variety of professional development opportunities as well as publications related to promising new ideas and research on best practice. In order to stay abreast of new knowledge related to teaching, teachers in many states are required to earn recertification credits by attending workshops and taking graduate courses. Many school systems have developed, with the assistance of veteran teachers, extensive staff development programs, peer coaching arrangements, and mentorships for new teachers. It is much rarer today than in past years to find new teachers being given the keys to their classroom and left alone to fend for themselves. Contemporary initiatives aim to transform schools into professional learning communities.

LESSONS FROM A HALF CENTURY OF REFORM

Any person or group committed to understanding and achieving educational change would be wise to consult the record of past reform efforts. This chapter's brief overview of some of the primary public ideas that have influenced reform over the past fifty years yields a variety of lessons. The first lesson is to beware of exaggerated claims. Those who claim that everything in education has changed, as well as those who argue that nothing has changed, are both wrong. Education is characterized by patterns of continuity and change. A certain amount of continuity, in fact, is probably essential for meaningful change to occur. An examination of efforts to respond to the public ideas discussed earlier reveals a mixed record of successes, failures, and unanticipated outcomes. What is crucial to remember is that as much can be learned about educational change from examining unrealized reforms as success stories.

Change Key

Beware of exaggerated claims regarding the historical records of educational change. Examples abound of successful as well as unsuccessful change. The history of reform is characterized by both continuity and change.

There are, of course, other lessons lurking in the record of educational reform efforts. In this section we shall consider several that relate to impetuses to change, relationships between different public ideas in education, shifts in the preferred unit of change, the constant possibility of unintended change, and the persistent confidence of reformers.

Impetuses to Educational Change

Our review of recent responses to public ideas suggests that the sources of much educational change lie outside the realm of public education. Sometimes the impetus is a perceived threat to national well-being, such as occurred after Soviet triumphs in space or the rise of powerful economies in Japan and Germany. In other instances, landmark court cases addressing long-standing social concerns provided the spark to ignite reformers. We can be sure of one thing—if it tickles the nation's conscience or pocketbook, expect the schools to cough.

Rightly or wrongly, public education has been regarded as the first line of defense against problems that threaten the nation. The cure for substance abuse is drug education. The remedy for political scandal is civic education. The antidote for a sagging economy is higher education standards. The solution to racial unrest is multicultural education. It seems that no matter what the problem, the schools are assumed to be able and willing to address it.

Reviewing impetuses to educational change reveals that educators frequently find themselves on the sidelines during the onset of major reform initiatives. Why this is so is open to conjecture. Some argue that educators are, by nature, reluctant to change. Others suggest that educators simply have grown too comfortable with the status quo. Still others maintain that educators do not command widespread respect among policy makers and politicians. In many cases, educators actually are regarded as part of the problem that reforms are supposed to address. Whatever the reasons, playing the role of bystanders has meant that educators frequently react to calls for change with caution or resistance. These defensive reactions, of course, only serve to confirm reformers' suspicions regarding the conservative nature of the education establishment.

When educators do take the initiative to propose changes, their motives sometimes are regarded as self-serving. When teachers insist on smaller class size, for example, critics deride the move as a way to reduce workload rather than improve learning. Any proposal for change, regardless of whether it derives from the initiative of educators or non-educators, also can be expected to elicit complaints from those whose children have fared well in school and those without children in school who must foot the bill for reform.

Change Key

The impetus for educational change frequently comes from sources outside of the public schools. This fact helps explain why educators often confront calls for reform with caution or resistance.

The Interplay of Public Ideas

Tracing the evolution of public ideas in education reveals several interesting patterns. Efforts to address a particular idea, such as educational excellence, set in motion forces that demand attention to other ideas. In the aftermath, for example, of national efforts to promote more rigorous academic content in the late fifties and again in the early eighties came pressure for equality of educational opportunity and programs to help at-risk students. On occasion, the rise of countervailing concerns has the effect of distracting educators from the original initiative for change and weakening reforms. Darling-Hammond (2000, p. 361), for instance, believes that the movement to expand educational choice has distilled efforts to improve the quality of public schools.

In other cases, however, the original initiative has merged with the counter-initiative, forming a hybrid set of reforms responsive to both public ideas. Such a marriage occurred during the nineties with the coalescence of movements for educational excellence, equal educational opportunity, and accountability. The call for higher standards to increase America's economic competitiveness was directed at *all* students, not just the most able. These higher standards then became the foundation for state accountability programs. Policy makers also linked accountability to the elimination of tracking and second-class diplomas, two key planks in platforms for educational equity and excellence.

One difficulty with the merging of different reform agendas is that the magnitude of change can be expanded so much that the likelihood of success is diminished. Confusion also can arise concerning the unit of change. Regarding the previous example involving the confluence of three initiatives in the nineties, educators were unsure whether the basic unit of change was the individual student who had to pass certain tests of curriculum standards in order to graduate; the individual school, which had to achieve a designated passing rate on state tests to achieve accreditation; or the school system, which was held responsible for seeing that accreditation standards were met for all schools under its jurisdiction. Some observers argued that denying some students diplomas because they failed mandated tests was a case of blaming the victims. Why should individual students be penalized because they happen to attend inadequate schools in inadequate school systems?

There is no reason, in theory, that efforts to address different public ideas cannot be compatible. Education, however, is big business in the United States. It is not immune to power politics. Public ideas related to education may reflect different business interests, political perspectives, value orientations, and special interest groups. Perhaps for this reason, observers have noted that American education seems to be characterized by reform cycles (Duke, 1987, pp. 2–6). We can count on the fact, for example, that any effort to improve high schools will generate demands for improving elementary and middle schools. Concern for the education of top-performing students will spawn cries for greater assistance for disadvantaged students. Raise the banner for back to basics, and overnight every content area will claim to be basic. When educators attempt to accommodate the demands of all groups pressing for change, they run the risk of leaving everyone dissatisfied.

Change Key

Efforts to change education in response to the desires of one group invariably give rise to pressure for change from other groups. It may not always be possible to accommodate the demands of all groups lobbying for change.

Shifts in the Preferred Unit of Change

In the wake of the Brown decision, the focus of educational change became the school and the school district. School officials, often under the direct supervision of the courts, were required to draft plans for desegregating schools, plans which eventually necessitated extensive within-district busing of students. When concern developed in the sixties for *how* disadvantaged students were being educated, as well as *where* they were being educated, the preferred unit of change shifted from the school to the classroom and special programs. Federal and state funds blended with local money to create a mélange of in-class, pullout, and parallel programs designed to help low-achieving students—many of whom came from poor backgrounds—acquire the basic skills needed to succeed in school.

Reformers, not surprisingly, eventually realized that supplementary programs were less likely to succeed if they were placed in ineffective schools. The late seventies and early eighties saw the rise of the so-called effective schools movement. Attention shifted to improving entire schools in an effort to serve the needs of disadvantaged students. Advocates for other public ideas, including educational excellence, also came to regard the school as the key unit of change. Initiatives to restructure, redesign, and reinvent schools proliferated following the publication of *A Nation at Risk* in 1983.

The beginnings of another shift in the preferred unit of change could be detected as the century drew to a close. Recognizing that good schools were unlikely to survive in poorly run school districts, reformers opened the aperture of change to take in entire school systems. Large school systems from Chicago to San Diego to Philadelphia were redesigned and restructured. States flexed their supervisory muscles by taking over poorly performing school districts. Contracts were signed with private corporations to operate clusters of schools and, in some cases, entire school districts.

Change Key

Different reform efforts may focus on different units of change. These units range from classrooms and supplementary programs to schools and school systems.

The Possibility of Unintended Change

The recent history of educational change indicates that reformers often develop fairly clear goals regarding what they hope to accomplish. The actual effects of change initiatives may turn out to be quite different from their intentions, however. Crystal balls that allow reformers to examine future results do not exist. Despite their efforts to predict the consequences of reforms, the record tells us that unintended effects, both desirable and undesirable, are possible and even likely.

Few advocates of school desegregation, for instance, anticipated that a mere two or three decades after the Brown decision many large urban school systems would be predominantly African American and Hispanic. Champions of statewide accountability programs based on high-stakes tests failed to foresee that dropout rates would rise, as many low-achieving students gave up the prospect of earning a diploma. Proponents of teacher professionalization reacted with dismay when some teachers resisted more rigorous and research-based teacher evaluation.

Because the changes that are sought are not always the changes that are achieved, students of educational change must look beyond the expressed goals of reformers. Being vigilant with regard to unintended byproducts of change is essential for those committed to conscientious reform.

Change Key

Educational change initiatives have the potential to produce unintended as well as intended effects. Efforts to determine the effects of change must include an examination of possible unanticipated byproducts.

Reformers' Persistent Confidence

One of the most striking features of the recent history of educational change is the persistent confidence of reformers that educational problems can be addressed and resolved by the very organizations and professionals who are accused of contributing to the problems in the first place. Paris (1995, p. 3) has explained this curious marriage of fault-finding and faith by noting that broad consensus exists regarding both the need for educational reform and the central importance of public education.

Reformers' confidence in educators' ability to right their own vessel, of course, is not boundless. The growth of homeschooling, voucher proposals, and private educational corporations indicates that some reformers have lost faith in public education. Still, public opinion polls consistently show that most parents are generally supportive of their children's schools. If they harbor misgivings, these concern other schools. Few individuals give serious consideration to dismantling the entire public school system. When problems arise, most people prefer to place their trust in educators and the possibilities of constructive educational change.

Change Key

The recent history of American education suggests that most people believe public schools are capable of correcting their problems.

CONCLUSION

Although education in the United States has been characterized by considerable continuity over the last half century, it would be mistaken to conclude that nothing ever changes when it comes to schooling. Important educational changes have taken place, and they frequently reflect significant public ideas. These ideas—including equal educational opportunity, educational excellence, accountability, choice, school safety, and professionalization—tend to derive from pressures outside of education. Among the changes that can be attributed to these public ideas are desegregation, compensatory education, mainstreaming of disabled students, equal funding for girls' and boys' athletics, bilingual education, magnet schools, detracking initiatives, programs for gifted students, Advanced Placement courses, statewide curriculum standards, subject-based standardized tests for graduation, alternative education, charter schools, antiharassment programs, crisis management plans, codes of student conduct, school security officers, inservice training for teachers, peer coaching, and expanded opportunities for teacher leadership. Although some observers might argue that some changes cancel out or undermine other changes, no one should dispute the fact that the topography of U.S. education is restless.

The brief overview of educational change in this chapter reveals a number of lessons that help us understand better the complexities of the change process. Educators' resistance to change may result, for example, from the fact that many proposals for reform originate outside of education. Another lesson concerns the fact that efforts to address one public idea invariably generate efforts to address other public ideas. In some cases, these efforts and counter-efforts coalesce to form a major reform initiative. In other instances, they remain distinct, serving to dilute reform and blunt the possibility of widespread change.

The unit of educational change has not remained stable over time. Depending on the reform initiative, the preferred unit has been the classroom, the program, the school, and the school system. Regardless of the unit of change or the nature of the desired change, the potential always exists for change efforts to produce unintended effects. These effects may be constructive or undesirable. Throughout the recent history of educational change, most reformers have remained confident, however, that educators are capable, with the right guidance and assistance, of improving themselves and their schools. Wholesale abandonment of public education is one change that has not been given serious consideration.

REFERENCES

Baldridge, J. Victor and Deal, Terrence. "The Basics of Change in Educational Organizations." In J. Victor Baldridge and Terrence Deal (eds.), *The Dynamics of Organizational Change in Education.* Berkeley: McCutchan, 1983, pp. 1–11.

Bolick, Clint. "A Bad IDEA Is Disabling Public Schools," *Education Week* (September 5, 2001), pp. 56, 63.

Brown, Shona L. and Eisenhardt, Kathleen M. "The Art of Continuous Change: Linking Complexity Theory and Time-paced Evolution in Relentlessly Shifting Organizations." *Administrative Science Quarterly,* Vol. 42 (1997), pp. 1–34.

Conant, James Bryant. *The American High School Today.* New York: McGraw-Hill, 1959.

Darling-Hammond, Linda. "Futures of Teaching in American Education," *Journal of Educational Change,* Vol. 1, no. 4 (December 2000), pp. 353–373.

Duke, Daniel L. *Creating Safe Schools for All Children.* Boston: Allyn & Bacon, 2002.

Duke, Daniel L. *A Design for Alana: Creating the Next Generation of American Schools.* Bloomington, IN: Phi Delta Kappa Educational Foundation, 2000.

Duke, Daniel L. *The Retransformation of the School.* Chicago: Nelson-Hall, 1978.

Duke, Daniel L. *School Leadership and Instructional Improvement.* New York: Random House, 1987.

Duke, Daniel L. *The School That Refused to Die.* Albany: State University of New York Press, 1995.

Duke, Daniel L. "What Is the Nature of Educational Excellence and Should We Try to Measure It?" *Phi Delta Kappan,* Vol. 66, no. 10 (June 1985), pp. 671–674.

Duke, Daniel L.; Grogan, Margaret; Tucker, Pamela; and Heinecke, Walter. *Educational Leadership in an Age of Accountability.* Albany: State University of New York Press, 2003.

"Elementary and Secondary Education Act, Title 1." In *The Jossey-Bass Reader on School Reform.* San Francisco: Jossey-Bass, 2001, pp. 107–127.

Goetz, Margaret E. "Redefining Government Roles in an Era of Standards-Based Reform," *Phi Delta Kappan,* Vol. 83, no. 1 (September 2001), pp. 62–66.

Henig, Jeffrey R. *Rethinking School Choice.* Princeton: Princeton University Press, 1994.

Hirsch, E. D. *The Schools We Need and Why We Don't Have Them.* New York: Doubleday, 1996.

Keizer, Garret. "Why We Hate Teachers." *Harper's* (Fall 2001), pp. 37–44.

Knapp, Michael S.; Stearns, Marian S.; Turnbull, Brenda J.; David, Jane L.; and Peterson, Susan M. "Cumulative Effects of Federal Education Policies at the Local Level." In Allen R. Odden (ed.), *Education Policy Implementation.* Albany, NY: State University of New York Press, 1991, pp. 105–124.

Lessinger, Leon M. "The Powerful Notion of Accountability in Education." In Leslie H. Browder, Jr. (ed.), *Emerging Patterns of Administrative Accountability.* Berkeley: McCutchan, 1971, pp. 62–73.

Maeroff, Gene I. *Education and Change: A Personal Critique.* Bloomington, IN: Phi Delta Kappa Educational Foundation, 2000.

Mirel, Jeffrey. "The Evolution of the New American Schools: From Revolution to Mainstream." Washington, DC: Fordham Foundation, 2001.

Nathan, Joe. *Charter Schools.* San Francisco: Jossey-Bass, 1996.

Paris, David C. *Ideology and Educational Reform.* Boulder, CO: Westview Press, 1995.

Sadker, Myra Pollack and Sadker, David Miller. *Teachers, Schools, and Society,* Second edition. New York: McGraw-Hill, 1991.

Sarason, Seymour B. *The Culture of the School and the Problem of Change.* Boston: Allyn & Bacon, 1971.

Timpane, Michael. "Some Political Aspects of Accountability Mandates." In Edith K. Mosher and Jennings L. Wagoner, Jr. (eds.), *The Changing Politics of Education.* Berkeley: McCutchan, 1978, pp. 181–186.

Toch, Thomas. *In the Name of Excellence.* New York: Oxford University Press, 1991.

Tyack, David and Cuban, Larry. *Tinkering toward Utopia.* Cambridge, MA: Harvard University Press, 1995.

Viadero, Debra. "Scholars Turn to Evaluating Charter Schools from the Inside," *Education Week* (November 21, 2001), p. 6.

Walling, Donovan R. (ed.). *Teachers As Leaders.* Bloomington, IN: Phi Delta Kappa Educational Foundation, 1994.

PART II

PREPARING FOR EDUCATIONAL CHANGE

Michael Fullan (1993) is fond of saying that change is a journey, not a blueprint. By this he means that change is nonlinear, unpredictable, and exciting. Although his observation certainly has validity, the fact remains that most people who engage in purposeful change proceed in a reasonably orderly manner. They determine that change is needed, they decide what the change should be, and they make plans to achieve the change. If, as Fullan warns, things do not turn out exactly as planned, it does not mean that people should abandon an orderly and thoughtful approach to change. Rather, they should remain flexible enough to make adjustments as they encounter the unexpected.

Part II examines the sources and substance of educational change. Where there is planned change, there is choice. The chapters in this section focus on the types of choices that are faced by those engaged in the process of educational change. The decision to emphasize options in the change process reflects a basic assumption of this book—that effective change is more likely to result from sensible choices than hasty reactions and impulsive acts. Sensible choices, in turn, are rooted in understanding— of the need for change, the appropriateness of various change options, and the process for achieving change.

Chapter 3 investigates the initial phase of the change process, when a need for educational change is identified and justified. Educators at this point may find themselves debating which needs to address first and how best to characterize these needs. Since needs and the changes they occasion must be "sold" to those whose support is required in order to achieve change, choices also must be made regarding the rationale for change. As Chapter 3 points out, considerable controversy and contention can arise regarding the reasons for proposing change.

Once a need for change is identified and accepted, work can begin on designing a change or set of changes to address the need. Chapter 4 looks at the Design Phase of the change process, including the range of educational change options and considerations in determining which options are best suited to particular needs.

The third step in preparing for educational change involves developing a plan to guide the implementation of change. Various approaches to planning are reviewed and analyzed in Chapter 5. It is important that change plans take into account such factors as organizational capacity, local culture, and the challenges of changing people.

QUESTIONS TO CONSIDER BEFORE READING PART II

1. Consider the current state of society. A variety of challenges confront the nation and the world. Which of these challenges can be addressed through the processes by which we educate young people? Which challenges are best left up to other institutions to address?

2. One person's need is another person's nightmare, it has been said. Can you think of any needs for educational change that are almost certain to generate opposition? How should such opposition be handled?

3. If you could create an ideal learning environment for young people, what would it look like? How would it operate? In what ways would your ideal learning environment differ from conventional schools?

4. An important step in the design of educational change involves identifying the key assumptions upon which conventional education is based. For example, it is assumed that education will take place in a school. Can you identify other key assumptions?

5. Think about the assumptions you identified in the preceding question. Should any of these assumptions be challenged? For what reasons?

6. Achieving educational change frequently requires that educators change. Changing adults can be a difficult process. What are some of the obstacles that impede efforts to change adults? Can you think of ways to overcome these obstacles?

7. Reflect on your own efforts to change behavior, acquire new skills, and alter beliefs. Have you encountered occasions when you were unable to achieve a desired change in yourself? What factors do you think accounted for your lack of success? Can you imagine a way to overcome these factors?

8. Imagine that you are a member of a group charged with the task of switching a high school from a seven-period day to a block schedule in which students take six double-length classes, three on one day and three on the next day. What should the plan for implementing such a new schedule include?

REFERENCE

Fullan, Michael G. *Change Forces.* London: Falmer Press, 1993.

IS THERE A NEED
FOR CHANGE?

MAJOR IDEAS

- Individuals possess different perspectives regarding the need for change.
- Determining that change is necessary is not the same as deciding what type of change is needed.
- Controversy and contention can characterize the process of justifying the need for change.
- A variety of decisions are involved in identifying a need for educational change.
- Change may be premised on a desire for restoration, accommodation, improvement, or transformation.
- One key to determining whether change is needed involves an awareness of the current situation.
- Educators may not always be able to address every need for change that is identified.
- Determining when a change is worth making is one of the most important judgments an educator can make.

Each year the University of Richmond holds a competition in which students suggest a single question important enough to serve as the foundation for a year's worth of courses, symposia, and guest lectures. The $25,000 prize in 2001 went to the undergraduate with this question—"Why change?" (Argetsinger, 2001). The student noted in her rationale that some human beings embrace change while others resist it. Although change may be constant, she went on to observe, how people choose to handle change varies greatly.

Much of the history of civilization can be understood by examining the circumstances under which people have decided to pursue or prevent change. In deciding how to respond to the perceived need for change, human beings reveal what they hold dear and what they disdain, their understanding of what their world is and what it should be, and their most basic values and fears. For present purposes, the decisions that individuals and groups make regarding the need for educational change serve as a window into how they think and feel—about their children and the children of others, the role of the state in educating the young, and the future of their society.

This chapter focuses on the process of determining if and under what circumstances educational change is needed. Deciding that change is needed may be closely tied to deciding what to change, but in this section these two important decisions will be treated separately. A case can be made, in fact, for decoupling the determination that change is needed from the choice of particular changes. Focusing too early on *what to change* can result in an overly hasty judgment regarding the need for change. In extreme cases, educators have been known, in fact, to commit to a particular reform or innovation *before* they have even determined that it is necessary.

The Discovery Phase of the educational change process is dominated by one central question—*Is there a current need for educational change*? If the question is answered in the affirmative, a way must be found to characterize the need and justify it. Needs for change are not always apparent. People frequently must be convinced that change is preferable to the status quo.

ISSUES IN DISCOVERING A NEED
FOR EDUCATIONAL CHANGE

The approach taken in this book is to consider the change process as a series of decisions. While certain circumstances may *require* educators to change, the process still entails many choices. My desire is to counter the notion that educators typically find themselves helpless victims of forces beyond their control. Studies of educational reform clearly indicate that every phase of the change process calls for educators to make important decisions affecting those involved in implementing change, those for whom change is intended, and even those who are expected to support and pay the bills for change. A partial list of decisions that may be faced during the Discovery Phase include the following:

- Do current or anticipated conditions call for educational change?
- How should the need for educational change be characterized?
- Is there a gap between education goals and actual performance?
- Does this gap justify a change in policies, programs, practices, or personnel?
- Should the purpose of educational change be restoration, accommodation, improvement, or transformation?
- How should the need for educational change be explained to those who must approve and support it?

Chapter 3 addresses these and other considerations that educators may face during the initial phase of the change process.

The Need for Change

At the risk of oversimplification, the need for change usually is revealed in one of two ways—the identification of *problems* or the discovery of *possibilities*. The distinction between problems and possibilities, of course, is somewhat artificial, because creative planners often convert the former into the latter. Still, the distinction is useful in the sense that changes that result from problem identification typically focus on the *elimination* of the problem, while changes that derive from the discovery of possibilities generally involve the *creation* of something new and desirable. Fritz (1989, p. 31) puts it thusly:

> There is a profound difference between problem solving and creating. Problem solving is taking action to have something go away—the problem. Creating is taking action to have something come into being—the creation. . . .
>
> The problem solvers propose elaborate schemes to define the problem, generate alternative solutions, and put the best solution into practice. If this process is successful, you might eliminate the problem. Then what you have is the absence of the problem you are solving. But what you do not have is the presence of a result you want to create.

Students of change have spent more time trying to understand problem-based change than possibility-based change. The literature on problem identification and problem solving, in fact, is enormous. One focus of attention has been the differentiation of types of problems. Whereas psychologists tend to address individual problems, such as fear of failure and low self-esteem, sociologists concentrate on social problems, such as discrimination and anomie. Horton and Leslie (1965, p. 4) defined a social problem as "a condition affecting a significant number of people in ways considered undesirable, about which it is felt something can be done through collective social action."

What is interesting about this definition is the fact that a problem begins as a *condition*. Unless people agree that the condition should be corrected, it remains a condition. In other words, people exercise choice when they opt to define a condition as a problem. Best (1995, p. 5) offers the following illustration:

> Suppose that no one noticed the declining ozone levels, or that politicians and the press refused to take the issue seriously. The objective condition (diminishing ozone) still would have had effects (more cancer, etc.) but it would not be on anyone's list of social problems. No condition is a social problem until someone considers it a social problem.

Schon (1983, p. 40) provides support for this position in his analysis of the challenges facing any service provider:

> In real-world practice, problems do not present themselves to the practitioner as givens. They must be constructed from the materials of problematic situations which are puzzling, troubling, and uncertain. In order to convert a problematic situation to a problem, a practitioner must do a certain kind of work. He must make sense of an uncertain situation that initially makes no sense.

Educational change tends to take place in organized social settings. These settings, or organizations, are characterized by various conditions. Schools, for example, have goals the achievement of which requires division of labor, coordination, control, and resources. The support of people within as well as outside the school is needed in order to be successful. Complete success is rare. Problems can arise at any time and in any part of an organization. Schein (1985, p. 9) maintains that all organizations must deal with two basic types of problems: external adaptation and internal integration.

External adaptation refers to the need of every organization, including schools and school systems, to exist in relative harmony with its neighbors. Educators face potential problems when they disregard the wishes of parents or the expectations of policy makers. At the same time that organizations are dealing with external adaptation, they also must ensure that those within the organization continue to address its goals. Internal integration becomes a problem when employees undermine or ignore each other's efforts and lose sight of the overall mission of the organization. High school principals sometimes find the coordination of instructional improvement efforts to be challenging because teachers identify more closely with their subject matter area than the school as a whole.

In thinking about efforts to change schools into more collaborative organizations, Barott and Raybould (1998, pp. 36–39) developed a typology of problems consisting of four components: first-order problems, difficulties, impasses, and second-order problems. In this scheme, problems are differentiated by the nature of efforts to resolve them. First-order problems deal with deviations from the norm. Their solution, consequently, involves returning things to normal. First-order problems are resolved, in other words, without altering the fundamental structure of the system. *Difficulties* describe problems for which there are no known solutions. Ways must be found to live with difficulties. *Impasses* occur when people get stuck dealing with situations in the same way on a repeating basis. Persistence of this kind can actually contribute to worsening circumstances. *Second-order problems* are closely related to impasses, in that the solutions to second-order problems actually *become* problems in their own right.

There is, of course, no one right way to characterize problems. They may be identified by their source, their magnitude, or their solution. What is important to realize, however, is that how a problem is characterized can be a matter of great consequence. The labels we attach to problems reveal our beliefs and biases regarding their origins and how they should be addressed. The extent to which particular problems can be effectively handled may be a function, in part, of how the problem is defined.

What Kind of Problem Is It?

I once was asked to conduct a study of two middle schools in an urban school district in the Northwest. Located in the same section of town, the two schools served students from similar backgrounds and socioeconomic groups. Both schools enrolled around six hundred students. The study was commissioned after school district officials learned that one middle school recorded more than two hundred suspensions in a year, while the other middle school did not suspend a single student during the same time period. The superintendent wanted to know why such a discrepancy existed in two schools that ostensibly were so similar.

During the course of my investigation, I heard a variety of reasons. Some individuals felt that the problem resided with the school with no suspensions. Accusations ranged from false reporting of data to lax discipline. Other individuals believed the problem belonged to the school with more than two hundred suspensions. Consensus regarding the nature of the second school's problem, however, did not exist. Some people saw the problem as a lack of parental support of school discipline, others blamed teachers for failing to provide engaging learning opportunities, and still others felt that the school had too many rules, thereby creating a hostile environment for young people. When educators cannot agree on what type of problem they are trying to resolve, the likelihood of a successful solution is diminished.

Various labels can be attached to problems associated with the process of education. As the preceding anecdote suggests, the same condition—substantial variation in numbers of suspensions between two schools—can be framed as various kinds of problems. Here, then, is another example of a choice point in the change process. What is the best or most appropriate way to characterize a problem?

The range of possibilities at first seems staggering. In an effort to narrow the options to a manageable number, Zaltman and Duncan (1977, p. 53) identified six basic types of problems with which organizations must deal:

Policy problems	Problems related to policy goals or the means for achieving the goals.
Organizational structure problems	Problems related to individuals' formal roles and the configuration of roles and groups in organizations.
Person problems	Problems related to how individuals perform their designated roles.
Production process problems	Problems related to the processes by which products are created and services are provided.
Channel problems	Problems related to the means used to distribute products and services.
Product problems	Problems related to the quality of the product or service and to unanticipated consequences of the product or service.

With a few adjustments, this list of possible problems could be used to map the territory of educational concerns. It might appear that such a classification system would greatly simplify the process of problem identification. Creating labels for problems, however, does not alter the fact that two people may examine the same condition and select two different labels for what they regard as the problem at hand.

How people choose to characterize a particular problem can be influenced by a variety of factors. In some cases, problem definition is governed by ideology or conviction. In the United States, for example, Republicans are known for framing problems in terms of too much government, whereas Democrats typically complain about too little government. Problem definition also may be influenced by resource availability. When funds are tight, people may be reluctant to define problems in ways that call for additional expenditures. Low salaries for teachers, for instance, may stand a greater chance of being identified as an educational problem during flush times than during periods of retrenchment. Yet another influence on problem definition involves the training and expertise of those responsible for defining the problem. If a communications specialist is hired to examine poor performance in a school, no one should be surprised when she discovers communication problems. That is what she is prepared to recognize. Schon (1983, pp. 44–45) has warned of the dangers that may result when we try to force problems to fit available expertise.

Problems are endemic to complex enterprises such as education. Put differently, the history of education is not characterized by great fluctuations between problem-rich and problem-free periods. Problems are always present. Where variation is detectable over time is in the types of educational problems that attract the most attention. The rise of interest in accountability ushered in an era when critics focused first on problems of purpose and subsequently on performance problems. At other times, problems of governance, resources, organization, and professional practice have garnered notice. Space does not permit an examination of all the types of problems that have been identified and used to justify educational change. It may be instructive, however, to focus on several examples in order to appreciate some of the issues involved in determining whether educational change is needed.

Problems of Purpose

Organizations exist to serve a purpose or fulfill a mission. Schools and school systems are no exception. Sometimes the purpose or mission is spelled out in formal statements of goals. In other cases, purpose and mission are implicit, no more than shared understandings. Under certain circumstances, the need for educational change may be associated with *problems of purpose*. Among these problems are the following:

- Unclear education goals
- Overly ambitious education goals
- Incompatible education goals
- Outdated education goals

Unclear Education Goals.   Educators in the United States have been assailed for being uncertain about what they are supposed to accomplish. Is the mission of schools to enable each student to achieve as much as he is capable of achieving? Should schools focus on narrowing the achievement gap between advantaged and disadvantaged students? Is the ultimate goal of public education to prepare young people for the workforce or equip them to pursue higher education? It is tempting, of course, to ask schools to achieve all of these purposes. Doing so reduces the risk of alienating any particular group served by educators. Expanding the schools' mission, however, can lead to loss of focus and ambiguity.

It is difficult to be effective when people are unclear about what they are supposed to accomplish. It may be impossible, under such circumstances, to establish meaningful priorities and allocate scarce resources intelligently. Whereas some theorists (McCaskey, 1982, p. 3) accept ambiguity of purpose as part of the organizational landscape, those responsible for contemporary education policy have worked hard to clarify the mission of public schools. The accountability movement, with its explicit standards of learning, statewide standardized tests, and politically determined passing rates, is testimony to this nationwide commitment to establish clear goals for educators.

Overly Ambitious Education Goals.   A second problem of purpose concerns the scope of education goals. The charge can be made that public schools try to accomplish too much. This problem may be a byproduct, in fact, of ambiguity of purpose. Uncertain of what schools are supposed to accomplish, policy makers simply assign schools the task of dealing with every new issue that arises. Over the past half century, schools have been asked to address racism, drug and alcohol abuse, teenage pregnancy, AIDS education, gun safety, diversity, moral decline, changes in the family, poverty, and threats to the economy. Schools are regarded as the first line of defense against low self-esteem, infectious disease, and child abuse—as well as ignorance.

Educators must share some of the blame for overly ambitious education goals. In many cases they have been only too willing to tackle new problems, motivated by a natural impulse to serve young people and a pragmatic desire for additional resources and influence. Being needed can be extremely gratifying.

Taking on too many goals, of course, entails risks. The narrower the aperture, the sharper the focus. Critics claim that educators are less likely to provide sound academic preparation when they assume responsibility for nonacademic goals. Others counter that it is impossible to separate academic preparation from the general welfare of young people. Children cannot learn effectively if their stomachs are empty or they fear for their safety or they are bored. All work and no play make Johnny hate school.

An overabundance of goals also increases the likelihood of conflicting goals. In other words, it is possible for efforts to accomplish one education goal to cancel out or undermine efforts to accomplish another education goal. In recent years, for example, some schools serving large numbers of students from poor homes have sought to raise student self-esteem. To do so, educators have adopted lessons that allow virtually every student to succeed. Some schools have even eliminated failing grades. The price to be paid, according to critics, is lower expectations and less academic rigor, problems which come back to haunt some disadvantaged students as they progress through the education system.

Incompatible Goals.   Another impetus for educational change involves education goals that are at odds with contemporary society. Schools exist within political, legal, cultural, social, and economic contexts. From time to time education goals come under fire for being out of step with the expectations, norms, or requirements of one or more of these encompassing contexts. Such a situation arose in the wake of the Brown decision when the Supreme Court struck down the principle of separate but equal. School systems that continued to insist they could address the educational needs of black and white students separately found themselves in violation of the law. Three decades after the Brown decision, public schools were thrust into the front lines of the nation's economic defenses. Educators were told that they needed to raise academic standards for all students if the United States was to compete effectively in a global economy (Marshall and Tucker, 1992).

When education goals are incompatible with political, legal, cultural, social, and economic realities, pressure mounts for change. New goals often lead to new policies, practices, and programs. One of the most dramatic examples of such change occurred when the federal government mandated changes in the educational opportunities available to students with special needs. School systems were compelled to redefine the goals of special education and then to implement policies, practices, and programs to ensure that these goals would be accomplished (McLaughlin and Rouse, 2000).

Outdated Goals. Education goals are expected to reflect existing conditions. If student performance in science currently is less than desired, it is reasonable to expect an education goal calling for improved achievement in science. Circumstances change, however. National priorities shift. The economy ebbs and flows. The school-age population fluctuates. Popular culture refuses to stand still. As a result, educators and those who make education policy continually debate whether education goals should be based on current or anticipated conditions.

In some ways, it is more prudent to set goals in light of current conditions. After all, it is at least possible to define current conditions with reasonable accuracy. Predicting the future is risky. Still, educators are engaged in preparing young people for tomorrow, not today. Basing goals on today's conditions increases the likelihood that tomorrow will look a lot like today. This prospect may be fine for students blessed with advantages, but not acceptable for students grappling with poverty, discrimination, and disabilities. History bears tragic testimony to the foolishness of assuming that tomorrow will be exactly like today.

One area where debate regarding the appropriateness of goals has been especially heated is vocational education. Traditionally, vocational education has constituted a safety net for students who struggled with academic work. Training for entry-level jobs offered those who were unlikely to attend college a solid foundation for earning a livelihood. Critics, however, point out that the nature of work is changing. Manufacturing jobs increasingly are being performed by machines. The future of the workforce lies in information processing and services, both of which require more academic preparation (Bottoms, Presson, and Johnson, 1992). Should education goals be changed to reflect the need to integrate rigorous academic preparation and vocational training?

Although most explicit education goals may need to be modified or changed outright as time passes, one implicit goal is likely to persist. All schools and school systems strive to survive, to continue to operate. The survival of public schools in the past could largely be taken for granted. Times have changed, and competition, not only from nonpublic schools but from schools of choice within public school systems, is the order of the day. Survival is becoming a matter of performance.

Performance Problems

Fifty years ago it was difficult to determine what schools actually accomplished. If data concerning student achievement and other performance categories were collected, they not shared with the public. How much was spent on each student often served as an approximate indication of school quality. Today, thanks largely to the accountability movement, a wealth of school and student performance data are available. These data allow the performance of individual schools to be tracked over time and the performance of different schools to be compared at a given point in time.

To find evidence that performance problems are providing the impetus for educational change, we need look no further than the Chicago Public Schools, one of the nation's largest school systems.

CASE STUDY
"NOWHERE TO GO BUT UP" IN CHICAGO

In 1987, U.S. Secretary of Education William Bennett labeled Chicago's schools the "worst in America." The comment was not simply an unsupported attack on a school system that had just experienced the longest teacher strike in its history. Bennett was able to base his condemnation on published data from Illinois' school report card. The data indicated that half of Chicago's high schools ranked in the lowest 1 percent of all high schools in the country on the basis of results of the American College Test.

Data regarding the low performance of Chicago schools had been accumulating for years. A citizen's guide published in 1984 showed that many Chicago high schools lost 50 percent or more of their students before graduation. Schools with large numbers of minority students were particularly hard hit. When the dropout problem was studied in depth, substantial variation in dropout rates across city schools was discovered. Dropout rates for individual schools ranged from 11 percent to 63 percent. In summarizing the performance problems of Chicago Public Schools, G. Alfred Hess (1991, p. 22) concluded,

> Thus, by several different educational measures, the Chicago Public Schools were seen to be failing in their charge to educate our young people to be effective and well-rounded citizens of the city. Dropout rates were high. Reading achievement was low. The problems to be overcome were great, but the system was not focused on solving these problems. It provided avenues for its most ambitious users to escape the worst of its schools, but that only depressed achievement and expectations in the schools on the lowest rungs.

In the wake of these revelations, a number of initiatives were implemented to restructure the organization, governance, and finances of Chicago Public Schools. The culmination of these efforts was the Chicago School Reform Act of 1988. The bill called for the decentralization

(continued)

CONTINUED

of the school system. Every school was to have a School Council with authority to hire principals, allocate resources, and undertake school improvement. Raising student performance was linked to greater involvement in school decision making by parents and teachers. In the event that local improvement efforts failed, the bill authorized sanctions that included state takeover of underachieving schools.

Much of the information for this case study was taken from G. Alfred Hess, *School Restructuring, Chicago Style*. Newbury Park, CA: Corwin Press, 1991.

The rational model of schools as organizations assumes that performance is guided by organization goals. Performance problems consequently are indicated by discrepancies between performance goals and actual performance. Until the advent of the accountability movement, schools and school systems rarely set goals in which actual performance targets were specified. Now such targets are expected and even mandated in certain jurisdictions.

Performance targets come in various forms. Some are based on student achievement on standardized tests. Targets or goals can involve raising the mean (average) test score, the percentage of all students passing a test, or the percentage of certain types of students passing a test. School systems with large numbers of poor and minority students may set targets that involve narrowing the gap in test performance between groups of students and reducing the percentage of failing scores.

CASE STUDY

A SCHOOL SYSTEM DRIVEN BY PERFORMANCE

When John Murphy became superintendent of North Carolina's Charlotte-Mecklenburg Schools, he inherited a set of performance problems that included relatively low scores on standardized tests and great disparities between the achievement of white and black students. To address these and other issues, he developed a strategic plan with a number of performance goals. These goals included the following:

- Increase the number of students who demonstrate competency over challenging subject matter in the five core areas of math, English, science, history, and geography as measured by the new criterion-referenced tests and a host of authentic assessments.
- Increase the percent of students who score in the top quartiles of national assessments in science, history, and geography.
- Increase the number of students who score at the top of the chart on national assessments in reading and math.

- Increase the number of students who score above the national average on SATs, ACTs, and international comparisons.
- Increase the number of students who are competent in a second language.
- Increase the number of students who take a rigorous college preparatory course of study, including algebra and geometry.
- Increase the number of students who are successful in securing high-skill jobs upon graduation after completing the apprenticeship program.
- Increase the number of poor and minority children who go to college.
- Increase the number of students who perform well in the first year of college.
- Increase the number of parents and employers who register satisfaction with the schools.
- Decrease the dropout rate.
- Decrease the gap in high school graduation rates between black and white students.
- Decrease suspension and expulsion rates.
- Decrease gap between black and white achievement rates on state, national, and international assessments.

In order to achieve these goals, Murphy implemented an ambitious change initiative that included bonuses for schools that made significant progress and sanctions for schools that did not. "Fluff courses" were eliminated, and counselors were directed to encourage students to enroll in higher level classes. Principals were expected to function as instructional leaders, monitoring student performance and discouraging "social promotions." Murphy's strategic plan also placed great emphasis on early childhood education and high levels of parental involvement in the education of their children.

Material for this case study was taken from John A. Murphy, "The Charlotte Process: An Executive Summary." Published by Charlotte-Mecklenburg Schools. Undated.

Besides performance on standardized tests, academic achievement targets may be based on grade-point averages, credit accumulation, percentages of students enrolled in particular academic courses (such as Algebra I) or academic tracks, and graduation rates. In some high-achieving schools, judgments about performance can involve the particular colleges to which students are admitted, the number and size of scholarships, and performance on Advanced Placement tests. The case study of Charlotte-Mecklenburg's strategic plan provides a good example of a diverse set of performance targets.

Performance problems are not limited to academic achievement. Schools routinely collect data on attendance, suspensions, expulsions, and serious crimes on campus. Since parents and policy makers often are very concerned about these matters, it is not unusual to find schools setting goals for improved attendance and reduced discipline problems. Some communities place such a high value on extracurricular activities that school goals may involve the level of student participation and even the success of athletic teams, music groups, and school publications.

While the determination that a particular school has performance problems may be based on comparisons with other schools, the safest comparisons are usually those that involve the past and present performance of the same school. With increased access to performance data on other schools, however, it is tempting to compare one school's performance with another's. Such between-school comparisons, however, can be misleading, since it is rarely the case that different schools are identical in terms of size, faculty training and experience, student background and socioeconomic status, resources, and quality of leadership. Because schools do not always exercise control over these variables, spotlighting performance differences between schools also can be unfair.

Despite the previous point, the fact remains that performance differences across schools exist for certain reasons. Some of these reasons can be addressed by educational change. One area where improvement is perennially desired is professional practice.

Problems of Professional Practice

The work of educating young people is carried on primarily by well-educated professionals applying their knowledge and skills in organized settings. A relationship is assumed to exist between what educators do and what students achieve. Were professional practice and student performance not linked, in fact, there would be little reason, other than a custodial one, to have schools. When performance problems are detected, it is therefore reasonable to look for related problems of professional practice.

This perspective reflects what some analysts refer to as the rational model of school organization. Wise (1983, p. 104) captures the essence of the rational model in the following statement:

> That model postulates that schools operate by setting goals, implementing programs to achieve these goals, and evaluating the extent to which the goals are attained. . . . Policies emanating from a belief in the rational model are designed to improve the operation of the goal-oriented process. Schemes which promise to increase accountability, efficiency, and effectiveness are imposed on the existing bureaucratic structure of the school in the anticipation that they will improve the school.

The preceding quote suggests that there are three types of problems related to professional practice—lack of accountability, ineffectiveness, and inefficiency. To this list should be added one additional problem—unethical conduct.

Accountability is a complex idea. It has various meanings. A teacher may lack accountability because of failure to follow the dictates of "best practice," noncompliance with school district policies, or failure to "give an accounting" of what was done to assist struggling students. Teachers are expected to assess student performance on a regular basis, provide feedback to students concerning how well they are learning required material, and assist students in overcoming learning difficulties. It may be unreasonable to expect teachers to guarantee that all students learn everything they are expected to learn, but they surely must do more than simply "cover" subject matter.

Ineffectiveness typically refers to failure to achieve designated performance goals. Determining that the cause of ineffectiveness is inadequate professional practice can be a relatively complex process. Judgments first must be made regarding whether students have made a genuine effort to learn what they were expected to learn and whether they actually were present for instruction. Assuming inadequate performance is not due to student-initiated problems, a judgment must be made concerning the appropriate focus of concern. Were performance goals not achieved because *particular* teachers failed to demonstrate good practice or is the problem faculty-wide in nature? It is one thing to discover that a few teachers have trouble keeping students on task and quite another to realize that an entire faculty lacks expertise in certain instructional essentials.

Another source of complexity involves the sheer range of knowledge and skills that fit under the rubric of professional practice. Effective teachers must demonstrate mastery of their subject, the willingness to work closely with colleagues, an understanding of how students learn, and skill in lesson planning, classroom management, assessment, diagnosis of learning problems, instructional delivery, and providing feedback. Pinpointing which particular aspects of professional practice may be responsible for performance problems is no easy task.

Another problem related to professional practice is inefficiency. Unlike ineffectiveness, inefficiency takes into account the cost of trying to accomplish performance goals. A teacher can be effective in achieving a goal, but also inefficient if the cost in terms of time and resources is so great that the achievement of other worthwhile goals is jeopardized. Schools do not exist in a world of unlimited resources. Choices must constantly be made regarding how best to use scarce resources. Reducing class size, for example, is inefficient if teachers continue to teach fifteen students the same way they taught twenty-five students, thereby failing to take advantage of smaller classes to provide more individual assistance.

Unethical practice may not always interfere with the achievement of performance goals, but it can pose serious problems for educators nonetheless. Educators depend on the support of those they serve. They risk losing that support when they mistreat students, take advantage of their position for personal gain, and fail to report problems of which they are aware. In recent years, pressure for improved student performance on standardized tests has led a few teachers and administrators to teach the test questions and even doctor test results. Because teachers' most important lessons often involve being role models for young people, when teachers behave unethically, the damage done to students can last a lifetime.

Four Basic Options

When it comes to characterizing the need for educational change, educators and policy makers must examine the nature of the problems they have identified, their understanding of how to address the problems, the resources available to them, and the prevailing political climate. As a result of such analysis, the need for change may be labeled in one of four ways: (1) need for restoration, (2) need for accommodation, (3) need for improvement, or (4) need for transformation.

Determining that a need for *restoration* exists presumes that drift from a desirable level of success has taken place. Individuals may have lost sight of important goals and values, or slippage in the quality of practice and performance may have occurred. Whatever the particular problem, restoration calls for a return to a previous level of success or state of operations. Change, under such circumstances, constitutes movement back to something that once existed, or at least was perceived to exist.

Deciding that *accommodation* is the appropriate response to problems involves the realization that existing expectations must be moderated. In other words, the nature of the problems is such that the achievement of current goals is highly unlikely. The focus of educational change, under such circumstances, is to minimize the negative impact of problems on performance.

A need for accommodation can result from a tax limitation measure such as California's Proposition 13. School systems suddenly find themselves facing budget cuts of 10 percent or more. Forced to reduce staff, eliminate programs, and defer the purchase of materials, district officials realize that current performance targets cannot be met. They propose a series of changes that they hope will limit the damage to core programs. By accommodating budget reductions in the short run, they hope eventually to refocus on accomplishing the full complement of school district goals.

A need for *improvement* is premised on the existence of a gap between goals and performance. Conditions are not so dire as in the case of accommodation. Resources are available to support educational change aimed at raising performance sufficiently to achieve existing goals. Improvement efforts frequently involve additional expenditures for staff development, new programs and materials, technology, and facility renovations. Unlike the need for restoration, improvement presumes that goals—or a desired state of operations—have not yet been achieved.

A need for *transformation* finds educators and policy makers questioning existing goals and, indeed, the entire structure of the educational system. More than improvement is needed. Transformational change often is justified in terms of dramatically changing conditions outside of education—new labor market demands, alienated segments of the population, shifts in the family structure, and the like.

Educational changes that respond to the needs for restoration, accommodation, improvement, and transformation are discussed in Chapter 4. The remainder of the present chapter looks at the initial steps in building an agenda for educational change.

IDENTIFYING A NEED FOR CHANGE

The first part of this chapter explored some of the issues involved in the Discovery Phase of educational change. The focus was on understanding the complexity of determining that change is needed. Complexity is not an acceptable excuse for inaction, however. Educators must be prepared to proceed with the change process despite their uncertainties. Approaching the initial phase of the change process in a systematic manner can help to alleviate many doubts and misgivings.

Five steps may be involved in the identification of a need for educational change. The first step often involves taking a careful look at the current situation. Rushing headlong into change without surveying the status quo can ensure disappointment and frustration. Armed with knowledge of what *is,* educators then must consider what *should be.* What should be may be incorporated in formal documents, such as mission statements and long-range plans, or implied in vague understandings and shared expectations. A third step, one that is not always taken but perhaps should be, involves considering what *could be.* It is not always sufficient to examine discrepancies between educational goals and actual performance. Great value can result from a serious examination of new possibilities. Based on these three initial steps, a determination must be made regarding whether or not change is needed. If change is deemed necessary, an explanation of why it is needed then must be developed. Justifying change is usually the final step in the Discovery Phase of educational change.

FIVE STEPS IN IDENTIFYING A NEED FOR EDUCATIONAL CHANGE

1. Carefully examine the current situation.
2. Review educational goals and expectations.
3. Consider new possibilities.
4. In light of the first three steps, determine if a need for educational change exists.
5. Develop a convincing and credible explanation of why change is needed.

Examining the Current Situation

Educators are prompted to examine the current situation for many reasons. A crisis demands taking a hard look at existing practices. A new policy or law must be implemented, and school officials are uncertain how it will affect operations. A computer company offers to donate a thousand new computers to a high school, and educators are unsure of how they should be used. A special interest group raises questions in the media about the performance of certain students. Impetuses such as these descend on educators from the outside and often without warning.

In other cases, examining the current situation occurs as part of organizational rituals and routines. An upcoming accreditation visit. An annual goal-setting process. The preparation of a School Improvement Plan required by the superintendent. When responding to outside impetuses, educators often examine the current situation for the purpose of *verification*—to ascertain whether a crisis actually exists or if the claims of a special interest group are valid. In the case of examinations prompted by organizational rituals and routines, the purpose is likely to be *troubleshooting*—the early detection of problems that may prevent the accomplishment of educational goals or diminish the effectiveness and efficiency of professional practice.

Whatever the reason, an examination of the current situation involves a variety of decisions. What are the parameters of "the current situation"? What sources of data should be tapped? Over what period of time should data be collected? Who should be involved in collecting data? Who should have access to the results of data collection and analysis?

Consider the first question—What are the parameters of the current situation? If we are examining a school where discipline problems have risen to levels that parents regard as a crisis, should the investigation be limited to what goes on in school, or should it include the local community as well? Does *current* refer to the point in time when the examination is conducted, or should data from the previous school year be included? If the precipitating concern is school discipline, should the inquiry be limited to student behavior problems, or should it include academic achievement? Answering questions such as these requires that everyone involved in the examination articulate their assumptions regarding the etiology and nature of discipline problems. Do they assume, for instance, that school discipline problems are related to how well students are doing in their school work and to what is happening in the community? If so, the parameters of their examination will be relatively broad.

Most of the educational activity discussed in this book takes place in organizational settings. In looking closely at any organization, Beckhard (1969, p. 26) recommends placing subsystems and organizational processes under the microscope:

> The development of a strategy for systematic improvement of an organization demands an examination of the present state of things. Such an analysis usually looks at two broad areas. One is a diagnosis of the various *subsystems* that make up the total organization system. These subsystems may be natural "teams" . . . or they may be levels such as top management, middle management, or the work force.
>
> The second area of diagnosis is the organization *processes* that are occurring. These include decision-making processes, communications patterns and styles, relationships between interfacing groups, the management of conflict, the setting of goals, and planning methods.

Once the parameters of the current situation have been agreed upon, it is necessary to consider what *sources* of data should be tapped. In this regard, it is important to bear in mind that the data eventually will be used to decide whether a need for change exists and to speculate on the reasons change is needed. Student performance data, such as test scores, can reveal a disparity between the achievement of different groups of students, but not point to the reasons *why* the disparity exists. Actual observations of classrooms, however, can address this concern by indicating how different groups of students use their time in class and how teachers interact with them. Data of this kind can be useful in developing an argument for change as well as designing a strategy to reduce the disparity.

When it comes to examining the current situation, the best advice is to rely on multiple sources of data. Some data already will be available. As a matter of routine, for example, most schools compile data on student grades, performance on standardized tests, credit accumulation, disciplinary referrals, and the like. Other sources of data include surveys and questionnaires, interviews, focus groups, case studies, and observations. Depending on the circumstances, individuals involved in collecting data on the current situation may want to consider the ideas noted in Figure 3.1.

FIGURE 3.1   Data Gathering Tips

1. Ask administrators and guidance counselors to keep track of questions that are frequently asked by students and parents. These questions can reveal important areas of concern.
2. Create a Student Cabinet or advisory group that meets regularly with the principal or a trusted staff member. Such a group is a source of ongoing information as well as a sounding board for interpretations of data.
3. Conduct exit interviews with students who graduate or drop out in order to learn about their experiences in school, school strengths and weaknesses, etc.
4. Review several years' teacher evaluations. In the aggregate, do the evaluations reveal similar concerns? Can shifts in areas of concern be detected over time?
5. Create a case review committee to examine, on a regular basis, randomly selected records of students with low grades. An effort should be made to determine what efforts have and have not been made to help these struggling students.
6. Conduct error analyses of tests to determine whether there are patterns to the mistakes made by students. These patterns may reveal areas where teaching is relatively weak.
7. Ask someone other than the teacher to debrief several students after they have completed a lesson or a unit. Determine what the students recall by asking them, "What did you learn in this lesson or unit?"
8. Conduct a postgraduation follow-up to determine how well former students feel they were prepared.
9. Gather data from employers who have hired recent graduates. Focus on how well students were prepared to carry out their responsibilities.
10. Ask teachers of different subjects to identify topics with which students tend to struggle the most. Find out what teachers have done to address these difficulties.

Gathering data in various ways from a variety of sources increases the likelihood that the complexity of the current situation will be captured accurately. It is important not only to describe *what is* as objectively and completely as possible, but also to understand how people perceive and make sense of *what is*. If teachers, administrators, counselors, students, and parents perceive the current situation differently, it may be one indication of problems that need to be addressed.

Change Key

In order to examine the current situation, it is important to rely on multiple sources of data and various means of collecting data.

Another piece of advice is to remember that at any given time educators in most schools already are dealing with a number of changes. Hardly a year goes by without new state mandates, new board policies, and new school initiatives. Such is the nature of contemporary education that standing still is rarely an option. Consequently, any examination of the current situation in a school or school system should include an inventory of change initiatives already in the process of being implemented. What advocates of change interpret as teacher resistance to new ideas and practices often is just the opposite. Teachers' willingness to entertain change is so great that occasionally new guests must be turned away. The capacity of individuals and groups to respond to petitions for reform is not limitless. Under certain circumstances, in fact, the change that educators may need the most is less change!

Change Key

An inventory of existing change initiatives should be a part of any effort to examine the status quo of a school or school system.

Although educators may be unable to respond to every need for change as it is discovered, they should not shrink from the obligation to carefully monitor what is going on in schools and classrooms. Ideally this monitoring would occur on a continuous basis, thereby increasing the likelihood that problems can be addressed before they mushroom into major difficulties. Burying one's head in the business of day-to-day activities should not become an excuse for ignoring the need for change. Lightfoot (1983, p. 309) captured the importance of being constantly aware of the existing situation when she characterized "good" schools:

> The search for "good" schools is elusive and disappointing if by goodness we mean something close to perfection. These portraits of good schools [in her book *The Good High School*] reveal imperfections, uncertainties, and vulnerabilities in each of them. In fact, one could argue that a consciousness about imperfections, and the willingness to address them and search for their origins and solutions is one of the important ingredients of goodness in schools.

Reviewing Goals and Expectations

Taking stock of current conditions may reveal problems that are so blatant and serious that no further analysis is required to determine that change is necessary. Educators need not review goals and expectations to know that complaints about high school students who are unable to read must be addressed. In other cases, however, data that have been collected on the current situation in a school or school system will have to be considered in light of educational goals and expectations before a decision can be made to initiate the change process. Such consideration is necessary because educators operate in a world of limited resources. There simply is not enough time, expertise, or money available to attend to every condition judged by someone to be problematic.

Reviewing goals and expectations constitutes a "status check" in its own right because espoused intentions do not always represent actual intentions. In some cases, formal goals no longer reflect what people regard as important. Organization theorists call this circumstance *goal displacement*. In other cases, goals are out of step with emerging conditions and need to be updated. *One of the first considerations in addressing the need for change should be whether or not goals and expectations need adjustment.*

Once educators are able to agree on a set of intentions, it can be used in two important ways. First, intentions can be compared with current performance in order to identify gaps. These gaps then serve as the basis for articulating various needs for change. Second, when a number of needs for change have been identified, the set of intentions may provide a useful basis for prioritization. The following case study offers an example of the value of school system goals in focusing on a particular need for change.

■ ■ ■ ■ ■ ▬▬▬▬▬▬▬▬▬▬▬▬▬▬▬▬▬▬▬▬▬▬▬▬▬▬▬▬▬▬▬▬

CASE STUDY

IS ENOUGH HELP AVAILABLE IN MIDDLE SCHOOLS?

A suburban school system invited me to conduct a comprehensive status check of its middle schools. Board members had received complaints from parents that some middle school students' needs were not being addressed as well as they should be. Assisted by a team of research assistants, I developed a study that looked at virtually every aspect of middle school education. Middle school principals were shadowed for a day. Focus groups were conducted with teachers, parents, and students. Teachers were observed introducing new lessons in grades six, seven, and eight. Case studies were conducted, with the assistance of guidance counselors, of students who had received a low grade at the end of the first semester.

After three months of data collection, a huge amount of data had been compiled. Analysis of the data revealed a variety of strengths and concerns. Among the concerns were the following:

- Principals held different views of what constituted good teaching.
- Middle schools offered various supplementary programs, but not all of them were effective.
- Only English teachers felt it was their responsibility to teach reading.
- Efforts to promote differentiated instruction had been only marginally successful.
- Many students who had been identified as gifted received little supplementary instruction.
- Students frequently felt that their concerns were not taken seriously by teachers and administrators.
- Students had few "breaks" during the school day.
- Middle schools offered few extracurricular activities.
- Struggling students who were not on an IEP often received little in the way of systematic assistance.
- Teachers used relatively few instructional interventions to help struggling students.

This list of concerns constituted an ambitious set of needs for change. Given a tight budget, the school district lacked the resources to address all of them. To determine how best to proceed, principals reviewed their annual school improvement plans. Every middle school's plan included a high-priority goal related to assisting students who fell through the

(continued)

CONTINUED

cracks. These were students who were struggling in one or more subjects, but who failed to qualify for special education services. Data from the middle school study indicated that a substantial number of these students were not receiving any customized academic interventions. Principals decided that a change was needed that would ensure teachers developed, implemented, and monitored assistance plans for all struggling students, not just those who qualified for special education.

Considering Unexplored Possibilities

If problems tend to be the ore mined when examining the current situation, then possibilities are the reward for digging into the future. When educators concentrate on identifying and eliminating problems, they rarely ask about what *could be*. In recent years, thinking about what could be has been referred to as *visioning*. In writing about the value of vision in the corporate world, Kotter (1996, pp. 68–69) observes,

> *Vision* refers to a picture of the future with some implicit or explicit commentary on why people should strive to create that future. In a change process, a good vision serves three important purposes. First, by clarifying the general direction for change . . . it simplifies hundreds or thousands of more detailed decisions. Second, it motivates people to take action in the right direction. . . . Third, it helps coordinate the actions of different people.

Imagine a group of educators being asked to plan a new school. They could proceed, of course, by simply copying an existing school. More likely, however, they would think about the shortcomings of existing schools and how these shortcomings might be eliminated in the new school. Planning in this way is certainly understandable, but the ultimate result, at best, will be a new school without the shortcomings of existing schools. A third strategy would be to consider what a school could be if planning were not tethered to the status quo.

An educational vision usually is slow to materialize during the change process. It may be triggered by many things—deeply held values, an ideological or faith-based commitment, a theory of learning, an image of what society can be, and so on. These triggers get people thinking about possibilities, which in turn leads to a merging of the Discovery and Design Phases. The new design or vision *becomes* the need for change, rather than a way to address the need for change. The next chapter is devoted to the design process. Suffice it to say for now that design calls for challenging sacred assumptions about educational purposes and practices. While examining the existing situation reveals a need for restoration, accommodation, or improvement, considering what could be often yields a need for transformation.

Skeptics question the value of vision. They maintain that locking one's sights on the horizon simply increases the likelihood of tripping over the next rock in the road. Attending too closely to what could be has the potential, of course, of leading people to overlook important and immediate problems that need to be addressed. Peterson (1986) has pointed out, however, that vision and "problem-finding" need not be mutually exclusive. In fact, based on his study of four principals, he noted that vision actually can enhance the identification of important problems (p. 94):

> Problem-finding will be influenced by the degree to which the manager has a clear and strongly-held idea of where the organization ought to go and what the strategic factors are in moving the organization forward. In contrast, principals whose vision is not clear and crystallized are more likely to engage in problemistic search, in firefighting rather than problem-finding and problem-solving.

Determining If a Need for Change Exists

Of all the decisions to be made during the Discovery Phase of the change process, the determination of whether or not change is needed is the most important. To reach this decision, educators should reflect on what has been learned from examining the current situation, reviewing educational goals and expectations, and considering future possibilities. Change may be called for if one or more of the following conditions is found to exist.

CONDITIONS THAT MAY CONSTITUTE A NEED FOR CHANGE

- Current educational goals are not being achieved.
- Reasonable progress toward achieving current educational goals is not being made.
- One or more stakeholder groups is dissatisfied with educational outcomes.
- Educational benefits are not being shared by all groups of students.
- Educational practices are not in compliance with policies or laws.
- Educational practices have been found to be harmful to certain groups of students.
- Conditions external to schools have changed sufficiently to warrant changes in educational goals and practices.
- New research and technology offer better ways to teach and learn.
- A change takes place in the resources available for education.

Deciding that educational change is needed may be the most important decision of the Discovery Phase, but it is not necessarily the most difficult. On occasion, educators may discover a number of reasons change is needed. Problems, after all, tend to run in packs. So, too, with possibilities. At a given point in time, however, it may be impossible to address all needs for change. How, then, should educators proceed?

CHALLENGE OF CHANGE

Competing Needs

Read any book on organizational effectiveness and we are likely to encounter a ringing endorsement for focus. Try to tackle too many problems or possibilities simultaneously, and the likelihood of success declines. Despite such advice, problems and possibilities, once recognized, are difficult to put aside. Evans (1996, p. 76) concludes that,

> the question is not just whether a specific problem or a specific improvement is important but also how important it is in comparison with others. However, prioritizing is difficult, for people are reluctant to neglect any goals, no matter how unrealistic it is to address them all. In fact, most schools seem unable to concentrate their energies, or else they are not allowed to.

There is no mystery why choosing to focus on certain needs for change and not others is a challenge. Schools are not immune from politics. Every problem and every possibility is likely to have supporters and opponents. Decide to focus on improving the remedial reading program instead of providing more opportunities for gifted students, and a group of parents of gifted students is likely to descend on the superintendent demanding attention to the needs of their children. Behind every commitment to address a need for change, or set it aside, is the first question of politics—Who benefits?

No formula exists to help educators choose among competing needs for change. Each decision must take into account local context, available resources, and potential sources of opposition and resistance. There are, in addition, several considerations that should be weighed when making a decision.

Success Breeds Success.   Although pressure may be felt to tackle the most difficult problem or the most serious need for change first, to do so can increase the probability of failure and thereby jeopardize subsequent change initiatives. Consequently, it may be prudent first to address a need for change with a reasonable prospect of success. The old adage that nothing succeeds like success has some validity. Demonstrating an ability to resolve a midlevel problem may provide just the confidence boost needed for educators next to confront a daunting problem.

Current or Anticipated Needs?   During the Discovery Phase of the change process, educators may identify both current needs and anticipated future needs. Because anticipated needs are based on assumptions about the future that may or may not be valid, current needs almost always win out. Ignoring needs that are likely to develop in the future has been shown, however, to be unwise educationally, economically, and politically. If educators are unable to address both current and anticipated needs simultaneously, they must at least consider creating a long-range plan with provisions for eventually dealing with anticipated needs.

Symptoms and Root Causes.   Among a set of identified needs for change, certain needs may be more important than other needs. The most important needs often are those which affect other needs. Addressing these *prerequisite needs* ultimately can lead to improvements in other areas of need. Low student achievement on word problems in mathematics, for example, may be related to reading comprehension problems. In other words, low achievement in mathematics could be a *symptom* of a more fundamental problem involving reading ability. Given limited resources, it may make sense first to address the *root cause*—reading comprehension—before tackling improvements in mathematics instruction. The ultimate failure of many change initiatives in education can be traced to a focus on symptoms rather than root causes of problems.

Deferring a Final Decision.   Although it is important to think about competing needs for change during the Discovery Phase, a final decision regarding which needs can and cannot be addressed may have to wait until the Design or Development Phase. Only when choices have been made regarding the nature of the changes to be made and the plans for implementing these changes may it be possible to determine which needs for change can and cannot be accommodated. Without a design and a plan, educators cannot generate a budget and a timeline for change. Both of these elements of the change process have a direct bearing on how much change can be undertaken.

Explaining Why Change Is Needed

Deciding that a need for change exists does not complete the work of the Discovery Phase. An identified need for change is not a need for change justified. Justification requires explaining *why* the need for change exists. As Deborah Stone (1989) has shown, competing explanations often characterize the initial phase of the change process. Competing explanations, or *causal stories* as she calls them, constitute a source of debate and contention. Those who succeed in having their causal story accepted often control subsequent decisions regarding what and how to change.

Let us consider an editorial written by George F. Will (2002), a well-known conservative columnist. Entitled "Broken Families and School Performance," the editorial used the occasion of President George W. Bush's victory on the No Child Left Behind Act to remind readers of the real causes of low student achievement. Citing work by Paul Barton, Will noted that variations in test performance largely could be explained by five factors: "number of days absent from school, number of hours spent watching television, number of pages read for homework, quantity and quality of reading material in the home and the presence of two parents in the home." Conspicuously absent in this causal story for poor performance were inadequate resources, insufficient educational research, and substandard teacher training. Accounting for student achievement problems in terms of deficiencies in families allowed Will to advance his case for greater emphasis on "family values" and to avoid the suggestion that education needs more money and government intervention.

Over the past century, the need for educational change has been explained in terms of a rich array of causal stories. Among the "causes" of inadequate academic performance, for example, have been the adolescent peer group, uninvolved parents, outdated and "dumbed down" curriculum, teachers who do not believe that all students are capable of learning, and antiquated teacher preparation programs. Several decades ago, I detected a trend in explanations for educational problems, which I termed the *depersonalization of blame* (Duke, 1978). Causes of educational problems, my argument went, had moved inexorably away from individual students who simply failed to apply themselves to a host of culprits, including dysfunctional families, negative peer group norms, poorly prepared teachers, schools designed for mediocrity, and confusing messages from mass media and popular culture.

Lee (2001, p. 3) sees a somewhat different shift in causal stories, from morality to the economy:

> Calls for school reform are usually issued in response to some problem. For much of our history, a pervasive moral decline has been invoked as a reason that schools should be changed. Although this "problem" has not left the lexicon of public discussions about education, in the last two decades the language surrounding the need for reforming schools has shifted. Currently, the rationale for reform—the problem to be fixed—is defined more often in economic than in moral terms.

Marshall and Tucker (1992) agree that economic changes account for much educational change. They argue that the United States fell victim to its own economic success. Convinced that economic dominance was evidence of the best system in the world, the United States had little incentive to change. In the eighties, however, the United States woke up to find Japan, Germany, and other countries challenging its preeminent position. A commitment to continuous improvement—educationally as well as economically—was seen as the only antidote to pernicious complacency.

How much educators have contributed to their own problems has been a matter of great and contentious debate. E. D. Hirsch (1996, p. 2) spared teachers while indicting faulty educational theories:

> When businesspeople, philanthropists, and parents turn to experts for guidance, they continue to hear the high-sounding, antiknowledge advice that has been offered for more than sixty years—the very prescriptions . . . that have produced the system's failures. These continually reformulated slogans have led to the total absence of a coherent, knowledge-based curriculum, but are nonetheless presented as novel theories based on the latest research and as remedies for the diseases they themselves have caused.

Others have noted that the past accomplishments of public schools are no guarantee of future success. Yesterday's performance is not necessarily sufficient to meet tomorrow's challenges. The following excerpt from *Thinking for a Living* (Marshall and Tucker, 1992, p. 79), a book that the Clinton administration found persuasive, is illustrative of this position:

> On balance, the performance of the [education] system had not deteriorated in anything like the measure that reformers claimed; in fact, it had changed little over the decades. But that was in fact the problem. The requirements the world was placing on school graduates were dramatically higher, but performance had stayed the same.

What is important to bear in mind, for present purposes, is not the validity of particular explanations for the need for educational change, but the fact that a key element of the Discovery Phase involves agreeing on a rationale for change. This rationale, by indicating what caused the need for change in the first place, points to the specific changes required to address the issues at hand. In other words, the rationale for change becomes a useful starting place for the Design Phase of the educational change process.

Rationales for change often derive from a "backward mapping" process. Individuals begin with an identified need for change and then work backward, trying to account for why and how the need developed. The backward mapping process initially may reveal symptoms of problems, rather than root causes. Persistence eventually can lead to the origins of problems; although educators are not always in a position to correct them. Educators, for example, may be unable to eliminate homelessness, but they can address the low academic performance of homeless children by providing them with a safe and supportive environment in which to do homework after school.

Creating a rationale for educational change can be a highly political process. It is not always prudent, for instance, to explain a need for change in terms of the failure of those who are expected to implement change. Accounting for inadequate student achievement in terms of teacher incompetence risks alienating the very individuals who will be asked to raise student achievement. It may be safer to lay the blame at the doorstep of teacher educators or policy makers who refuse to raise teacher salaries. One of the most difficult decisions to be made during the entire change process concerns whether or not to base a rationale on an open and honest sharing of the "real" reasons why change is needed. While politically understandable, efforts to launder explanations so as not to upset key stakeholders may deflect attention away from important areas in desperate need of change.

CONCLUSION

There is no substitute for a compelling need for change. Innovative designs and detailed plans cannot compensate for a need for change that people regard with skepticism. The failure of Littleton's restructuring initiative, described in the Introduction, can be explained in terms of the absence of a compelling need. Littleton High School already was remarkably successful. Many parents questioned why sweeping change was required when student achievement and graduation rates already were impressive. Littleton educators failed to make a convincing argument that tomorrow's workforce would require knowledge and skills that today's high school was not addressing.

In taking a close look at the Discovery Phase of the educational change process, Chapter 3 has identified various decisions involved in determining whether a compelling need for change exists. Initial decisions concern whether or not to take a close look at the current situation and, if so, how to conduct such an inquiry. Subsequent decisions involve determining when a *condition* constitutes a *problem* and how best to characterize the problem. A need for change, it was noted, may emerge from an exploration of possibilities as well as an examination of problems. Deciding when to consider what *could be* as well as what *should be* constitutes another Discovery Phase decision. When multiple needs for change are identified, choices may have to be made regarding which needs can and should be addressed first. Finally, a rationale for educational change must be created. When efforts to improve schools run into difficulties, they often can be traced to inadequate decisions during the Discovery Phase.

■ ■ ■ ■ ■

APPLYING WHAT YOU KNOW
DO THE DATA DICTATE A NEED FOR CHANGE?

School districts increasingly are data driven. In other words, decisions regarding what and when to change must be based on actual data rather than speculation and curiosity. The types of data that may be consulted include student achievement data, surveys, and needs assessments. This exercise involves a suburban school system of 14,000 students. In response to school board concerns regarding the quality of the educational program for middle school students, the superintendent initiated a review process that called for the collection of various kinds of data. When all the data had been collected, the Middle School Steering Committee, consisting of middle school administrators, teachers, and parents, was asked to review the data and determine whether the school district needed to change any policies, programs, or practices related to the operation of the district's five middle schools.

Imagine that you are a member of the Middle School Steering Committee. Consider the data presented below. As you review each table, determine whether there are indications that changes may be needed in any or all of the middle schools.

The first source of data is student grades in mathematics, language arts, science, and social studies for the previous school year. Table A contains the percentages of students at each middle school who received Ds or Fs for the year. These percentages have been relatively stable for the last three years.

TABLE A   Students with Ds and Fs at the End of the School Year

MIDDLE SCHOOL	Math D (%)	Math F (%)	Language Arts D (%)	Language Arts F (%)	Science D (%)	Science F (%)	Social Studies D (%)	Social Studies F (%)	TOTAL ENROLLMENT
1	4	6	7	5	4	2	5	4	435
2	8	4	5	3	8	5	7	5	600
3	8	3	10	5	10	7	7	6	503
4	7	4	7	6	9	4	7	5	629
5	8	4	9	3	10	6	4	3	610

Another source of data was interviews with middle school administrators, teachers, students, and parents. Consultants were hired to conduct the interviews, and they chose individuals representing different grade levels, subject matter areas, and ability groups. The results of the interviews are presented in Tables B and C. Table B indicates the strengths of each middle school as perceived by each group—administrators, teachers, students, and parents. Table C presents these groups' perceptions of problems and areas of concern.

TABLE B   Perceived Strengths of Middle School
(A = Administrators; P = Parents; S = Students; T = Teachers)

	MIDDLE SCHOOL				
STRENGTH	1	2	3	4	5
Development of programs for students requiring academic help	AT	AT		AT	AT
Development of programs for gifted students	PT	T			
Improved test scores on state tests			AT	A	AT
Guidance program	T	T		P	T
Exploratory courses				PS	
Club/athletic opportunities			AT		
Continuum of special ed. services			T		T
School leadership		P		PS	P
Teamwork/teaming	A		P	T	
Positive school climate	AP		T		
Students feel safe at school	P	P	ATS	ST	
School has high academic standards/expectations		P	A	P	
Communication between school and home		P	P	P	
Teacher instruction in . . .					
General topics				P	
Language arts	PS	P	S		
Mathematics	P	P			
Science	PS	P		S	
Social studies	P	P			
Physical education	P	P	AT		S
Practical arts		P			
Gifted education	P				

The last source of data involved observations of teaching. Trained observers visited classrooms in each middle school and observed teachers introducing a new lesson in sixth grade science, seventh grade standard (low-level) mathematics, and eighth grade advanced language arts. Using a set of research-based indicators of effective teaching, they rated each teacher on ten items. Table D summarizes the results by grade level, but not by individual middle school.

After reviewing the four tables, you may want to address some of the following questions related to the Discovery Phase of the change process:

1. Based on Tables A, B, and C, are particular middle schools facing problems that are not present in other middle schools?
2. How would you characterize or label any problems that you found in the data? Do your labels correspond to any of those found in the chapter?
3. In considering all four tables, can you identify any problems that need to be addressed in all five middle schools? How would you characterize or label these problems?

(continued)

CONTINUED

TABLE C   Perceived Problems and Areas of Concern
(A = Administrators; P = Parents; S = Students; T = Teachers)

PROBLEM/CONCERN	MIDDLE SCHOOL				
	1	2	3	4	5
Staffing Concerns					
Lack of adequate staffing		AT	P	T	
Concerns about . . .					
Foreign language instruction	P				P
Art instruction	AP	P			
Technology program	PS				P
Science instruction	S	S			S
Need for more differentiation of instruction		A	AT		
Boring teachers; lessons that are not enjoyable	S	S	S	S	ATS
Some teachers don't explain things well	S		S	S	
Additional help is needed for poor readers		AT			
Poor teachers are allowed to remain in the classroom	S		P		S
Safety and Discipline Concerns					
Bullying	T	P		S	
Attendance problems			AT		
Small number of students cause most of the major discipline problems		AT			
Concerns Related to Parents					
School-home communication is inadequate	P		APT	T	AP
Lack of parent/community involvement	A	AT		A	
Concerns with School Organization					
Not enough heterogeneous grouping		AT			AT
Teaming has not been fully or adequately implemented		AT			AT
Concerns with School Policies					
Too much daily homework	ST		AT		
Concerns with Outcomes					
Achievement gap between minority and non-minority students			AT		
Concerns with Extra-Curricular Activities					
Lack of clubs and activities before and after school			AS	P	AT

4. Review your list of data-based problems. How would you go about prioritizing the list in the event that you are unable to address all problems simultaneously?
5. Would you recommend addressing the need for change on a school-by-school basis or by initiating a district-wide effort to improve middle school education?
6. In taking a close look at the current status of middle schools in this school district, what additional sources of data would you find useful?

Table D   Evidence of Good Teaching Practices

Research-based teaching practices that have been shown to be effective	6TH GRADE SCIENCE Number of teachers $N = 9$	7TH GRADE STANDARD MATH Number of teachers $N = 8$	8TH GRADE ADVANCED L.A. Number of teachers $N = 9$
Teacher helps students understand importance of topic/subject	5.5	5.0	5.0
Students are told what they need to know/do in order to meet unit objectives	6.5	4.0	8.0
Teacher determines what students already know about topic/subject	5.5	3.0	6.0
Teacher succeeds in stimulating students' interest in topic	6.0	5.0	6.0
A variety of different instructional methods are used	7.0	5.5	5.0
Teacher attempts to engage all students in the lesson	6.5	6.5	6.5
Directions for seat work and assignments are clear	6.0	3.5	7.5
Students have a chance to ask for assistance and clarification	8.0	7.5	7.5
Rules and routines have been established to reduce wasted time and promote order	7.0	6.0	4.5
Students are treated with care and respect	9.0	7.5	7.5
Highest possible rating*	9.0	8.0	9.0

*Each teacher who consistently demonstrated an effective teaching practice was given a 1.0 rating. Each teacher who occasionally demonstrated an effective teaching practice was given a .5 rating.

REFERENCES

Argetsinger, Amy. "College Student Hits Jackpot by Asking $25,000 Question." *Washington Post* (April 25, 2001), pp. B-1, B-4.

Barrott, James E. and Raybould, Rebecca. "Changing Schools into Collaborative Organizations." In Diana G. Pounder (ed.), *Restructuring Schools for Collaboration.* Albany: State University of New York Press, 1998, pp. 27–42.

Beckhard, Richard. *Organization Development: Strategies and Models.* Reading, MA: Addison-Wesley, 1969.

Best, Joel. *Images of Issues,* 2nd edition. New York: Aldine De Gruyter, 1995.

Bottoms, Gene; Presson, Alice; and Johnson, Mary. *Making High Schools Work.* Atlanta: Southern Regional Education Board, 1992.

Duke, Daniel L. "The Etiology of Student Misbehavior and the Depersonalization of Blame," *Review of Educational Research,* Vol. 48, no. 3 (Summer 1978), pp. 415–437.

Evans, Robert. *The Human Side of School Change.* San Francisco: Jossey-Bass, 1996.

Fritz, Robert. *The Path of Least Resistance.* New York: Fawcett Columbine, 1989.

Hess, G. Alfred, Jr. *School Restructuring, Chicago Style.* Newbury Park, CA: Corwin Press, 1991.

Hirsch, E. D. *The Schools We Need and Why We Don't Have Them.* New York: Doubleday, 1996.

Horton, Paul B. and Leslie, Gerald R. *The Sociology of Social Problems.* New York: Appleton-Century-Crifts, 1965.

Lee, Valerie E. *Restructuring High Schools for Equity and Excellence.* New York: Teachers College Press, 2001.

Lightfoot, Sara Lawrence. *The Good High School.* New York: Basic Books, 1983.

Marshall, Ray and Tucker, Marc. *Thinking for a Living.* New York: Basic Books, 1992.

McCaskey, Michael B. *The Executive Challenge.* Boston: Pitman, 1982.

McLaughlin, Margaret J. and Rousoe, Martyn (eds.). *Special Education and School Reform in the United States and Britain.* London: Routledge, 2000.

Murphy, John A. "The Charlotte Process: An Executive Summary." Charlotte: Charlotte-Mecklenburg Public Schools, undated.

Peterson, Kent D. "Vision and Problem Finding in Principals' Work: Values and Cognition in Administration," *Peabody Journal of Education,* Vol. 63, no. 1 (1986), pp. 87–105.

Schein, Edgar H. *Organizational Culture and Leadership.* San Francisco: Jossey-Bass, 1985.

Schon, Donald A. *The Reflective Practitioner.* New York: Basic Books, 1983.

Stone, Deborah. "Causal Stories and the Formation of Policy Agendas," *Political Science Quarterly,* Vol. 104, no. 2 (1989), pp. 281–300.

Will, George F. "Broken Families and School Performance," *Washington Post* (January 6, 2002), p. B-7.

Wise, Arthur. "Why Educational Policies Often Fail: The Hyperrationalization Hypothesis." In J. Victor Baldridge and Terrence Deal (eds.), *The Dynamics of Organizational Change in Education.* Berkeley: McCutchan, 1983, pp. 93–113.

Zaltman, Gerald and Duncan, Robert. *Strategies for Planned Change.* New York: Wiley, 1977.

WHAT CHANGE IS NEEDED?

MAJOR IDEAS

- The Design Phase of the educational change process involves determining what needs to change in order to address identified educational needs.
- Educators may choose to adopt, adapt, or create a design for educational change.
- Six criteria characterize a good design for change.
- Designs for change can be differentiated by purpose, unit, nature, and magnitude.
- Creating a design for educational change is an iterative process involving the identification and challenging of prevailing assumptions, exploring and assessing a wide range of possible changes, and thinking systemically.

Determining that a need for change exists is only the beginning of the change process. In this chapter we investigate the challenges associated with deciding what to change in order to address educational needs. This part of the process is referred to as the Design Phase.

The term *design* connotes a model of something that eventually will be implemented. During the Design Phase, models of educational change are created, adopted, or adapted to address particular needs. The design process may be as simple as choosing an existing educational program or as complex as developing the framework for an entirely new approach to learning. No matter what the nature of the design, however, certain conditions should be met. Six criteria of good educational design are discussed at the beginning of the chapter.

Designs for educational change can be characterized in a number of ways. Drawing on the dimensions of change presented in Chapter 1, several different ways to classify designs are introduced. Understanding the range of design choices can help educators select an appropriate design for a particular educational need.

Chapter 4 concludes by examining *how* good designs for educational change are created. Three aspects of the design process are highlighted: challenging assumptions, exploring options, and thinking systemically. Undertaking these processes increases the likelihood that a good match between a *design* and a *need for change* will be achieved.

ELEMENTS OF A GOOD DESIGN
FOR EDUCATIONAL CHANGE

A new lesson plan is a design for educational change. So, too, is a reorganization scheme for an entire school system. Whether each is a *good* design for educational change depends on a variety of factors. Some of the most important of these factors are addressed in this section. Before exploring the elements of a good design for educational change, however, it is important to understand why the term *design* is used to describe this phase of the change process.

The Idea of Design

Until recently, those who used the term *design* tended to be artists, architects, and engineers. Organization theorists began to use design in the seventies to describe the "decision process to bring about a coherence between the goals or purposes for which the organization exists, the patterns of division of labor and interunit coordination and the people who do the work" (Galbraith, 1977, p. 5). Their intent was to impress upon organization leaders the fact that their organizations could be arranged and configured in many ways. Choices existed concerning goals, modes of organization, processes for accomplishing tasks, roles, and other organizational components. Thinking like a designer came to imply the thorough and careful examination of possibilities, rather than the tacit acceptance of a single form or structure.

Educators also became attracted to the idea of design. At first, the term was linked primarily to instruction, but by the mid-nineties design was being used to describe the restructuring of entire schools and school systems (Duke, 2000; McDonald, 1996; Stringfield, Ross, and Smith, 1996). It should be noted, though, that different meanings often were attached to educational design.

Lack of consensus regarding the meaning of design should come as no surprise. The *Random House College Dictionary* (1984, p. 360), for example, offers fifteen definitions of design, ranging from "an outline sketch, or plan" to "the organization or structure of formal elements in a work of art" to "intention." Schon (1983, p. 78) considered design to be "a reflective conversation with the situation." Duke, Bradley, Butin, Grogan, and Gillespie (1998, p. 159) focused specifically on *educational design,* maintaining that it is "the process of creating the means by which educational intentions can be achieved within a specified context."

Part of the confusion associated with the term *design* is that it can be either a noun or a verb. For present purposes, design will be used as a noun to describe the product of the Design Phase of the educational change process. This product represents a *model* of what educators (or others involved in the Design Phase) intend as a change in current arrangements. The model constitutes a potential *solution* to a need for change.

Over seven decades ago, Waller (1932, p. 448) warned educators of the challenges associated with trying to come up with solutions to problems:

> It is easier to diagnose social ills than it is to cure them. And it is easier far to criticize institutions than to suggest remedies for the evils that are in them. It is also possible to be more scientific while criticizing, for criticism may rest upon established facts, whereas remedies are largely unknown and untried. Yet our task of social reconstruction in the schools is great and it presses.

Not every educational change initiative, of course, aims at such a daunting target as "social reconstruction," but Waller's admonition still holds. Identifying educational needs typically is an easier matter than effectively addressing them. Because of the difficulties associated with design, many educators prefer to *adopt* or *adapt* existing designs rather than to *create* a new design. Adoption involves the wholesale importing of a change from another setting, as is the case when a faculty decides to purchase an existing reading program and implement it exactly as prescribed by the designers. If they prefer to implement certain elements of the reading program and modify or set aside other elements, in light of local circumstances, *adaptation* rather than *adoption* has occurred.

Creating a new design—say for an elementary reading program—may be too ambitious for any one school or school system. Still, the belief persists that the likelihood of effective change is increased when local educators play an active role in the Design Phase. Designs that derive from external sources or that are imposed on educators often are subject to substantial resistance. Implementation issues of this kind are addressed in Chapters 6 and 7.

One last clarification is necessary. Designs for educational change should be distinguished from factors that enable the designs to be implemented. Imagine that a school is having problems getting a majority of its students to pass a new state test. To address this need, the school's administration and faculty create a design for a new type of summer school, one with a combination of small tutorials and instruction in test-taking skills. To implement this *design*—the new summer school—it will be necessary to secure additional funds, develop new policies and regulations, and train teachers. These *enabling* factors are not part of the design itself. Rather, they are what will be required to implement the new summer school. As such, they belong in the implementation plan—the focus of the next chapter.

Six Features of a Good Design

Educators are fond of arguing that there is no one best way to educate people. Similarly, there probably is no one best design for addressing educational needs. This assertion does not mean, however, that all designs are equal. Clearly, some designs for educational change are better than others. A good design for educational change should satisfy at least six conditions.

Change Key

A good design for educational change is one that—

1. Addresses legitimate educational needs
2. Reflects a clear understanding of how people learn
3. Is supported by research and professional judgment
4. Takes into account local conditions
5. Enables educational needs to be addressed without adversely affecting any particular group of learners
6. Enables educational needs to be addressed as efficiently as possible without sacrificing effectiveness

Legitimate Educational Needs.   If all educational needs are being addressed effectively, efficiently, and ethically, and if sufficient resources continue to be available, there is little reason to engage in the process of change. These, of course, are big "ifs." Few schools will take the risk of boasting that they are meeting all educational needs. The fact that virtually every school can do a better job of addressing educational needs does not mean, however, that all so-called improvements actually address legitimate educational needs. Some designs for educational change are intended to enhance the reputation of an ambitious leader, while other designs derive more from partisan politics and ideological commitments than true educational needs. Slavin (1989, p. 752) has gone so far as to contend that "education resembles such fields as fashion and design, in which change mirrors shifts in taste and social climate and is not usually thought of as true progress."

The *legitimacy* of an educational need depends on two primary factors—the will of the people and the interests of the state. In a democratic society, these two factors are expected to complement each other. History, though, suggests that such compatibility cannot always be assumed. Vigilance is required, lest educational needs reflect *only* the interests of the party in power or just the will of people with influence.

Although schools take on a variety of noneducational responsibilities, ranging from child care to inoculations against infectious diseases, it is fair to argue that their primary responsibility is to enable young people to acquire the knowledge and skills necessary to become contributing members of society. Teaching and learning are the functions that allow this goal to be achieved. An educational need therefore can be considered to be legitimate when it is associated, directly or indirectly, with effective teaching and learning.

An Understanding of How People Learn.   If the central mission of educational institutions is learning, their operation should reflect what is known about how learning occurs. Consequently, designs for educational change also should be based on an understanding of the learning process. Because knowledge about learning is constantly being refined and revised, educators cannot rely exclusively on what they studied in college. The past three decades, for example, have seen cognitive research (Bransford, Brown, and Cocking, 1999), constructivist views of learning, and the theory of multiple intelligences (Gardner, 1999) rise up to challenge behaviorism. Learners no longer are considered to be passive recipients whose learning is largely a function of external stimuli and reinforcement. Educators are coming to realize that learners construct knowledge, that they draw heavily on prior understandings, and that much learning results from social interaction. Learning is highly situated, meaning that what is learned cannot be separated from the circumstances in which it is learned. In the past, educators tended to focus on the acquisition of knowledge, but they increasingly recognize that the application of knowledge is a more reliable indication that what has been learned also has been understood.

Not every educational reform, of course, relates directly to learning. Many change initiatives involve the conditions that enable productive learning to occur. For changes that do bear directly on learning—such as new instructional methods and interventions for struggling students—the questions below illustrate some criteria that can be used to evaluate designs for educational change.

- Are opportunities provided for students to apply what they learn?
- Does instruction take into account students' prior knowledge?
- Does instruction recognize the importance of social interaction?
- Are efforts made to select content that is meaningful to students?
- Are students actively engaged in the learning process?
- Does instruction address different learning styles and intelligences?

Each year brings new thinking about the nature of learning, but it would be a mistake to assume that educators agree on all aspects of the learning process. Controversy surrounds such matters as readiness to learn, motivation, and the proper role of incentives. For this reason, the second element of a good design for educational change—an understanding of how people learn—should be supported by the third element—research and professional judgment.

Research and Professional Judgment.   Educational reforms sometimes appear to be little more than experiments based on calculated guesses, anecdotal evidence, and questionable endorsements. Slavin (1989, p. 753) is critical of educators who "rarely wait for or demand hard evidence before adopting new practices on a wide scale." Such disregard for the value of rigorous research and evaluation data contributes, according to Slavin, to faddism and the pendular nature of educational change. Good designs for educational change are supported by high-quality research and evaluation data and the prevailing judgment of professional educators.

Thanks to decades of systematic inquiry into the components of effective teaching and effective schools, contemporary educators can be much clearer than their predecessors about the conditions that sustain productive learning. Studies of effective schools, for example, have yielded seven correlates that serve as useful guidelines for reformers (Taylor, 2002, p. 377). Effective schools are characterized by—

- Clearly stated and focused school mission
- Safe and orderly climate for learning
- High expectations for students, teachers, and administrators
- Opportunity to learn and student time-on-task
- Instructional leadership by all administrators and staff members
- Frequent monitoring of student progress
- Positive home/school relations

In one of the most comprehensive syntheses of research related to school improvement, Berliner and Biddle (1995, pp. 281–342) offer a number of principles for designing sound educational change initiatives. Among their recommendations are the following:

- Reduce the size of our largest schools.
- Rethink and redesign the system for evaluating student achievement.
- Abandon the age-graded classroom.
- Strengthen the ties between communities and their schools.
- Strengthen the professional status of teachers and other educators.

One way to achieve Berliner and Biddle's last recommendation is to acknowledge the value of educators' professional judgment. Too often, though, teachers and administrators are made to feel that their experience and insight are of little importance in determining how to improve schooling. The truth is that reflective educators are able to recognize local circumstances and unique situations that can affect educational change that researchers may underestimate or overlook. Good designs for educational change should draw on both the latest research and the most respected professional judgment.

Awareness of Local Conditions.   One reason why it is important to involve educators in the Design Phase is because they have acquired an understanding of the local context in which educational change must be achieved. To ignore context is to court resistance, disappointment, and failure.

Schools, school systems, and communities typically are characterized by cultures with particular beliefs, norms, understandings, and traditions. These aspects of local culture influence how educators and others regard proposals for change. Sarason (1982, pp. 96–98) has written that any attempt to introduce change is likely to challenge "existing regularities." Existing regularities range from how time and space are allocated to how people are expected to behave under certain circumstances. He warns educators to avoid assuming that educational change poses no threat to local culture.

What if there is a legitimate need for educational change, but local conditions are unfavorable for reform? Good designs for educational change should take local conditions, however inhospitable, into account, but not necessarily allow such conditions to scuttle change entirely. Slavin (1998, pp. 1302–1307) recognizes that schools vary in their "readiness for reform." In his tripartite scheme, some schools are ready and willing to change, other schools are interested in improving but unprepared to generate their own designs for change, and still other schools are unreceptive to change because they feel a good job already is being done. Change is possible in each setting, but the design and implementation plan will need to be different.

Local factors that may affect the design process include available resources and change initiatives already in progress. It may be difficult to tackle an ambitious new design when funding for schools is declining or educators are engaged in other time-consuming improvement efforts. Past experience with change also can color people's reaction to new designs. A school that has tried unsuccessfully on several occasions to switch from letter grades to narrative report cards is less likely, for obvious reasons, to embrace a proposal to change how student progress is recorded.

Avoiding Adverse Effects.   The admonition to physicians to "do no harm" applies equally well to designers of educational reforms. Duke and Canady (1991, p. 7) express a similar idea when they define a good school policy as one "that increases the likelihood that school goals will be achieved without adversely affecting any particular group of students." Particular policies may not benefit or please everyone, but they at least should not cause any group of students to be disadvantaged.

This notion of a good school policy can be applied to other areas of change, including programs and practices. Consider a high school that establishes a new honors track for very bright students. If the cost of creating the honors track is to increase the size of non-honors classes, a case can be made that one group of students is benefiting at the expense of another group. It should be noted that adverse effects are based on the consequences for a group, not individuals. A particular change, such as a new suspension policy or a new grading procedure, may adversely affect a particular student who refuses to obey school rules or complete assignments. What is essential, however, is that the policy or procedure does not place a certain definable group, such as low-achieving students or African American students, at greater risk than they were before.

This criterion of a good design for educational change requires educators to anticipate the possible consequences of reforms before implementing them. It is not possible, of course, to foresee all the potential adverse effects of educational change. When Virginia policy makers implemented new high-stakes tests and required schools to achieve 70 percent passing rates in order to receive state accreditation, no one anticipated that some schools would establish triage systems that focused instructional interventions on students who were close to passing the tests and left lower-achieving students to fend for themselves (Duke and Tucker, 2003). Because the true impact of some reforms can only be determined once they are in effect, implementation plans may need to include a pilot test during which unanticipated problems can be ironed out.

Efficiency.   Educators are constantly bedeviled by inadequate resources. Nowhere is this more apparent than the Design Phase of educational change. It is tempting for designers to dream, and, in fact, creating visions of "ideal" learning environments can be helpful for stimulating the imagination and challenging sacred assumptions. High expectations are just as important in designing educational change as they are in prodding students to do their best.

At the same time, educators cannot afford to be wasteful or to disregard the impact of high-cost reforms on existing programs. To a great extent, educational finance is a zero-sum game. When resources are devoted to new initiatives, current programs may be affected in negative ways. Consequently, designs for educational change should enable educational needs to be addressed as efficiently as possible without sacrificing effectiveness.

It may be desirable, for example, for all instruction to take place on a tutorial basis—one teacher to one student. Resources are insufficient, at least under current conditions, to permit this arrangement as a general rule. Educators, therefore, seek to determine the smallest number of students per class that can be accommodated with existing resources. Breakthroughs in technology, however, may enable educators one day to achieve the equivalent of tutorials for every student.

Assessing the efficiency of a particular design should involve consulting with schools and school systems that have tried and evaluated similar designs. Ultimately, though, trial and error may be the only way to determine conclusively whether designated needs can be addressed effectively for less cost. Those in the best position to make such judgments are often the educators involved in actually implementing new designs.

AN ABUNDANCE OF DESIGN POSSIBILITIES

An almost infinite variety of designs for educational change exists. To make the design process more manageable, it is useful to consider different ways to distinguish designs. The dimensions of change that were presented in Chapter 1 provide various bases for differentiating designs, including purpose, unit of change, nature of change, and magnitude of change.

Designs for Different Purposes

Designs for educational change, in the final analysis, are intended to ensure that educational institutions continue to operate. Besides survival, however, four general purposes for educational change were identified in the preceding chapter. These included restoration, accommodation, improvement, and transformation. Each calls for a somewhat different type of design.

Restoration.   When educators create designs for the purpose of restoration, they hope to foster changes that result in a return to prior conditions and practices. The so-called back-to-basics movement of the seventies and eighties represented a loosely organized national movement to replace the progressive educational experiments of the sixties with traditional subject matter and instruction. Advocates of back to basics deplored the proliferation of dumbed down elective courses and new teaching techniques, the displacement of rigor for relevance, and the erosion of adult authority in schools.

Designs for educational change that aim for restoration are relatively uncreative. The intent is to model reform after that which previously existed, not to generate new programs and practices. It is intriguing to consider the possibility that one day educators may long to restore the progressive programs and practices of the sixties. In some ways, the contemporary spread of charter schools and alternative schools harks back to this period. Designers of current initiatives are reluctant, however, to trace their efforts back to a period that still suffers from negative associations. History teaches us, however, that one generation's scapegoat may become the next generation's salvation.

■ ■ ■ ■ ■ ▬▬▬

CASE STUDY
KENSINGTON SCHOOL RETURNS TO THE FOLD

Kensington Elementary School (a pseudonym) has been the focus of one of the most carefully conducted longitudinal studies of educational change ever undertaken (Smith and Keith, 1971; Smith, Prunty, Dwyer, and Kleine, 1987; Smith, Dwyer, Prunty, and Kleine, 1988). For almost two decades, researchers tracked the evolution of an innovative elementary school in the Midwest. When Kensington opened, it instantly became a showcase for many of the progressive ideas of the sixties. An open-space facility, the very architecture of the school was designed to promote team teaching and active learning. Described as a "learner-centered environment," Kensington stressed democratic pupil–teacher decision making, ungradedness, and curricular flexibility. The school's design for learning embraced concepts, skills, and values, not just facts, and relied on teachers and students to initiate experiences that promoted the learning of desired content.

Over the next fifteen years, a series of planned changes converted Kensington to an elementary school just like other elementary schools in Milford School District. Instead of striving to develop all facets of its students, the school adopted a conventional focus on preparing students for junior high school. The innovative multiage, nongraded teams were replaced by self-contained, graded classes. Hands-on learning activities gave way to textbooks, the same textbooks used in other Milford schools. Even Kensington's physical structure was brought into line with older schools, as interior walls were installed to eliminate the open-space design.

The restoration of Kensington did not mean returning to a prior state, since the school began as an experiment. Instead, restoration entailed changes designed to bring Kensington into line with programs and practices at other Milford elementary schools. This conversion process did not take place at one point in time, but rather was achieved incrementally over a number of years. Reflecting on this process, the researchers explain why Kensington was the focus of restoration (Smith, Prunty, Dwyer, and Kleine, 1987, p. 286).

> It is almost as if central office school administration on the one hand or individual schools on the other hand are on a leash, lightly held by the community. The staffs and their schools can wander about with a fair amount of freedom, but eventually, perhaps mostly in time of crisis, for example, changing populations, declining population, or loss of economic resources, the leash is tightened, freedom lessens, and the system becomes more tightly coupled.

Accommodation. When schools and school systems are faced with unusual challenges, such as a dramatic reduction in funding or an unprecedented influx of new students, they may be compelled to come up with designs that involve cutting back on services. The intention is to introduce changes that will minimize the negative impact of altered circumstances. Designs for the purpose of accommodation, such as the one in the case study below, frequently begin with a prioritization of current functions. Savings are then calculated for low-priority functions. When educators are clear on the resources available, reductions can be made in functions that have not been deemed to be high priorities. In certain instances, designs for the purpose of accommodation actually may result in the discovery of new and better ways to deliver educational services.

■ ■ ■ ■ ■ ▬▬▬▬▬▬▬▬▬▬

CASE STUDY
**AN OREGON SCHOOL DISTRICT
COPES WITH RETRENCHMENT**

In November of 1990, Oregon voters approved a measure limiting the taxing authority of localities. Ballot Measure 5 jeopardized the ability of school districts to offer a full range of educational services. While some districts panicked, North Clackamas dusted off a design for orderly retrenchment—the Education Assurance Plan (EAP)—that had been developed for just such a contingency. The heart of the EAP was a set of program priorities and a process for making decisions related to budget cuts. Priority 1 programs included curriculum areas mandated by the state and directly related to promotion and graduation requirements. These included core curriculum subjects, such as reading and mathematics, and required programs for gifted and talented students and special education students. Any changes made as a result of Ballot Measure 5 had to avoid adversely affecting these programs. Priority 2 programs were regarded as essential, but not required. Career education, computer literacy, and technical education fell under this heading. Priority 3 programs, including band, orchestra, and outdoor education, were judged to be nonessential. The EAP provided a starting place for deliberations regarding retrenchment and resulting changes. The final design involved a number of adjustments, with some programs being shifted from one classification to another and additional prioritization of noninstructional programs. To preserve the integrity of required programs, district officials decided to eliminate outdoor education, orchestra, and elementary vocal music. Other cuts were made in elementary instructional assistants, secretarial assistants, senior high athletics, and elementary physical education. While budget cutting is never a pleasant experience, the EAP allowed North Clackamas to protect core programs and minimize rancor and uncertainty.

This case was based on a study by Daniel L. Duke and Timothy J. Carman, "Implementing an Orderly Budget Reduction Process: A Case Study," *Record in Educational Administration*, Vol. 13, no. 2 (Spring/Summer 1993), pp. 85–90.

Improvement. When U.S. citizens are polled regarding public education, they tend to give higher grades to schools in their own community than to the nation's schools in general (Rose and Gallup, 2001, pp. 43–44). The vast majority of people prefer to focus on improving existing schools and school systems rather than finding alternatives, such as providing parents with vouchers that can be used for private or parochial schools (Rose and Gallup, p. 44). Educators in many U.S. schools are engaged in a continuous process of improvement. Of all the purposes for educational change, improvement is probably the most popular.

Hopkins (2001, pp. 172–173) offers a scheme for classifying school improvement designs. Type I designs are intended to help failing schools become moderately effective. Key elements of Type I designs are a clear focus on a limited number of basic curricular and organizational concerns and a high level of external support. Type II designs seek to help moderately effective schools become more effective. Key elements include the refinement of priorities and attention to specific aspects of teaching and learning. Type III designs enable effective schools to remain so. Key elements involve building awareness of new practices and developing local support networks.

Designs for improvement are primarily concerned with achieving existing education goals. They address discrepancies between current and desired performance, students who fail to benefit fully from their schooling, and better ways to use existing resources. Designs for improvement may involve various units of change, from classrooms to entire school systems. They may target a single subject or encompass the whole K–12 curriculum. Some designs deal directly with improved teaching and learning, while others concentrate on the organizational conditions likely to support teaching and learning. The latter may entail a reorganization scheme involving the creation of teacher teams, a school safety initiative, or an effort to restructure school decision making. The following case study illustrates a design for improvement that addressed teaching and learning in both direct and indirect ways.

■ ■ ■ ■ ■ ▬▬▬▬▬▬▬▬▬▬▬▬▬▬▬▬▬▬▬▬▬▬▬▬▬▬▬▬▬▬

CASE STUDY
RESPONDING TO LOW ACHIEVEMENT
AND OVERCROWDING

Faced with rapidly increasing enrollments and subsequent overcrowding, increasing numbers of at-risk students, and declining test scores, three California elementary schools were funded to initiate school improvements, including a year-round schedule. The schedule called for students to attend school in 60-day blocks, separated by 15-day intersessions. Students in need of additional academic assistance were expected to attend school during intersession, while other students received a break. This 60–15 cycle was repeated three times during the school year. All students shared a common summer vacation of one month. The calendar was based on research that indicated shorter breaks reduced student loss of learning.

The year-round schedule not only provided a way to deal with overcrowding, but it allowed educators to address the needs of at-risk students more effectively. Among the elements of the so-called Orchard Plan for school improvement were the following:

■ Shift from 180 to 223 days of instruction
■ Reorganization of categorical funding to support intersession courses for academic assistance and enrichment

(continued)

CONTINUED

- Creation of five tracks of students, with only four of the five tracks present at any one time
- Reduction of class size by two to three students as a result of the student tracks
- Contract extension of 20 percent for teachers (resulting in 20 percent higher salaries)
- Restructuring of curriculum into smaller units with built-in review and more careful monitoring of student progress
- Development of team teaching and small-group learning

In a study of the impact of this improvement design, Gandara and Fish (1994) found that all three schools demonstrated increases in student achievement, a high level of parent and teacher satisfaction, and greater efficiency in the use of school facilities. It is therefore possible for one design for educational change to address several needs simultaneously.

This case study was based on Patricia Gandara and Judy Fish, "Year-Round Schooling as an Avenue to Major Structural Reform," *Educational Evaluation and Policy Analysis,* Vol. 16, no. 1 (Spring 1994), pp. 67–85.

Transformation. Designs for transformation constitute dramatic departures from convention. Constrained only by the limits of imagination, these designs typically challenge prevailing assumptions about teaching and learning. Kensington Elementary School, in the preceding case study, represented a transformational design for educational change when it first opened. Milford educators sought to alter what and how students learned as well as how teachers worked together and how the school was organized.

A transformational design is intended to do more than improve performance on existing goals. The goals themselves come under scrutiny. Educational policies and practices and the conditions under which learning takes place are reexamined. Transformational designs reflect awareness of the inseparability of ends and means. The work of John Dewey (1959) provides a good example of the thinking that supports transformational design. Dewey argued that the education of citizens for a democratic society should take place in schools that themselves were models of democracy. For the schools of Dewey's time—or today—to be models of democracy, sweeping changes would be needed in governance, instructional practices, and curriculum emphasis. The following case study provides a recent example of transformational design.

CASE STUDY

FRANKLIN COUNTY MAKES MIDDLE SCHOOL MEANINGFUL

Possessing only half the funds needed to replace the old middle school, educators in Franklin County, Virginia, wondered what could be done to relieve overcrowding while also addressing the county's high dropout rate. They realized that the seeds of dropping out were sown at the end of middle school, when many students lost interest in academic subjects. What was needed, they reasoned, was a set of experiences that showed students how what they learned could lead to interesting careers. The result was the Center for Applied Technology and Career Exploration (CATCE), a truly transformational design.

All eighth graders in Franklin County spend a semester at CATCE and a semester at the old middle school. When students are at CATCE they choose three six-week-long career modules from a set of eight possibilities. The modules range from Environmental Science to Manufacturing. Each module is team taught by two instructors, one certificated middle school teacher and one individual from an occupation related to the module's focus. The instructors jointly develop each six-week module around a practical problem likely to interest young adolescents. Students, who are referred to as interns, might concentrate on identifying and cleaning up a toxic spill in a local stream in Environmental Science or design a garage for a local family in Architecture. Instructors want interns to learn to solve real problems and, in so doing, make contributions to their community.

Knowing that eighth graders are not particularly fond of school, CATCE was purposely designed to be as different as possible from a conventional school. The facility looks more like a high-tech office building than a school. There are no bells, no gymnasium, no cafeteria, no media center, no lockers, and no desks. Interns spend most of each day for six weeks in a module, which occupies a large room divided into different work areas, depending on the focus of the module. Every intern shares a work station and a computer with another intern. They track their own progress and record it on a computer disk portfolio. Dress is dictated by the day's activities, and interns go to the commons for lunch whenever they reach a stopping point in their work for the day. The learning environment is intended to be as close as possible to a workplace for adults. Educators expect interns to acquire an interest in one or more careers, learn to work together productively in teams, and develop personal responsibility.

See Daniel L. Duke, "Designing Schools to Foster Teaching and Learning," *Orbit,* Vol. 30, no. 1 (1999), pp. 6–8.

Designs for Different Units

Educational change can take place at various levels, ranging from an individual classroom or program to an entire school or school system. Designs for classrooms and small groups of students, the most basic units of design, may involve a variety of elements, including—

> Curriculum content
> Instructional methods and technology
> Assessment techniques and grading criteria
> Classroom management strategies
> Learning activities and task structures
> Routines and procedures
> Rules and responsibilities
> Class or group size (number of students)

Formats for grouping students for instruction
Supplementary instructional personnel

In recent years, designs for educational change at the classroom level have involved such innovations as computer technology, cooperative learning, problem-based instruction, performance-based assessment, experiential learning, and teacher teams.[1] The physical design of classrooms has been altered in some instances to accommodate more active learning and provide space for a variety of different activities. Instead of a single instructor, classrooms may be staffed by a regular education and a special education teacher or a teacher assisted by an aide or volunteers. Many designs for classrooms derive from concern for students who are not experiencing academic success. These designs call for differentiated instruction, flexible grouping, tutoring, and instructional materials that match the reading levels of different students.

■ ■ ■ ■ ■ ▬▬▬▬▬▬▬▬▬▬▬▬▬▬▬▬▬▬▬▬▬▬▬▬▬▬▬▬▬▬▬▬▬▬▬▬▬

CASE STUDY

THE KAMEHAMEHA ELEMENTARY EDUCATION PROGRAM (KEEP)

Based on a fifteen-year research-and-development program devoted to improving the cognitive and educational development of at-risk Hawaiian students, KEEP has been implemented in a number of elementary classrooms across the United States. It draws on the work of Soviet psychologist Lev Vygotsky and stresses learning based on providing less capable students with graduated assistance, and a clear idea of the ultimate goals of learning activities. Learning, for purposes of KEEP, is defined as "assisted performance."

Tharp and Gallimore (1988, p. 118) provide a thumbnail sketch of the design of a KEEP classroom:

> The KEEP classroom is an open area that is functionally divided into several activity settings, or "centers." . . . A rotational system schedules each child into five of these centers each day for about 20 minutes each. Over a week's time, each child may attend as many as 12 different centers—library center, game center, listening-skills center, and so forth.

When students are working in a center, they often receive assistance from other students who are further ahead on an activity. The primary interaction between students and the teacher occurs in Center One, which involves five or six students of a similar achievement level in reading and language development. Every child attends Center One every day for twenty minutes in order to receive formal reading instruction and assistance from the teacher. Reading lessons revolve around the discussion of a story.

Roland G. Tharp and Ronald Gallimore, *Rousing Minds to Life* (Cambridge, UK: Cambridge University Press, 1988).

▬▬▬▬▬▬▬▬▬▬▬▬▬▬▬▬▬▬▬▬▬▬▬▬▬▬▬▬▬▬▬▬▬▬▬▬▬▬▬

[1]A useful source of information on different elements of classroom design is the latest edition of Thomas L. Good and Jere E. Brophy's *Looking in Classrooms* (New York: Harper & Row).

Designs for classrooms have been characterized in various ways. These characterizations sometimes take the form of a dichotomy, such as learner-centered classrooms versus teacher-centered classrooms. One of the two options typically is treated as far more desirable than the other. Among the design options expressed as dichotomies are the following:

Learner-centered	Teacher-centered
Heterogeneously grouped	Homogeneously grouped
Open classroom	Closed classroom
Graded classroom	Ungraded classroom
Structured classroom	Unstructured classroom
Content-based	Process-based instruction
Phonics	Whole language instruction

Dichotomies such as these probably are more useful for rhetorical purposes than design purposes. Most designs that take into account practical issues such as variations among students and resource limitations tend to be located along the continuum between extremes. A class, for example, can consist of a heterogeneous group of students, but they may be divided by ability for particular lessons. Teachers often blend highly structured lessons for crucial content with less structured lessons intended to encourage students to develop independent learning skills.

Programs. Another unit of design is the program. Under this rubric can be found a variety of arrangements, including academic departments, supplementary programs for students with particular characteristics, and extracurricular activities. For the smallest programs, the dividing line between a program and a classroom may blur, as in the case of an in-school suspension room or weekly pullout program for gifted students. A similar convergence occurs at the opposite end of the spectrum, where large programs may be indistinguishable from small schools. Examples include alternative programs for struggling students and schools-within-a-school offering highly focused academic work.

Programs may be differentiated in various ways besides their size. Some programs deal with the regular academic curriculum, whereas other programs are characterized as cocurricular or extracurricular. Programs may be intended for purposes of enrichment, acceleration, remediation, rehabilitation, therapeutic intervention, prevention, or isolation (in cases involving serious disciplinary infractions). Some programs operate during regular school hours, whereas other programs run before or after school or in the summer. It would be difficult to catalogue all of the program possibilities in this brief section. Programs, it should be noted, have become one of the most popular units of design for educational change.

To appreciate the range of design options for a particular program, let us consider one academic area—the Mathematics Department of a large high school. The list below represents some of the program design changes that could be placed on the drawing board:

- Change the goals and objectives for particular mathematics courses or the entire mathematics program.
- Add or delete content for mathematics courses.
- Update content or correct inaccurate content.
- Integrate technology (computers, graphing calculators) with math curriculum.
- Re-organize content for a particular course.
- Integrate content across several courses (such as Algebra I and Geometry).
- Integrate content between a mathematics and a nonmathematics course (such as algorithms in Algebra I and Chemistry).
- Differentiate course content by level of difficulty, in order to facilitate within-class ability grouping.
- Add or delete mathematics courses from the list of course offerings.
- Alter the sequence in which courses are taken.
- Lengthen courses (such as extending Algebra II to three semesters from two).
- Increase graduation requirements in mathematics.

These design changes deal primarily with the mathematics curriculum. Add to this list other categories of change, such as new instructional methods and assessment techniques, and the design possibilities for mathematics education mushroom.

Schools.   One of the most popular units of design for educational change is the school. Since the advent of effective schools research in the seventies, educators have been told that the school is the key to effective classrooms and programs (Wideen, 1994, p. 112). Initiate an innovative program in a weak school and the likelihood of success is substantially diminished. Over the past few decades reforms have sought to restructure, reculture, and reinvent existing schools. In addition, momentum has built to create new schools, including charter, focus, and alternative schools.

School designs, like classroom and program designs, may be based on a variety of factors. The nature of curriculum offerings represents one basis for design differentiation. Besides comprehensive schools that try to accommodate various student interests, different types of specialty schools have been created. Areas of specialization can be linked to careers, as in the case of vocational–technical schools and career academies, and to academic clusters, as in the case of magnet schools focusing on science or Governors' schools concentrating on international affairs. The focus of specialization in other schools is not the curriculum, but the type of student to be served. These schools may be designed for students who have been expelled or who have serious emotional problems, highly gifted students, and students who are not experiencing success in conventional academic settings.

■ ■ ■ ■ ■

CASE STUDY

A HOME BASE FOR CHILDREN WITHOUT A HOME

Pappas Elementary School in Phoenix, Arizona, fills a unique void. The four-year-old public school was designed for homeless children. Besides teaching the content required by the state, Pappas provides students with hot breakfasts, monthly supplies of socks and underwear, showers, dental care, and medicine. Buses run flexible routes each day, since students do not always return to the same destination. Because each student's family circumstances are unstable, the school is prepared to send emergency food supplies to parents, refer families to agencies for assistance, and provide transportation to medical facilities.

While critics argue that homeless children are unlawfully segregated at Pappas, advocates for the school contend that the needs of homeless children require unusual measures and a special school design. The school serves a transitional purpose while homeless families locate a permanent residence and parents secure stable employment. Teachers and counselors at the school are specially trained to deal with the problems of homelessness.

Melissa Morrison, "School Is a Home for Children without One," *Washington Post* (January 9, 2001), p. A–11.

School designs also can be based on structural features. Elementary schools, for example, may consist of self-contained classrooms or they may be departmentalized (usually just for the upper elementary grades). Some elementary schools are organized into teams, with a team consisting of a "family" of classrooms covering kindergarten through fifth grade. Many middle schools also are characterized by some form of team-based design, and some high schools have begun to experiment with teacher teams as well, particularly for ninth graders and at-risk students.

Size also is a distinguishing feature of schools. Schools range from one-room schools with fewer than twenty students to mega-schools with over five thousand students. To deal with the negative impact of large enrollments, some high schools are subdivided into semi-autonomous houses or academies. Several urban school systems have converted large comprehensive high schools into multiplex schools, actually several separate schools located at the same site. "Virtual schools," where students do not actually congregate in one place, but maintain contact with teachers and each other via computer links, have begun to operate in recent years.

Other features of schools can serve as a basis for design differentiation. One of the most ubiquitous distinguishing features involves the age of students or the grade levels included in the school (a proxy for age in most cases). The names elementary, middle, and high school, however, do not adequately capture the variations in grade level combinations found for each category. Enrollment policies are another distinguishing feature. Students may be assigned to some schools, choose to attend other schools, and have to pass an entrance exam to qualify for still other schools.

It is rarely the case that a design for changing an existing school involves altering every aspect of the school. Sometimes the focus of change is the daily schedule or the yearly calendar. Although switching from a seven-period-day to a block schedule or from a nine-month calendar to year-round school targets only one design element, educators generally understand that such changes are likely to affect what and how they teach, staffing, extra-curricular activities, resource allocation, and much more.

Large Units of Change.   Educational change initiatives sometimes extend beyond the school to encompass entire school districts, intermediate units, state systems of education, and even the federal system of education. In some cases, these initiatives focus primarily on classrooms, programs, and schools, while in other instances they deal with the complex bureaucratic structure of education. It is not unusual, for example, to hear of a new superintendent proposing a reorganization plan for the central office. New governors like to restructure state departments of education. Some of the most comprehensive educational changes have occurred recently, as part of the nationwide movement to improve accountability. Many states have introduced curriculum standards, standardized tests, school accreditation requirements, and report cards on school performance. These changes have a trickle-down effect, eventually touching every school and every classroom.

Designs for educational change at the district level and above often involve such matters as school finance, curriculum offerings, graduation requirements, decision-making processes, and the evaluation of schools and educational personnel. Reforms oscillate between greater centralization and greater decentralization of control, more rigorous and more flexible standards and requirements, and more and less standardized forms of evaluation. When money is in ample supply, school systems tend to expand their size and services, while program and personnel reductions are the norm during tight money times. It is probably fair to say that the likelihood of dramatic change lessens as the unit of change grows larger. On occasion, however, sweeping change has resulted from federal and state initiatives. The passage of Public Law 94-142, the Education for All Handicapped Children Act, is a vivid example.

Different Elements of Educational Design

In Chapter 2, the *nature* or focus of particular changes was divided into two categories—things and people. For present purposes, *elements of design* refer to things. The preceding section addressed units of change, such as classrooms and schools. While these entities may be considered *things* in a literal sense, the fact is that classrooms and schools are not actually changed in many cases, at least not in their totality. Instead, certain elements of classrooms and schools are changed—such as how students are grouped or the length of the school day. If enough of these changes in the elements of educational design are made, or if the changes are perceived to be important enough, we may regard the changes as transformational.

In considering the range of educational design elements, it is helpful to think about learners. For individuals or groups of learners, the following can be changed:

- The purposes and goals of learning
- The content of learning
- When learning takes place
- Where learning takes place
- How learners are organized and instructed
- The conditions under which learning takes place
- The criteria and methods for determining what has been learned

When researchers analyzed the design elements in proposals for New American Schools grants, they came up with a set of possible changes that was similar in many respects to the above list (Bodily, 1996, pp. 294–295):

- Curriculum and instruction
- Standards
- Assessments
- Student grouping
- Community involvement
- Integration of social services
- Governance
- Professional development
- Structure, staffing, and allocation of staff time

For each of these elements of educational design, a variety of specific changes is possible. Let us consider student grouping, for example. Grouping can occur within a class or on a course-by-course basis. Students may be grouped on the basis of interests (as in the case of magnet schools and career academies), overall ability (as in the case of programs for gifted and talented students), ability in a specific subject or skill (as in the case of Advanced Placement courses and reading groups in elementary classes), and disabling condition (as in the case of a class for seriously emotionally disturbed students). In recent years, grouping students who are at risk of experiencing academic problems has grown in popularity. An example is a ninth grade transition program in which students with marginal academic records from middle school are assigned to the same core team of teachers in the ninth grade. Student grouping can be highly flexible, with frequent movement between groups, or relatively stable, with little mobility. Traditionally, grouping tended to place students with certain similarities together. When such practices came under fire as a form of de facto segregation, educators began to constitute student groups on the basis of heterogeneity. The mainstreaming of disabled students is one example of this trend. At the same time, however, some educators have made a strong case for creating learning groups made up exclusively of boys or girls. Mathematics classes designed just for girls and elementary classes made up entirely of African American boys are two examples that have been tried in recent years.

The choices related to student grouping are only a small fraction of the possibilities for educational change. These possibilities include single changes and different combinations of design elements.

Designs of Different Magnitude

Educational designs can be differentiated by magnitude in various ways. Slavin (1998, pp. 1300–1302), for instance, identifies two basic designs: (1) systemic reforms that apply to all schools and involve changes in assessment, accountability, standards, and governance, and (2) school-based reforms that focus on creating a model school and then exporting the model to interested localities. Furthermore, he finds three variations on the school-based reform design: organizational development models, comprehensive reform models, and single-subject innovations. Organizational development models, including Sizer's (1992) Coalition of Essential Schools and Levin's (1987) Accelerated Schools, call for involving school staffs in developing their own design for school change. These designs typically build on exemplary reform programs created by experts. Comprehensive reform models are more prescriptive and include Slavin's own Success for All program. Schools that adopt these models are provided with instructional materials, teachers' manuals, staff development training, and evaluations. Single-subject models focus on one curriculum area and, often, a particular cluster of grades. Reading Recovery is an example of such a model.

Another design classification scheme comes from a RAND study of New American Schools. Bodilly (1996, p. 297–298) identifies three types of educational design: core designs, comprehensive designs, and systemic designs. The designs are distinguished by the number and type of design elements and the number of collaborators involved in developing the design at a site. Core designs, such as Expeditionary Learning and Roots and Wings, focus on school partnerships and emphasize "changes in elements associated with the core of schooling: curriculum, instruction, standards, assessments, student groupings, community involvement, and professional development" (Bodilly, 1996, p. 297). Comprehensive designs involve additional elements, such as integrated youth services, new forms of governance, and staffing changes. Community Learning Centers and the Los Angeles Learning Center exemplify this type of design. Systemic designs, such as the National Alliance for Restructuring Education, call for changes in *all* design elements and widespread collaboration. These designs go beyond individual schools to encompass entire school systems.

Research on the desirability of particular types of design is far from conclusive. Muncey and McQuillan (1996, pp. 157–158) found that comprehensive change in members of the Coalition of Essential Schools was more likely to "take root and endure" than less ambitious initiatives. On the other hand, Lee (2001, p. 75), in a study of high school reform, concluded that "the simultaneous implementation of many restructuring reforms . . . did not increase either effectiveness or equity." Recent research on so-called "whole-school reform" raises questions regarding the wisdom of trying to extend successful initiatives from original sites to other schools in a given jurisdiction (Viadero, 2001). Schlechty (2001) contends that designs for educational change, in order to address the range of current problems, must encompass entire school districts.

Additional Design Options

Designs for educational change can be differentiated in other ways as well. For example, the duration of anticipated design implementation can be a distinguishing characteristic. Reforms may range from short-term to long-term designs. Another basis for differentiation involves the level of local involvement in the design process. A distinction in this case may be made between off-the-shelf designs or prototypes that can be imported as is to a site, designs that blend external models and local creativity, and designs that are totally developed at the local level. Earlier these options were referred to as adoption, adaptation, and creation.

In a study of different reform development processes, Datnow (2000) cautions educators against designs that do not include some level of local participation. The ultimate success of a design may depend, she maintains, on "buy-in" by those expected to implement the design. The best way to achieve such acceptance is to make certain that local educators and community members participate in all phases of the change process.

KEY ASPECTS OF THE EDUCATIONAL DESIGN PROCESS

The desired outcome of the Design Phase of the educational change process is a design that addresses an identified need or set of needs. Six characteristics of a good design for educational change were presented earlier to help individuals involved in the design process. In this section, additional guidance regarding the design process is provided. The discussion applies specifically to the creation or adaptation of designs. A design that is adopted as is entails little or no design work.

Creating a design for educational change is usually a highly iterative process. This means that design does not follow a fixed sequence of steps. Despite the unpredictable nature of design, steps can be taken to ensure a worthwhile outcome. The design process is most productive when it is characterized by (1) the identification and interrogation of prevailing assumptions, (2) the exploration and assessment of a wide range of possible changes, and (3) systemic thinking (Duke, 2000, pp. 13–14). Each of these dimensions of design will be examined more closely.

Identifying and Interrogating Assumptions

The fate of educational change is tied to two sets of assumptions—those held by the individuals involved in designing change and those held by the individuals who are subject to the change once it is implemented. Of the first group, Evans (1996, p. 9) has noted:

> The typical pattern when reform fails has been to blame teachers rather than designers; it now appears, however, that the designers' assumptions are often at the core of the chronic failure of change efforts.

Designers are advised to interrogate their assumptions about the change process in general and the object of their change efforts—usually schools and teachers. Do designers, for example, assume that the change process is a purely objective enterprise where desired ends are specified and means are then selected because they are likely to lead to these ends? Or do they recognize that change can be a political process, characterized by conflict, winners, and losers? Designers with experience in the private sector sometimes assume that public schools respond to the same change processes as private corporations. They fail to appreciate the major differences in mission, resources, and governance between public and private entities. Sarason (1982, pp. 95–117) has taken designers to task for assuming that the desirability and intended outcomes of proposed changes are clear to everyone. He attributed the failure of the New Math initiative in the sixties, for example, to confusion regarding the goals of curriculum change. Was New Math supposed to raise mathematics achievement, change the way students understood mathematics, or encourage more young people to pursue careers in mathematics?

Metz (1990) took a careful look at the disappointing results of the post–*A Nation At Risk* reform movement and concluded that change agents had failed to examine their own assumptions about schools and school improvement. For example, she noted that reformers assumed adults would and should determine what happens in schools. Students were regarded as "passive agents who will learn, if only they are taught" (p. 146). Metz (p. 146) went on to contrast this assumption with the reality of schools:

> In practice, teachers must adjust their teaching to a multitude of characteristics of their students. The whole point of teaching—and of schools—is to create changes in students . . . American students come to high school with a wide variety of academic skills, general knowledge, attitudes, cognitive styles, cultural beliefs, and ambitions. Schools and classroom teachers who take no account of these factors are likely to be unsuccessful in creating the changes they plan.

Senge (1990, pp. 174–204) popularized the term *mental model* as a reference to the collection of assumptions that influence how individuals make sense of the world around them. Of mental models, he wrote (p. 175):

> Mental models can be simple generalizations such as "people are untrustworthy," or they can be complex theories, such as my assumptions about why members of my family interact as they do. But what is most important to grasp is that mental models are *active*—they shape how we act. If we believe people are untrustworthy, we act differently from the way we would if we believed they were trustworthy.

How many school principals have missed opportunities to improve instructional performance by veteran teachers because they held the view that old dogs cannot be taught new tricks? Beliefs of this kind need to be recast as hypotheses and tested as part of the design process. What is the evidence that veteran teachers cannot change? Are we unduly influenced by the negative reactions to reform of a few older teachers? Have we asked older teachers to discuss the conditions under which they are most and least likely to grow as professionals? Failure to challenge assumptions, as Sarason (1982) has shown, can result in changes that turn out to be remarkably similar to the status quo.

Change Key

Individuals involved in the educational change process need to examine their own beliefs and assumptions about change and schools.

Understanding our own assumptions and mental models about change and schools is necessary, but not sufficient alone to ensure a productive design process. It is also crucial for designers to understand the assumptions and mental models of those who are expected to implement change initiatives. In this regard, there is no substitute for listening carefully to what these individuals have to say about proposed designs. It is not unusual, for example, to discover that many educators assume that the way things *are* is the way they *should be*. Change efforts that ignore such a belief court failure.

Change Key

Individuals involved in the educational change process need to identify and challenge prevailing assumptions held by those expected to implement change.

Trying to identify educators' assumptions *before* a tentative design for change has been created may prove fruitless. Only when confronted by a concrete proposal for change are strongly held beliefs and mental models likely to surface. For this reason, it is best to wait until the design process is well under way before determining whether particular assumptions occasion modifications in the initial design or whether these assumptions need to be challenged. In a monograph on creating the next generation of U.S. schools, eight popular assumptions about schools that may present obstacles to transformational change efforts were identified (Duke, 2000, p. 29):

- The central activity of school is teaching.
- The purpose of teaching is the acquisition of knowledge.
- Students must be graded on how well they acquire knowledge.
- All students must acquire the same basic knowledge.
- All students must acquire basic knowledge in the same amount of time.
- All students must acquire basic knowledge in the same sequence and combination.
- All students must acquire basic knowledge in the same place.
- The needs of all students can be accommodated under one roof.

This list of assumptions captures what Sarason (1982, p. 96) has termed the "existing regularities" of schooling. The justifications for such fixed features are rarely questioned. Who would suggest that students be allowed to take *only* science courses in a given year, rather than one science, one mathematics, one English, and one social studies course? Who would think that students might spend time in several different learning environments during the same school year? Assumptions such as those listed above constitute the commonplaces of public education, the things most people take for granted.

Despite the ubiquitousness of these assumptions, examples can be found of educators who are challenging them. In Franklin County, Virginia, the notion that middle school had to be one place was challenged by the creation of the Center for Applied Technology and Career Exploration (see earlier case study). Eighth graders in Franklin County now spend one semester at the traditional middle school and one semester at CATCE. When students are at CATCE, the focus of activity is on the application, rather than just the acquisition, of knowledge. In many school systems across the country, educators are beginning to vary the amount of time that different students are engaged in learning, thereby challenging the assumption that time must be held constant across all students. Students who fall behind their classmates are provided with before- and after-school tutorials, Saturday and summer school programs, and double-blocked courses in subjects where extra help is needed.

When the design process reveals assumptions that threaten the prospects for successful change, designers should consider altering these beliefs. New beliefs actually may become part of the design for change. Assumptions and beliefs help make up what some scholars refer to as organizational culture (Sarason, 1982; Schein, 1985). Changing the culture of a school, of course, is no simple task. School cultures take years to develop, and they are very resistant to change (Duke, 1995). Without shifts in school culture, however, substantive improvement in education may be difficult (Rossman, Corbett, and Firestone, 1988, p. 15).

Maehr and Midgley (1996) have studied what is involved in changing school culture, and they maintain that cultural change ultimately involves a shift in thinking (p. 201):

> At the essence of culture change . . . is a fundamental transformation in persons, especially in the way they think of themselves, their choices, their actions, and their purposes in acting. . . . In schools, administrators, teachers, and ultimately and primarily students need to think differently about schooling.

Among the categories of thought that Maehr and Midgley (1996, p. 201) contend must undergo change are perceptions of options and alternatives:

> People's actions are largely a result of the options they think they have. . . . What is or is not an option depends . . . upon the norms and patterns of the groups to which the individual belongs and of which she wishes to remain a member.

It should be no surprise that how people think about options influences how they approach the change process. The fewer options that are considered during the Design

Phase, the less the likelihood of successful change. It is to the subject of options, then, that we now turn.

Exploring Possibilities

The failure of many educational change initiatives can be traced, in part, to the absence of a systematic and thorough exploration of possible design elements. Sometimes a wide range of options is not considered because of time pressure and fiscal constraints. In other cases, leaders already have committed to a particular change, and they have no desire to risk the discovery of an attractive alternative. How many times have local educators watched a principal or superintendent try to import a pet program or practice because it worked in her previous location or she heard glowing reports about it at a conference? In many cases, the simple fact that a design is available at an opportune time leads to its being chosen without any serious consideration of other possibilities. In this regard, Slavin (1998, p. 1309) has noted,

> One general problem of innovation is that school staffs choose a model of reform because it happens to be available at the point when a school is ready and able to make a change. Rarely do schools make considered choices among a set of attractive options to find a match between the model's characteristics and the school's needs and capabilities. . . . This results in frequent mismatches between innovative models and implementing schools.

Various approaches have been taken to encourage educators to consider a variety of possible designs before committing to one. In its efforts to promote reform in under-performing schools and school systems, New American Schools presents a menu of seven possible reform models that have passed its review process. Some states and school districts host design fairs where various innovations are introduced. The goal is to build educators' awareness of design possibilities before they attempt to adopt, adapt, or create a design for educational change.

Change Key

Prior to choosing a design for educational change, educators should identify and evaluate a variety of design options.

In considering design possibilities, educators are advised to seek evidence that particular options have been tried and that they achieve desired results (Slavin, 1998, p. 1310). It can be helpful to visit sites where options have been implemented and discuss their strengths and weaknesses with local educators, students, and other stakeholders. Educators are fond of saying that there is no one best way to teach or run a school. While this observation may be valid, there clearly are ineffective and inappropriate educational programs and practices. Time is always at a premium in public education, but the time that is wasted on failed change initiatives more than justifies an investment of extra time for fact-finding at the beginning of the change process.

CHALLENGE OF CHANGE

Devotion to One Option

Sarason (1971, p. 224) argues that an educator's "affection for particular alternatives is the most effective barrier to coming up with alternatives." When the educator in question occupies a leadership role, the impact on the change process can be particularly harmful. Janis (1972), in his studies of groupthink, has documented the chilling effect of a leader's premature commitment to a particular course of action. By disclosing their preferences for particular options early in the design process, leaders can suppress the identification of worthy alternatives that merit serious consideration.

The goal of the Design Phase is to choose a design that stands the greatest chance of addressing the educational needs that have been identified. The likelihood of choosing the best design—regardless of whether it is created, adapted, or adopted—is increased by considering as many design options as possible. For this to happen, the Design Phase should involve the identification and examination of design options that address agreed upon educational needs. It is worth noting that the assumptions held by designers can serve to artificially limit the range of options under consideration. Hoy and Sweetland (2001) have pointed out, in this regard, that many educators automatically assume that aspects of bureaucratic school structure inhibit rather than enhance improvement efforts. The researchers make the case that certain structural design elements actually can facilitate school improvement. By examining their assumptions prior to generating a set of design options, designers can free themselves of limiting beliefs.

Systemic Thinking

The process of creating designs for educational change does not lend itself to prescriptions and formulas. Identifying assumptions and exploring possibilities are important aspects of the process, but they should not be treated as steps in a linear process leading to a design. In some cases, an initial design may serve as a starting place, an impetus to reflect on assumptions. Reflection then may lead to a revised design and subsequent exploration of options. In other cases, the process may begin with an exploration of design options and an examination of assumptions. Only at the very end of the process does a design finally emerge.

Despite the highly variable nature of the design process, one thread runs throughout the creation of successful designs. *Designers think systemically.* Senge (1990, p. 68) characterizes systemic thinking as "seeing wholes" and focusing on "interrelationships rather than things." He contends that thinking systemically involves *feedback* that allows designers to understand how actions reinforce or neutralize each other (p. 73). Thus, if we want to change teaching methods in order to help underachieving students, it is not enough to consider how certain methods affect students. We must also understand how these methods affect teachers. Learning environments consist of ongoing interactions between teachers and students as well as among students. Designers must recognize that what students do shapes what teachers do and vice versa. As Senge puts it, "Every influence is both cause and effect" (p. 75).

Thinking systemically may require some educators to discard the assumption that *someone* has to be responsible for a problem requiring reform. By appreciating the interrelationships between people, designers can come to realize that "everyone shares responsibility for problems generated by a system" (Senge, 1990, p. 78). A design for improving reading achievement that only targets language arts teachers is probably not a good design. Every subject involves reading; therefore every teacher is, to some extent, a reading teacher. So, too, are parents and classmates.

Change Key

Successful designs for educational change result from systemic thinking—from an appreciation of the interrelationships between and among design elements and those who work and learn in schools.

In applying the notion of systemic thinking to educational design, McDonald (1996, pp. 16–19) focuses on three essential elements of schools—core beliefs, functions involving the distribution of resources and power, and connections with the world beyond the school. It is not enough to concentrate on only one of these elements. *Systemic design,* as he terms the process, requires understanding and addressing all three (McDonald, 1996, pp. 17–18):

> one cannot hope to redesign the whole school without dealing in depth with issues of belief; issues involving the distribution of power, energy, and information within the school; and issues involving the schools' links to outside values and ideas.

The message for designers is clear. No element of design should be assumed to operate independently of other elements. No individual who works in a school should be assumed to function independently of other individuals. Despite the conventional wisdom that teachers close their doors and do whatever they want, and the scholarship that characterizes schools as "loosely coupled" organizations, interactions and interrelationships pervade schools. What happens in schools also must not be divorced from what happens in homes, neighborhoods, communities, and society in general. A primary obligation for designers is to anticipate and investigate the relationships between and among elements of their designs and the context in which the designs are to be implemented.

CONCLUSION

Faced with needs for change, educators can decide to adopt an existing design outright, adapt it, or create one of their own. Whatever course they choose, they need to understand the principles of good educational design. Good designs address legitimate educational needs, reflect a clear understanding of how people learn, derive support from research and professional judgment, and take into account local conditions. In addition, good designs do not come at the expense of particular groups of learners or entail unreasonable expense.

Designs for educational change can be differentiated according to various characteristics, including purpose, unit of change, and magnitude of change. A rich array of design elements are available, depending on the focus of change efforts. Given all the choices that may be called for during the Design Phase, educators need to approach the design process in a thoughtful and systematic way. This entails identifying and interrogating assumptions regarding how change is achieved and the nature of schooling. Successful design often depends on exploring and assessing a wide range of possible changes before committing to a particular design. Sensitivity to the interrelationships between and among design elements, or what is referred to as systemic thinking, is a third important component of the design process. The central message of Chapter 4 is that good designs for educational change are not accidents; they are the result of reflection, imagination, and analysis.

■ ■ ■ ■ ■

APPLYING WHAT YOU KNOW
DESIGNING A NEW ELEMENTARY
SCHOOL FOR BATTLEFIELD

Battlefield School District serves a working class community near a large city. Burdened with two overcrowded and outdated elementary schools, school officials convinced taxpayers to support a bond issue that would allow them to replace the facilities. Approved funding, however, only permitted construction of one new elementary school. The new school would need to accommodate a thousand students in pre-kindergarten through fifth grade.

Parents and teachers expressed concern over the large size of the proposed school. Many agreed with Jan Rollins, a veteran teacher, when she spoke at a public hearing on the new school—"Young children need an environment in which they can feel safe and where everybody knows who they are. An elementary school with a thousand students is more like a factory than a school. Can you imagine sending a first grader to the office by herself in a building the size of the one we'll have to build?"

At the recommendation of the architect who had been hired to design the new school, a committee of teachers and parents was formed to offer suggestions regarding the physical design and the educational program for the new school. The superintendent asked the committee to address the school size issue and offer suggestions on how to reduce the negative effects of a big elementary facility. In addition, he challenged the group to use the planning of the new school as an opportunity to rethink the entire educational program for Battlefield elementary students. She noted that Battlefield students were falling behind their neighbors in reading and mathematics achievement, use of technology, and opportunities for academic enrichment.

At the behest of the school board, the committee was presented with a set of specific design guidelines to help them in planning the new school. The guidelines included the following:

The New Battlefield Elementary School Should—
- Prepare students to do well on state tests in reading and mathematics
- Promote teacher cooperation and collaboration
- Encourage active community involvement
- Expose students to the latest technology
- Provide all students with challenging learning activities and timely assistance
- Accommodate the needs of an increasingly diverse student body
- Serve as a symbol of the community's commitment to learning
- Reflect research-based "best practices"

The assistant superintendent for instruction provided the committee with a list of "research-based best practices" for early childhood and elementary education. The list consisted of these items:

- Teachers believe all students can learn.
- Faster learners have opportunities to learn at their own pace.
- Students receive continuous feedback.
- Students are expected to apply what they learn.
- Teachers understand how to adjust instruction for students who are not experiencing success.
- Students spend a significant amount of time every day on reading.
- Students are exposed to a variety of sources of stimulation and encouraged to complete hands-on projects.

The superintendent instructed committee members to begin by generating as many creative ideas as they could imagine. She encouraged them to challenge conventional ways of designing schools and delivering educational services.

What would be your recommendations for the new elementary school if you were a member of the committee? More specifically,

1. Are there ways that a school can be designed and organized to reduce the negative effects of large size?
2. Are there relationships between how well students learn and the settings in which they learn? If so, what are these relationships?

(continued)

CONTINUED

3. In what ways should students be exposed to new technology? At what age should this exposure begin?

4. How crucial is it for elementary students to be taught by one teacher in a self-contained classroom? Are there alternatives to self-contained classrooms that should be considered?

5. How should differences of opinion on the planning committee be handled? What if parents and teachers on the committee disagree about the best way to design the new school and its educational program?

REFERENCES

Berliner, David C. and Biddle, Bruce J. *The Manufactured Crisis.* Reading, MA: Addison-Wesley, 1995.

Bodilly, Susan. "Lessons Learned." In Sam Stringfield, Steven Ross, and Lana Smith (eds.), *Bold Plans for School Restructuring.* Mahwah, NJ: Erlbaum, 1996, pp. 289–324.

Bransford, John D.; Brown, Ann L.; and Cocking, Rodney R. (eds.). *How People Learn.* Washington, DC: National Academy Press, 1999.

Datnow, Amanda. "Power and Politics in the Adoption of School Reform Models," *Educational Evaluation and Policy Analysis,* Vol. 22, no. 4 (Winter 2000), pp. 357–374.

Dewey, John. "The School and Society." In John Dewey, *Dewey on Education.* New York: Teachers College Press, 1959, pp. 33–90.

Duke, Daniel L. *A Design for Alana: Creating the Next Generation of American Schools.* Bloomington, IN: Phi Delta Kappa Educational Foundation, 2000.

Duke, Daniel L. "Designing Schools to Foster Teaching and Learning," *Orbit,* Vol. 30, no. 1 (1999), pp. 6–8.

Duke, Daniel L. *The School That Refused to Die.* Albany: State University of New York Press, 1995.

Duke, Daniel L.; Bradley, William; Butin, Dan; Grogan, Margaret; and Gillespie, Monica. "Rethinking Educational Design in New School Construction," *International Journal of Educational Reform,* Vol. 7, no. 2 (April 1998), pp. 158–167.

Duke, Daniel L. and Canady, Robert Lynn. *School Policy.* New York: McGraw-Hill, 1991.

Duke, Daniel L. and Carman, Timothy J. "Implementing an Orderly Budget Reduction Process: A Case Study," *Record in Educational Administration,* Vol. 13, no. 2 (Spring/Summer 1993), pp. 85–90.

Duke, Daniel L. and Tucker, Pamela. "Initial Responses of Virginia High Schools to the Accountability Plan." In Duke, Daniel L.; Grogan, Margaret; Tucker, Pamela; and Heinecke, Walter (eds.), *Educational Leadership in an Age of Accountability.* Albany: State University of New York Press, 2003.

Evans, Robert. *The Human Side of School Change.* San Francisco: Jossey-Bass, 1996.

Galbraith, Jay R. *Organization Design.* Reading, MA: Addison-Wesley, 1977.

Gandara, Patricia and Fish, Judy. "Year-Round Schooling as an Avenue to Major Structural Reform," *Educational Evaluation and Policy Analysis,* Vol. 16, no. 1 (Spring 1994), pp. 67–85.

Gardner, Howard. *Intelligence Reframed.* New York: Basic Books, 1999.

Good, Thomas L. and Brophy, Jere E. *Looking in Classrooms,* 4th edition. New York: Harper & Row, 1987.

Hopkins, David. *School Improvement for Real.* London: Routledge/Falmer, 2001.

Hoy, Wayne K. and Sweetland, Scott R. "Designing Better Schools: The Meaning and Measure of Enabling School Structures," *Educational Administration Quarterly,* Vol. 37, no. 3 (August 2001), pp. 296–321.

Janis, Irving L. *Victims of Groupthink.* Boston: Houghton Mifflin, 1972.

Lee, Valerie E. *Restructuring High Schools for Equity and Excellence.* New York: Teachers College Press, 2001.

Levin, Henry M. "Accelerated Schools for Disadvantaged Students," *Educational Leadership,* Vol. 44, no. 6 (1987), pp. 19–21.

Maehr, Martin L. and Midgley, Carol. *Transforming School Cultures.* Boulder, CO: Westview Press, 1996.

McDonald, Joseph P. *Redesigning School.* San Francisco: Jossey-Bass, 1996.

Metz, Mary Haywood. "Hidden Assumptions Preventing Real Reform." In Samuel B. Bacharach (ed.), *Education Reform.* Boston: Allyn & Bacon, 1990, pp. 141–154.

Morrison, Melissa. "School Is a Home for Children without One," *Washington Post* (January 9, 2001), p. A-11.

Muncey, Donna E. and McQuillan, Patrick J. *Reform and Resistance in Schools and Classrooms.* New Haven: Yale University Press, 1996.

Random House College Dictionary, revised edition. New York: Random House, 1984.

Rose, Lowell C. and Gallup, Alec M. "The 33rd Annual Phi Delta Kappa/Gallup Poll of the Public's Attitudes toward the Public Schools," *Phi Delta Kappan,* Vol. 83, no. 1 (September 2001), pp. 41–58.

Rossman, Gretchen B.; Corbett, H. Dickson; and Firestone, William A. *Change and Effectiveness in Schools.* Albany: State University of New York Press, 1988.

Sarason, Seymour B. *The Culture of the School and the Problem of Change.* Boston: Allyn & Bacon, 1971.

Sarason, Seymour B. *The Culture of the School and the Problem of Change,* 2nd edition. Boston: Allyn & Bacon, 1982.

Schein, Edgar H. *Organizational Culture and Leadership.* San Francisco: Jossey-Bass, 1985.

Schlechty, Phillip C. "Assessing District Capacity." In *The Jossey-Bass Reader on School Reform.* San Francisco: Jossey-Bass, 2001, pp. 361–381.

Schon, Donald A. *The Reflective Practitioner.* New York: Basic Books, 1983.

Senge, Peter M. *The Fifth Discipline.* New York: Doubleday Currency, 1990.

Sizer, Ted. *Horace's School.* New York: Houghton Mifflin, 1992.

Slavin, Robert E. "PET and the Pendulum: Faddism in Education and How to Stop It," *Phi Delta Kappan,* Vol. 71, no. 10 (June 1989), pp. 752–758.

Slavin, Robert E. "Sand, Bricks, and Seeds: School Change Strategies and Readiness for Reform." In Andy Hargreaves, Ann Lieberman, Michael Fullan, and David Hopkins (eds.), *International Handbook of Educational Change.* Dordrecht: Kluwer, 1998, pp. 1299–1313.

Smith, Louis M.; Dwyer, David C.; Prunty, John J.; and Kleine, Paul F. *Innovation and Change in Schooling: History, Politics, and Agency.* New York: Falmer, 1988.

Smith, Louis M. and Keith, Pat M. *Anatomy of Educational Innovation.* New York: Wiley, 1971.

Smith, Louis M.; Prunty, John P.; Dwyer, David C.; and Kleine, Paul F. *The Fate of an Innovative School.* New York: Falmer, 1987.

Stringfield, Sam; Ross, Steven; and Smith, Lana. *Bold Plans for School Restructuring.* Mahwah, NJ: Erlbaum, 1996.

Taylor, Barbara O. "The Effective Schools Process: Alive and Well," *Phi Delta Kappan,* Vol. 83, no. 5 (January 2002), p. 375–378.

Tharp, Roland G. and Gallimore, Ronald. *Rousing Minds to Life.* Cambridge, UK: Cambridge University Press, 1988.

Viadero, Debra. "Whole-School Projects Show Mixed Results," *Education Week* (November 7, 2001), p. 1, pp. 24–25.

Waller, Willard. *The Sociology of Teaching.* New York: Wiley, 1932.

Wideen, M. F. *The Struggle for Change.* London: Falmer, 1994.

■ ■ ■ ■ ■

CHAPTER 5

PREPARING TO ACHIEVE EDUCATIONAL CHANGE

MAJOR IDEAS

■ Creating a design for educational change does not ensure that change will occur.

■ Planning for change calls for determining individual readiness, organizational capacity, and community support.

■ A variety of implementation strategies are available to guide educators as they develop an implementation plan.

■ A sound implementation plan specifies the steps required to implement a design, including provisions for staff development, organization development, and the mobilization of resources.

■ Care should be taken that implementation plans do not become ends in themselves. Flexibility is important.

■ Implementation plans should include provisions for formative evaluation and feedback.

A design for educational change is no better than the plan that is developed to implement the design. Promising reforms have run aground because educators failed to anticipate resistance, allocate sufficient time for training, and secure adequate funding. Once a design has been chosen, it is necessary to draft an implementation plan to guide the process of achieving change. The drafting of this plan is referred to as the Development Phase of the educational change process.

A good implementation plan is based on a careful assessment of preparedness, including the readiness for change of those who must implement the design, the capacity of the school and school system to support and sustain change, and the willingness of the community to underwrite and nurture change. The plan should prescribe the steps that will be necessary to move the design from the drawing board to the classroom or school. These steps typically include provisions for staff and organization development and the mobilization of resources and external support. A realistic timeline for the achievement of these steps and a program for ongoing evaluation and feedback also are important components of the plan.

Chapter 5 is divided into two sections. The first examines the foundation upon which a good implementation plan is based. This foundation involves a thorough assessment of the factors that need to be in place to facilitate successful implementation—individual readiness, organizational capacity, and community capacity. The second section discusses different implementation strategies and the components of a sound implementation plan. The most important of these components—staff development—receives special attention.

THE FOUNDATION OF A GOOD IMPLEMENTATION PLAN

It is tempting for educators to feel that the hard work of change has been completed when they have identified a need for change and selected a design that addresses the need. In fact, they have only begun. The next phase of the process involves developing an implementation plan—a set of guidelines for seeing that the design is actually put in place. These plans also may be referred to as *action plans, change execution plans, school improvement plans,* or *strategic plans.* It is important to remember that implementation plans are not the designs themselves, but the provisions for moving the designs from the drawing board to the school, classroom, or other unit of change.

It has been said that we cannot understand something until we try to change it. By the same token, a case can be made that we cannot change something, at least not successfully change something, unless we understand it. The foundation of any good implementation plan is a careful and thorough assessment of readiness for and resistance to change. Put differently, Kanter, Stein, and Jick (1992, p. 507) contend that a change execution plan must be based on "a thorough understanding of the actual situation." Readiness for change can be examined from three distinct perspectives—(1) the individuals who are expected to implement change, (2) the organization in which change is to be implemented, and (3) the external environment in which the organization exists. In order to focus the upcoming discussion, teachers will be the individuals, schools the organizations, and local communities the external environment involved in educational change. The extent to which individual teachers are prepared to implement a specific design will be referred to as **readiness for change.** The extent to which a school and a community are prepared for change are functions of what will be called **organizational capacity** and **community capacity.** Successful educational change is most likely when teachers are ready to change, schools are organized to enable change to happen, and communities are mobilized to support change.

Key Terms

Readiness for change   The extent to which individual educators are able and willing to implement change.

Organizational capacity   The extent to which a school or other educational organization is prepared to implement and sustain change.

Community capacity   The extent to which a community is prepared to support change.

Readiness for Change

Readiness for change is a function of two factors—commitment and competence. Individuals must be willing to implement a new policy, program, or practice, but willingness alone may be insufficient. Implementing a new policy, program, or practice may require individuals to undergo change themselves, including the acquisition of new skills, knowledge, and beliefs. When competence is present but commitment is lacking, new designs for educational change may never leave the drawing board. When commitment is unaccompanied by competence, the result can be personal frustration and failed reform.

Kottler (2001, pp. 49–50) contends that people become committed to change for four reasons. First, they recognize that things are not working and that some kind of change is needed. Boredom also can be an impetus to change. Normal growth and development, along with the need to cope with the consequences of aging, serve as a third reason. Finally, critical incidents and unforeseen events may compel people to change.

Assessing readiness for change requires understanding resistance as well as commitment. Zaltman and Duncan (1977, p. 63) define resistance as "any conduct that serves to maintain the status quo in the face of pressure to alter the status quo." Lewin (1951) recognized the central role of resistance in his model of "force field analysis." Drawing on the laws of physics, Lewin argued that individuals, and by extrapolation organizations, will remain at rest unless the forces for change exceed the forces for stability. Quinn, Faerman, Thompson, and McGrath (1996, p. 366) offer examples of possible driving forces (forces for change) and resisting forces that might be identified in a force field analysis of an organization:

DRIVING FORCES	RESISTING FORCES
Social change in society	Perceived threats to power
Economic change in society	Routine and structure
Improved efficiency	Resource limitations
Technological advances	Preference for tradition
Expansion	Reluctance to take risks

It is not only the number of driving and resisting forces, but the relative strength of each that must be determined in order to reach a conclusion regarding readiness to change. Among the options available to developers of implementation plans are the following:

- Increase the strength of driving forces
- Add new driving forces
- Decrease the strength of resisting forces
- Remove some of the resisting forces
- Determine whether any of the resisting forces can be changed into driving forces (Quinn, Faerman, Thompson, and McGrath, 1996, p. 367)

Chapter 7 explores the special role of leadership in overcoming resistance and pro-moting commitment to change.

Resistance to change can be differentiated in several ways. Resistance, for ex-ample, can be general or selective. General resistance manifests itself in opposition to any and all suggestions for change. Selective resistance, on the other hand, is reserved for proposed changes of certain kinds or in certain areas. An example of selective re-sistance is found in a study by Mitman and Lambert (1993) of instructional reform in seventeen California middle schools. When some of these schools attempted to elim-inate homogeneously grouped classes, teachers accepted the move for all subjects except mathematics. Apparently, they believed that de-tracking represented a con-structive change for most subjects, but not for mathematics, where the range of stu-dent abilities and achievement was perceived to be especially great.

Resistance also can be distinguished by the nature of the particular concerns. Hall and Hord (2001, p. 72) note that resistance early in the change process is likely to derive from *personal* concerns: "There is uncertainty about what will be expected and self-doubts about one's ability to succeed with the new way. There may also be some grieving over the loss of things that were currently being done successfully." Further along in the change process, however, concerns often become more *profes-sional* in nature. Questions arise, for instance, regarding the effectiveness of certain reforms and their impact on students.

Students of change have identified a variety of reasons individuals resist change. Table 5.1 presents the work of three researchers (Duke, 1993; Kanter, 1991; and Kottler,

TABLE 5.1   Why People Resist Change

DUKE (1993)	KANTER (1991)	KOTTLER (2001)
Lack of awareness of possible changes	Loss of control	Lack of awareness that change is needed
Disillusionment with failed change	Excess uncertainty	Inability to decide what needs to be done
Distrust of change agents	Shock of unexpected change	Lack of understanding of what is expected
Pessimism	Change can threaten familiar routines and habits	Inability to do what is expected
High comfort level with current practice	Loss of face	Lack of willingness to give up what is perceived as valuable
Preoccupation with other concerns	Concerns about future competence	Reinforcement for remaining the same
Stress	Ripple effects (impacts of change on other projects, personal life, etc.)	Lack of belief that what is offered is better than the status quo
Fear of failure/fear of success		Feeling threatened by the anticipated outcome
Impatience	More work	Low personal tolerance for change
Poor time management	Past resentments	Tendency to cooperate in a way that is different from what others prefer or expect
	Change creates winners and losers	

2001). Despite the fact that Duke focused on educators, Kanter on employees in the private sector, and Kottler on individuals involved in counseling, the three lists overlap in a number of ways. By focusing on reasons that were cited by at least two of the three researchers, it is possible to come up with a master list containing nine general reasons people resist change:

1. Commitment to the status quo
2. Lack of awareness
3. Heightened anxiety
4. Potential disruption and discomfort
5. Risk of failure
6. Potential impact on personal life
7. Increased work
8. Threat to job security
9. Work-related alienation

Resistance can arise at any stage in the change process. Some of the reasons listed above, however, may be more likely to influence individuals during the Discovery or Design Phases than the Development or Implementation Phases. Let us look more closely at each of the nine reasons for resistance.

Commitment to the Status Quo.   Anyone who has ever lobbied for change doubtless realizes that some individuals see no compelling reason to abandon the status quo. Kottler (2001) notes that people may not believe that the proposed change represents an improvement over current practice. Sometimes this reasoning is difficult for outsiders to understand, as in the case of someone who refuses to abandon an abusive relationship because the prospect of being alone is so terrifying. Teachers, too, may be unwilling to entertain new ideas because the familiar is preferable to the unknown. In other cases, teachers may have received considerable praise for what they are doing. Why, then, should they take the risk of changing their practice? Kanter (1991, p. 678) observes that reform proposals may be perceived as an indictment of the work people have been doing. It is no wonder that many individuals are motivated to resist change. Such action is an understandable effort to protect their past efforts and egos.

Lack of Awareness.   When individuals do not possess a clear understanding of a proposed change, they may be more inclined to resist it. Sometimes impressions of a reform are based on negative rumors and hearsay. Failure to clarify such impressions can sink a new program or practice before it sets sail. Kottler (2001, p. 51) notes a second awareness problem. Individuals may be unaware that a need for change exists. When this lack of awareness concerns their own need to change, people are sometimes said to be in denial. Individuals simply cannot see that problems requiring correction derive from their own actions or shortcomings. In other cases, lack of awareness is a function of restricted exposure. Teachers who instruct students in honors and Advanced Placement courses may fail to appreciate the struggles faced by low-achieving students. As a consequence, they see no need to change instructional and grouping practices.

Heightened Anxiety.   Change often occasions anxiety. Kanter (1991), for example, argues that employees may equate change with loss of control. Interestingly, her antidote for loss of control—more options for those involved in change—also may be a source of anxiety. Duke (1993, p. 711) recognizes that too much choice can be stressful:

> Providing teachers with various growth options puts them in the position of having to make a decision about the kind of professional they want to become. The blame for professional stagnation can no longer be laid at another's doorstep.

Faced with various choices related to possible changes, some teachers become stressed over which choice to make. Kottler (2001, p. 51) observes,

> A person may readily acknowledge that something needs to change but he or she can't decide which course of action to take. The individual remains frozen, torn between choices, unable or unwilling to risk being wrong.

Change produces anxiety and subsequent resistance for other reasons as well. Kanter (1991, pp. 676–677) points out that some people are shocked when change comes without warning. Uncertainty often attends change and can give rise to anxiety. Kottler (2001, p. 52) contends, in this regard, that people may *want* to change, but become resistant because they lack an understanding of what is expected of them under conditions of change.

Potential Disruption and Discomfort.   The reasons people resist change are not just imagined. In actuality, change can play havoc with the normal operation of schools and classrooms. Duke (1993, p. 710) notes that teachers work hard to develop routines for dealing with predictable circumstances. Such routines, in fact, constitute an indication of instructional effectiveness. Kanter (1991, p. 677) observes that a "great deal of work in organizations is simply habitual" and that most people "could not function very well in life if [they] were not engaged in a high proportion of . . . habitual activities." Change poses a direct threat to behavior patterns that have developed over years of practice and that constitute a comfort zone for individuals. Resistance is particularly likely when they feel that these behavior patterns have been responsible for their successful practice.

Risk of Failure.   All three lists in Table 5.1 acknowledge that concern over possible failure is a source of resistance to change. Individuals faced with designs for change may feel that they lack the skills necessary to implement them. In recent years, for instance, many veteran teachers have worried that they did not possess the competence to integrate new technology into their lesson plans. Duke (1993, p. 711) suggests that it may be the perceived consequences of failure, rather than failure itself, that causes some individuals to be alarmed by change proposals. If a possible consequence of failure to achieve successful change is the loss of colleagues' respect or public embarrassment, teachers may do all they can to avoid change.

Like failure, success also can be a source of fear. Teachers who find themselves in school cultures where mediocrity is the norm may be unwilling to risk the disdain of their colleagues that can result from embracing change and successfully implementing new practices. Once again, it is the perceived consequences of success, rather than success itself, that discourages individuals from embracing reform efforts.

Potential Impact on Personal Life.   Many persons might be more tolerant of change if its impact were limited to the workplace. Kanter (1991, p. 680), however, indicates that new designs can have ripple effects that adversely affect people's personal lives and families. Change invariably entails more worry and more work, both of which can exert a negative effect on life outside of the workplace. The timing of change also can become an issue. If change is proposed at a time when individuals are preoccupied with personal concerns—such as illness or dysfunctional relationships—they may lack sufficient energy to react favorably to it. Work-related concerns also can deflect attention from change. Individuals who are new to their job or heavily involved in a special project can feel overwhelmed at the prospect of having another item added to an already packed agenda. People do not have an unlimited capacity to meet new demands.

Increased Work.   Many change initiatives promise to simplify work and save time, but the actual experience of change often causes people to wonder. Reform invariably is accompanied by more meetings, more training, more paperwork, and more worry. The increased workload affects everyone, from top-level leaders to rank-and-file employees. If people already feel pressed, they are unlikely to welcome change with open arms.

Among those who may be most adversely affected by the additional demands associated with educational change are new teachers. Hall and Hord (2001, pp. 58–59) drew on the research of Frances Fuller to develop their Stages of Concern model. The model recognizes that the level of concern for change can vary among teachers and others facing change. New teachers, according to Fuller's research, initially focus on *self concerns,* or what they need to do in order to make a smooth adjustment to their job. When self concerns have been taken care of, new teachers shift to *task concerns,* or what they must do to manage the various responsibilities associated with teaching. *Impact concerns,* such as whether students are learning what they need to learn, attract attention only when self and task concerns have been addressed adequately. Fuller's findings suggest that new teachers may not regard change as being of paramount importance unless it involves self or task concerns. Any additional effort related to implementing new programs and practices may be resented and resisted until matters of prior importance have been resolved.

Threat to Job Security.   One of the most obvious reasons people resist change is because it can threaten their employment status. Kanter (1991, p. 681) contends that change creates winners and losers. Individuals who are unable to adjust to reform or who lack the skills to perform well under new conditions find themselves in a vulnerable position. In certain situations, reconfiguring existing programs or creating new ones results in the elimination of jobs. Achieving more with less, or the desire for greater efficiency, is an important impetus for change in many organizations. Schools are no exception. When computers were first placed in classrooms, some teachers worried that they eventually would be replaced by technology. Under such circumstances, their resistance was understandable.

Work-Related Alienation.   When employees do not feel good about working conditions or their supervisors, they are less likely to support change. Duke (1993, p. 710) reports that teachers may become cynical about new programs and practices after they experience a number of abandoned reform efforts. It is bewildering to see high hopes dashed and hard work wasted because of the departure of a sponsoring administrator or a shift in school board policy. Distrust is another source of alienation (Duke, 1993, p. 710). Past experience leads some teachers to question the need for change and the motives of those proposing it. Administrators have been known to appropriate reforms in order to advance their own career interests. Kanter (1991, p. 681) notes the chilling effect of "past resentments" and points to the fact that anyone "who has ever had a gripe against the organization is likely to resist the organization telling them that they now have to do something new."

Assessing Readiness for Change.   In order to determine the extent to which individuals—in this case, teachers—are prepared to implement a new design for educational change, it is necessary to collect data. Observations of teaching can help identify the nature of current practice and preferred classroom routines, thereby suggesting areas where instruction and classroom management may need to change. Conducting a force-field analysis, as discussed earlier, can pinpoint sources of support for and resistance to change. Data for such an analysis can be collected by surveys or from interviews and focus groups.

Hall and Hord (2001, pp. 68–72) have developed a widely used questionnaire to facilitate the assessment of individuals' readiness for reform. Their Stages of Concern Questionnaire contains thirty-five items keyed to the seven stages of concern. These empirically based stages range from the awareness stage, where individuals feel little concern for change, to the refocusing stage, where individuals fully embrace change and seek to improve upon it.

Instruments such as the Stages of Concern Questionnaire are helpful in determining the range of readiness for change that characterizes a faculty or other group. To really understand the specific reasons why people resist change, however, requires listening to them. Interviews and focus groups provide opportunities to explore the actual sources of people's concerns and what steps might be taken to reduce them. Such information should be a foundational element of any implementation plan.

Organizational Capacity

An organization can be full of people who are ready and willing to embark on a course of reform, yet the organization itself can present obstacles to change. The extent to which an organization, such as a school, is prepared to implement and sustain change is sometimes referred to as *organizational capacity*. Experts have investigated the key elements of organizational capacity. The work of several will be examined.

Barriers to Change.   Zaltman and Duncan (1977, pp. 75–80), in their landmark book, *Strategies for Planned Change,* identified four organizational barriers to change. The first barrier was the threat change can pose to the power and influence of various parts of an organization. Just as change can create individual winners and losers, it can lead to a redistribution of benefits among organizational units. Loss of benefits, whether perceived or real, leads to resistance. Organizational structure constituted the second barrier. Such structural elements as communication channels, division of labor, rules and procedures, and authority patterns can serve to inhibit innovation and reform. The third barrier involved the behavior of top-level administrators, particularly their unwillingness to support change. The last organizational barrier concerned the climate for change. For Zaltman and Duncan, climate for change was embodied in organization members' perceptions of the change process, including the perceived need for change and the organization's potential for change.

Organizational Innovativeness.   In another important book on change, *Diffusion of Innovations,* Rogers (1995, pp. 379–383) presented various structural characteristics that influence an organization's innovativeness. Centralization (the degree to which power and control are concentrated in the hands of relatively few individuals) and formalization (the degree to which the behavior of employees is guided by rules and procedures) were inversely related to innovativeness. Structural characteristics that were positively associated with innovativeness included complexity (the degree to which employees possess a high degree of specialized knowledge), interconnectedness (the degree to which organizational units are linked by interpersonal networks), organizational slack (the degree to which uncommitted resources are available to promote change), and organizational size. Regarding the last item, Rogers found, perhaps surprisingly, that larger organizations tend to be more innovative. This tendency may be related to access to greater resources.

Organizational Capacity in Schools.   Evans (1996, pp. 119–144) identified six organizational traits that "one would wish for in a school where innovation is to occur." His list includes the following variables:

- *Occupational framework.* The structure of the profession and its influences on the school—the nature of the work, the norms of practitioners, their social status and prevailing outlook
- *Politics.* The trust, consensus, and autonomy the school enjoys and its ability to maintain informed, supportive constituencies
- *History.* The school's previous experience with innovation
- *Stress.* The level of demand on the school vis-à-vis its organizational strengths
- *Finances.* The school's wherewithal to underwrite reform
- *Culture.* The supportiveness of the school's underlying ethos and shared assumptions

Evans recognized the fact that these variables can be related to each other. A history of failed efforts to innovate, for example, is likely to affect the nature of a school's politics and culture.

Conditions for Sustained Development.   Drawing on research from a British project—"Improving the Quality of Education for All" (IQEA), Hopkins (2001, pp. 96–104) found that six conditions were associated with a school's capacity for sustained development:

- A commitment to staff development
- Practical efforts to involve staff, students, and the community in school policies and decisions
- Transformational leadership approaches
- Effective coordination strategies
- Serious attention to the potential benefits of inquiry and reflection
- A commitment to collaborative planning activity.

Based on these conditions, Hopkins offers six propositions regarding the establishment of a school culture conducive to continuous improvement. All of the propositions in some way concern how teachers can develop and function collectively, rather than as isolated individuals.

While Hopkins' focus was the school, Firestone (1989) considered capacity at the level of the school district. He defined the capacity to use reform as "the extent to which the district has the knowledge, skills, personnel, and other resources necessary to carry out decisions" (p. 157). Three problems must be confronted, according to Firestone, in order to activate a district's capacity to use reform. Personnel must be mobilized to carry out decisions, various functions must be performed in order to implement decisions, and linkages must be forged between and among individual schools in the district. Firestone's work identifies some of the conditions that must be in place before comprehensive change across an entire school system can be implemented.

A Trio of Critical Components.   If we survey the work of Zaltman and Duncan, Rogers, Evans, and Hopkins, three essential elements of organizational capacity emerge: (1) a facilitative organizational structure, (2) an organizational culture that supports change, and (3) adequate resources to initiate and nurture change. To assess the organizational capacity of a school or school system, it may be helpful to identify indicators for each of these elements.

Change Key

A school or school system's organizational capacity for change is a function of three factors:

1. A facilitative organizational structure
2. An organizational culture that supports change
3. Adequate resources to initiate and nurture change.

Indicators of a Facilitative Structure.   It is tempting to regard organizational structure as an inevitable impediment to innovation and improvement. Terms like bureaucracy, control, and regulation often are treated as if they were antithetical to change. Hoy and Sweetland (2001) remind educators, however, that school structure can be enabling as well as inhibiting when it comes to designing better schools. Focusing on two aspects of structure, formalization and centralization, they identify various ways that rules, procedures, and hierarchy actually can promote change. When rules and procedures, for example, serve to enable change, they encourage people to—

- Engage in interactive dialogue
- View problems as opportunities
- Foster trust
- Value differences
- Learn from mistakes
- Delight in the unexpected
- Facilitate problem solving (p. 299)

When the hierarchical structure of a school paves the way for successful change, it—

- Facilitates problem solving
- Enables cooperation
- Promotes collaboration and flexibility

- Encourages innovation
- Protects participants (p. 301)

Three aspects of organizational structure are particularly important when it comes to supporting change. Schools and school systems need to (1) recognize and reward people for engaging in efforts to improve performance, (2) encourage cooperation and collaboration, and (3) provide opportunities for those who are expected to implement change to contribute to decisions regarding change. Obviously if teachers as a group feel that the costs of pursuing change outweigh the benefits, they will be less likely to support it. Successful change also is a function of collective effort (Barth, 1991, pp. 126–127; Hall and Hord, 2001, p. 15). When organizational structure discourages teamwork and sharing across departments and units, change becomes more difficult. Lastly, change can be undermined when teachers and other staff members do not feel involved in determining the nature of change and how it will be achieved. Any assessment of organizational capacity, therefore, should address the following questions:

1. Are teachers recognized and rewarded for supporting change?
2. Does school structure encourage and support teamwork and collaboration across units?
3. Are teachers involved in making decisions related to change?

Indicators of a Supportive Culture.   Schools and school systems are characterized by organizational cultures. These cultures may be relatively robust or ill-defined, unitary or fragmented into subcultures, and resistant to or supportive of change. Organizational culture conveys a sense of what is and is not valued as well as expectations regarding appropriate behavior and beliefs. In other words, organizational culture provides a normative structure within which individuals undertake educational activities. Scott (2002, pp. 16–17) maintains that normative structure consists of values, norms, and role expectations, which he defines as follows:

> *Values* are the criteria employed in selecting the goals of behavior; *norms* are the generalized rules governing behavior that specify, in particular, appropriate means for pursuing goals; and *roles* are expectations for or evaluative standards employed in assessing the behavior of occupants of specific social positions.

A school or school system culture that is supportive of change is characterized by the expectation that teachers and administrators continually search for new and better ways to promote effective teaching and learning. Improvement is valued in such a culture, and norms encourage individuals and groups to question traditional practice and challenge assumptions about what, where, when, and how to learn. Cultures that embrace change reinforce the importance of collegiality and collaboration, but also recognize that these characteristics can lead to groupthink and resistance to reform (Leithwood, 1995; Leithwood, Steinbach, and Ryan, 1997). When teachers value the open expression of new ideas and welcome divergent views, they are more likely to be receptive to change.

In cultures that resist change, convention is valued above improvement. Preserving tradition becomes an end in itself. Individuals are socialized to distrust change and those who press for it. High social status is accorded to *gatekeepers*—persons who ensure that all new ideas and reform proposals are challenged. Loyalty is defined in terms of support for the status quo and its champions.

The following questions may need to be answered in order to assess the extent to which a school or school system's culture supports change:

1. Are teachers and administrators expected to continually search for new and better ways to teach and learn?
2. Is a positive value placed on experimentation, improvement, and reform?
3. Do teachers and administrators feel free to question current policies, programs, and practices?
4. Are new ideas and divergent views greeted with an open mind and a desire to understand?

Indicators of Adequate Resources.   In planning for educational change, two resources are of primary importance—time and money. Since time, unless it involves contributions by volunteers, must be reimbursed, money is a key to readiness for change and must be part of any assessment of organizational capacity. Monk and Plecki (1999, p. 505) put it thusly:

> Knowledge about the costs of educational reform strategies for school improvement are crucial to decision-making about the types of strategies to be implemented and the level of resources that will be devoted to any particular set of reform efforts.

When Littleton launched its Directions 2000 initiative (see Introduction), district officials estimated that 1.2 million dollars over and above the district budget would be required. Much of the money was needed for teacher training, new materials, and release time for teachers assigned to develop integrated curriculum. Unable to obtain these funds from the local tax base, Littleton created a foundation to assist in raising money from individual and corporate donors.

The case of Littleton suggests that change may occasion the need for new resources as well as the reallocation of existing resources. Some designs call for additional personnel, extended school days and school years, and new technology. Other designs rely on existing personnel, but call for extensive staff and professional development and faculty collaboration. Training often focuses on the use of new instructional materials, technology, curriculum, teaching methods, and assessment techniques. Teachers may need to visit sites where new practices are in place and enroll in graduate courses to receive advanced instruction. Time is needed for teachers to meet together in teams and departments and conduct collaborative planning, curriculum development, and troubleshooting.

The cost of teacher development can be substantial. Although private corporations may devote up to one-tenth of their annual operating budgets to on-the-job training, school districts rarely exceed 1 percent. Marshall and Tucker (1992, p. 127) recommend that an amount equal to 4 percent of annual salaries and wages be set aside for the continuing education of school staff members.

Although the largest expenditures related to change are likely to be incurred early in the implementation process, it is often the case that resources continue to be needed. Newly hired teachers require the same training that veterans initially received. Formative evaluation may reveal that certain aspects of a design must be altered, a process that can involve hiring consultants and reimbursing teachers for additional planning time. At some point after implementation, a summative evaluation of reforms probably will be needed. Such an evaluation, especially if conducted by external evaluators, entails further expenditures. When budgeting for change, educators need to look beyond the initial period of implementation and set aside sufficient resources for continuing staff development, planning, and evaluation.

Effective educational change not only depends on adequate resources, but on the flexibility to make on-site adjustments in how resources are allocated to support reform (Hill, Campbell, and Harvey, 2000, p. 69). Individuals who are closest to the "chalkface" of change are typically in the best position to determine how to use available resources. It is impossible to predict in advance the exact course of implementation efforts. Shifts in personnel, unanticipated mandates, and other unforeseen developments may necessitate alterations in implementation plans. Precious time and momentum can be lost when such alterations must be approved by those far removed from the site of change. Teacher contracts and school district bureaucracy can limit flexibility, especially when they restrict opportunities for after-school training and collaborative decision making (Solomon, 1995, p. 164).

In order to assess the adequacy of resources available to support change, the following questions should be asked:

1. Are funds available for the training, planning, and materials required to initiate change?
2. Is it possible to encumber funds to sustain change after the initial implementation period and cover the costs of evaluating the effects of change?
3. Will individuals close to the site of implementation be able to make necessary adjustments in the allocation of resources for change?

Community Capacity

Schools and school systems do not exist in a vacuum where they are insulated from the stresses and strains of community life. Educators depend on local communities for political and financial support. While the approval of teachers and administrators is necessary, research consistently indicates that the fate of educational change ultimately may rest with the community (Louis, Toole, and Hargreaves, 1999,

p. 270). Preparing for educational change therefore needs to involve an assessment of *community capacity*—the extent to which a community is prepared to support change.

The story of Littleton's Directions 2000 initiative suggests that assessing community capacity can be tricky. Educational leaders in Littleton thought that they had covered all their bases. Parents and business leaders were involved in planning Directions 2000 and raising funds to support it. The school system hired a public relations firm to spread the word about reforms. Small gatherings were held in local homes so that school district personnel could explain the details of Directions 2000 to parents. All indications were that the Littleton community was ready and willing to embrace the bold initiative. Only when the first high school seniors actually faced the prospect of not graduating because they had failed new performance-based evaluations did substantial resistance surface. Community members complained that they had not fully understood what the school system was attempting to do or how their children would be affected. The message of Littleton is clear—community support should never be taken for granted by educators interested in change. Assessing community capacity needs to begin early and continue throughout the change process.

What should educators look for as indicators of community capacity? One essential component is a clear understanding of proposed changes and their implications for students, parents, and the community. Littleton educators learned the hard way that initial support for change does not necessarily imply understanding. Fullan (1991, p. 227) underscores the challenge of understanding change:

> If teachers and administrators who spend 40 to 60 hours a week immersed in the educational world have trouble comprehending the meaning of educational change, imagine what it is like for the parent. Highly educated parents are bewildered; what of the less educated ones who have always felt uncomfortable in dealing with the school?

Understanding change may not ensure support for change, but support without understanding is equivalent to an undetonated mine. It could explode at any time, with disastrous consequences for reform efforts. The likelihood that community members will understand change is increased when educators articulate clear goals and avoid the use of educational jargon. Efforts must be made to explain change to non-English-speaking parents in their native language. Parents will want to know the consequences of change for their children; taxpayers will be concerned about the costs of change.

A second indicator of community capacity is the extent to which community members already are involved in their schools. Local support for change is more likely in communities characterized by high levels of citizen participation in schools. Parent volunteers, school–business partnerships, and active Parent–Teacher Associations are evidence of participation and support.

Community capacity also is a function of social capital. Social capital, according to Coleman (1988), involves three components—trusting relationships, social networks, and community norms. A community's social capital is high when most community members trust that obligations and expectations will be met, when social relations facilitate rather than impede access to information to help individuals achieve their goals, and when community norms reward and reinforce constructive, improvement-oriented behavior. A study of school and community improvement efforts in Chicago found that social capital played a key role in the change process (Kahne, O'Brien, Brown, and Quinn, 2001, p. 456):

> In short, the study underscores the extent to which broad and coherent school reform requires not only trusting/committed relationships and effective social networks, but also the degree to which these relationships and networks must align with a coherent set of norms and priorities to which members are held accountable.

The researchers go on to note that achieving such alignment can be challenging, since there is an "inherent tension between accountability and trust."

Schlechty (2001, p. 372) believes that the success of many school improvement initiatives may depend on the ability of educators to forge links with other youth-serving agencies in the community. A goal of every school district, he argues, should be "to encourage and support the creation of new relationships between and among agencies and groups that provide services to children and youth, in order to ensure that each child has the support needed to succeed in the school and the community" (p. 372). The implication of Schlechty's recommendation is clear—educating young people requires more expertise and support than can be found in school. Similar thinking led the New American Schools program to designate as one of its primary objectives the creation of "a services and support system that strengthens community and family engagement in the school, reduces health and other non-academic barriers to learning, and promotes family stability" (Stringfield, Ross, and Smith, 1996, p. 19).

THE COMPONENTS OF A GOOD IMPLEMENTATION PLAN

In thinking about how best to go about implementing a design for educational change, a number of questions must be considered. Should the design be subdivided into components and implemented in stages or should the entire design be implemented at one time? Should implementation commence with volunteers or should everyone be required to participate? Should the design be implemented on a pilot basis and then revised in light of experience or fully implemented right off the bat? Questions such as these call for educators to develop an *implementation strategy* before crafting the actual *implementation plan*. An **implementation strategy** represents a general approach to achieving change. This approach should take into account an assessment of individuals' readiness for change, organizational capacity, and community capacity. A good implementation strategy, in other words, is developed with a particular context in mind. An **implementation plan** is a structured sequence of specific steps for achieving a particular design for change. The nature and number of these steps presumably depend on the type of implementation strategy that is chosen.

Key Terms

Implementation strategy   An overall approach to achieving change in a particular setting at a particular time.

Implementation plan   A structured sequence of specific steps for achieving a particular design for change.

Implementation Strategies

When Virginia developed its comprehensive statewide educational accountability program, the decision was made to phase it in gradually, allowing time to finetune different elements of the design and gradually acclimate teachers, students, and parents (Duke, Grogan, Tucker, and Heinecke, 2003). High-stakes tests to determine how well students were learning the new state Standards of Learning were initially administered on a trial basis, so that test items could be validated and passing scores could be determined. The tests were initiated in 1996, but no student could be denied graduation, based on state test results, until 2004. No school could be denied accreditation until 2007. In the years leading up to these dates of full implementation, School Performance Report Cards for every Virginia school were published and distributed to parents and newspapers, thereby forewarning communities that some schools might be at risk. Adjustments in the Standards of Accreditation for schools continued to be made as different elements of the state plan were implemented.

Virginia's choice of an implementation strategy was characterized by *delayed consequences* and *sequenced implementation.* This combination allowed aspects of the accountability program, such as passing scores on tests and technical assistance for low-achieving schools, to be adjusted, thereby minimizing political pressure to scrap the reforms. By contrast, Littleton, Colorado, failed to sequence the implementation of its new performance expectations and evaluation procedures. All nineteen performance-based graduation requirements were introduced simultaneously. In addition, the advent of negative consequences for students was not delayed long enough. Students had only a few years to gear up for new graduation requirements and assessments.

Delayed consequences and sequenced implementation are two of a variety of strategies that educators can employ to increase the likelihood of successful educational change. Another popular strategy involves *piloting* new designs. Unlike sequenced implementation, piloting calls for implementation of the complete design, but only on a trial basis by a limited number of individuals or schools. Piloting allows unforeseen problems to be detected and corrected before full implementation begins, thereby saving resources, unnecessary aggravation, and negative publicity.

A strategy that often is coupled with piloting is *voluntary participation.* Instead of telling individuals or schools that they must implement a new design, they are permitted to volunteer to participate. This strategy can reduce resistance to change, while allowing unforeseen implementation problems to be handled. Voluntary participation, however, is not without problems. Volunteers, be they individual teachers or entire schools, cannot be assumed to be typical. As a result, their experience with change may not necessarily predict the results of full implementation, should all teachers or schools eventually be required to participate at a later date. Memphis, Tennessee, encountered major difficulties when its superintendent attempted to move from voluntary participation in the New American Schools program to required participation by all schools in the city (Viadero, 2001).

What the superintendent tried to do in Memphis was a strategy referred to as *scaling up.* Scaling up calls for the initial identification of a small number of sites for change (schools, districts, communities). These sites may be chosen because they have the greatest need for help, demonstrated willingness to participate, and/or high likelihood of successful implementation of a new design. The intention is for these vanguard sites to become models for subsequent implementation efforts (Stringfield, Ross, and Smith, 1996, pp. 13–16).

When substantial resistance to change is expected, it may be prudent not just to delay the consequences of reform, but to delay the reform itself. This strategy of *postponement* is not an admission of defeat, but a course of action consciously chosen to permit time to rally support for change before the commencement of implementation. Hopkins (2001, p. 112) maintains that it is foolhardy to embark on implementation until both internal and external conditions are conducive to change.

Although the benefits of considering implementation strategies prior to developing an implementation plan seem obvious, evidence exists that educators do not always do so. When Rand researchers studied the New American Schools initial planning documents, they found that implementation strategies received relatively little attention (Bodilly, 1996, pp. 316–317). Primary emphasis was given to the designs for change. Design teams devoted relatively little thought to how designs actually would be introduced to participating schools. Consultants for New American Schools eventually saw to it that planners were apprised of the importance of coupling designs with carefully chosen implementation strategies.

EXAMPLES OF IMPLEMENTATION STRATEGIES

- *Postponement.*   Delay implementation until internal and/or external support for change can be generated.
- *Delayed consequences.*   Proceed with implementation, but delay the impact of change until people learn about and adjust to it.

- *Sequenced implementation.*   Implement new design in segments, rather than all at once.
- *Piloting.*   Implement the complete design, but on a limited or trial basis initially.
- *Voluntary participation.*   Initially implement new design with individuals or sites that choose to participate.
- *Scaling up.*   Begin implementation with carefully selected sites, then use sites as models to guide subsequent implementation.

Components of an Implementation Plan

Once an implementation strategy or strategies have been determined, work can begin on the development of an implementation plan. The primary purpose of this plan is to provide guidance to those involved in implementing a design for educational change. A good implementation plan is less a recipe than a roadmap. Rather than specifying every ingredient of the change process in great detail, it marks the ultimate destination and important points along the way. How educators get from one point to another may be plotted initially, but midjourney corrections should be expected. No plan, however well conceived, can anticipate every new development and contingency.

Plans, of course, will vary in length and content, depending on the nature and magnitude of the desired change. Figure 5.1 contains an actual implementation plan for an elementary school in Virginia.

The sample implementation plan consists of various components. Goal 1 represents a district-wide goal adopted by the board of education. The two specific objectives refer to the need for change—the failure of a small number of students to pass new state tests in English and mathematics. The objectives contain targets that can be used as a basis for evaluating the success of the design for change. The design consists of five activities, including differentiated instruction, after-school tutoring, mentors to help students with homework, parent contact, and a homework Help Desk. For each activity, the plan specifies the individuals who are responsible for implementation and anticipated dates for initiation and completion. Following the activities are a statement of staff development needs related to implementation, benchmarks for the assessment of progress in February, targets for the year-end evaluation, and places for signatures by key individuals.

The format for the sample implementation plan corresponds well with a list of essential components of a school improvement plan by Bullard and Taylor (1993, p. 284). Their list contains six components:

1. Goal statements . . . and evidence that the goals represent problem areas that require improvement
2. Specific activities or strategies designed to achieve the goals, including staff development plans
3. Personnel responsibilities for implementing each activity

FIGURE 5.1   Sample Implementation Plan

Goal 1:	All K–5 students will master the essential curriculum and achieve at levels consistent with their academic potential.
Objective 1:	70% (14 of 20) of students eligible for Remediation Recovery in English will pass the SOL retake test in the Spring, 2005.
Objective 2:	70% (9 of 13) of students eligible for Remediation Recovery in Mathematics will pass the SOL retake test in the Spring, 2005.

		DATE INITIATED		DATE COMPLETED	
ACTIVITY	STAFF RESPONSIBLE (NAME/POSITION)	ANTICIPATED	ACTUAL	ANTICIPATED	ACTUAL
Differentiation of instruction in regular classroom based on assessed needs of students	Principal K–5 teachers	8/2004		6/2005	
Fall and Spring after-school tutoring in small groups or 1:1, based on needs of individual students	4th grade teacher Administrative intern Literacy specialist Principal	10/2004		5/2005	
Provide mentors after school one day a week for purpose of providing homework help and emotional support for achieving in school	Principal Parent Counselor Administrative intern	10/2004		5/2005	
Parent contact/support through variety of channels, including letters and home visits	Principal Family support Counselor Administrative intern Classroom teachers	9/2004		6/2005	
Establish "Early Morning" homework "Help Desk" available 30 minutes before school to assist students with homework questions	Principal PTO Volunteer Coordinator	11/2004		5/2005	

Staff Development Support Needed (Details included in the School-Based Professional Development Planning Document):

Differentiation of Instruction Class (10 hours)
A. Anticipated Evidence of Attainment:
   90% of eligible students will be enrolled in appropriate intervention program. These students will show one-half year of growth based on QRI and Running Record Assessments
B. Actual Evidence of Attainment:

(continued)

FIGURE 5.1   Continued

Year-End Evidence of Progress Attainment:
A. Anticipated Evidence of Attainment:
   70% of students eligible to take the SOL retake test in English and Math will pass.
B. Actual Evidence of Attainment:

Final Review:

Principal	Date

Assistant Superintendent for Instruction	Date

Superintendent	Date

---

4. Resources and materials needed from within the school, as well as from area and central offices
5. Formative evaluation strategies such as timelines or checkpoints to assess progress throughout the year
6. Summative evaluation strategies, expressed in terms of student outcomes whenever possible, to determine if goals have been reached

Besides the components noted by Bullard and Taylor, an implementation plan also may need to provide for *continuous feedback* related to the implementation of various design elements, *organization development* to facilitate activities required for implementation, and *community awareness* regarding the progress of change efforts. Benchmarks and midpoint formative evaluations are helpful, but are not substitutes for the ongoing sharing of information. Effective implementation often requires adjustments and finetuning in light of unanticipated problems and unexpected insights attending implementation. In order to make these midstream course corrections, a steady flow of information is needed from those directly involved in and affected by implementation. At the same time, people who are not directly involved, including parents and educators at other sites in the system, need to be kept apprised of progress. These external stakeholders constitute important sources of support for change initiatives. Leaving them out of the loop increases the likelihood of misunderstanding and resistance to change.

In order to promote the continuous sharing of information on the progress of implementation, both within and outside schools and school systems, implementation plans may need to include provisions for organization development. Schools and school systems are not necessarily designed to encourage individuals to troubleshoot, collaborate, and coordinate efforts to change. By establishing teams, designating channels of communication, scheduling regular briefings and updates, and authorizing steering groups to monitor change initiatives, educational leaders can create an infrastructure to support and sustain change.

**Change Key
Characteristics of a Good Implementation Plan**

An implementation plan should include—

- Specific objectives
- Activities required to implement the design
- Provisions for training needed to implement the design
- A timeline specifying when various implementation activities should begin and end
- A list of resources needed to complete implementation
- Personnel responsibilities related to various implementation activities
- Provisions for continuous feedback and formative evaluation
- Provisions for organization development to support implementation
- Summative evaluation guidelines
- Provisions for keeping stakeholders informed on the progress of implementation

Staff Development

Of all the components of an implementation plan, staff development is by far the most important. The point often has been made—education is unlikely to change unless educators change (Hall and Hord, 2001, pp. 7–8; Sarason, 1982, p. 107). Pasmore and Fagans (1992, p. 391) put it thusly: "There can be no sustained organizational development without individual development and that individual development is predicated upon the creation of an organizational context in which . . . people can experience, reflect, experiment, and learn." Fullan (1991, p. 167), in addressing the first challenge of change for principals, could be addressing all educators when he writes:

> The starting point for improvement is not system change, not change in others around us, but change in ourselves. There is a tendency to externalize the problem and to look for blockages or solutions at other levels of the system.

Various terms are used to describe the process of helping educators to change—on-the-job-training, inservice education, professional development, and staff development. Staff development is preferred for present purposes because it is the most encompassing term. Staff development may involve training, in the sense of skill development linked to particular work functions, or education in a broader sense, referring to the cultivation of understanding and professional judgment. Educational change may require teachers and administrators to become familiar with new materials, master new skills, and learn new curriculum content. New policies, procedures, and routines may need to be studied and assimilated. The typology of professional development goals in Table 5.2 suggests the range of possible goals for staff development.

TABLE 5.2 Typology of Professional Development Goals

GOAL	TYPE	EXAMPLE
1.0	**Prerequisite Goal**	Accomplish activities necessary to work on professional development goal, such as awareness-building, fund-raising, time management
2.0	**Acquisition Goal**	
	2.1 Acquire new skill	Learn to speak Spanish
	2.2 Acquire new knowledge	Learn the work of a new author
3.0	**Developmental Goal**	
	3.1 Develop/refine existing skill	Become a better public speaker
	3.2 Develop/refine existing knowledge	Update knowledge of post-Soviet Russia
	3.3 Develop/refine attitudes or attributes	Increase sensitivity to the needs of special education students
4.0	**Application Goal**	
	4.1 Apply existing skill or knowledge to familiar situation	Use existing knowledge of drama to enhance language arts course
	4.2 Apply new skill or knowledge to familiar situation	Use recently acquired knowledge of computers to enhance geometry class
	4.3 Apply existing skill or knowledge to new situation	Use existing knowledge of drama to motivate students in a new dropout prevention program
	4.4 Apply new skill or knowledge to new situation	Use recently acquired knowledge of computers to challenge students in a new thinking skills program

Source: Daniel L. Duke et al. *Journeys of Discovery.* Federal Way, Washington: Washington Education Association, 1994, p. 20.

Skills and knowledge are not the only possible foci for staff development. Under certain circumstances, it may be very important for educators to change their beliefs and assumptions about teaching, learning, students, and related topics. Evans (1996, p. 65) offers the following example:

> The mainstreaming of special needs students involves new materials, a greater range of curriculum goals, and a wider variety of teaching approaches—but what it demands most is a new conceptualization of learning and teaching, one that radically broadens a teacher's definition of her responsibility. She must accept special needs students as properly hers and capable of meaningful learning, not as "special ed kids" who really belong in a separate class.

Beliefs or Behavior?

One of the unresolved issues in educational change is whether beliefs must change before behavior changes. Is it possible, for instance, for a regular education teacher to acquire and apply instructional strategies for mainstreamed special education students without first embracing the belief that *all* students, regardless of their status and circumstances, are capable of mastering challenging content? If the regular education teacher learns new instructional strategies without changing her beliefs about special education students, is she likely to apply them very effectively?

Although definitive research on the relationship between educational beliefs and behavior does not exist, several experts maintain that it is not essential for beliefs to change before behavior changes (Fullan, 1991, p. 91; McLaughlin, 1990, p. 13). Rossman, Corbett, and Firestone (1988, p. 128) reported on a high school where teachers changed practice despite their continuing opposition to reforms. Why they did so was traced to increased monitoring by supervisors and constant emphasis on new expectations for teachers. When behavior changes while beliefs remain opposed to the change, the spectre of coercion invariably arises. Most students of change would agree that it is preferable for individuals to believe in the changes they are called on to make.

Staff development might not be such a critical component of implementation plans if educational leaders were able to staff new initiatives with individuals hired especially to meet the requirements of these initiatives. In most cases, however, leaders must achieve change with existing personnel. Staff development, therefore, is essential. A variety of ways are available for accomplishing staff development. The following case study describes several.

■ ■ ■ ■ ■

CASE STUDY

STAFF DEVELOPMENT FOR SCHOOL IMPROVEMENT IN AN ONTARIO ELEMENTARY SCHOOL

Leithwood, Jantzi, and Steinbach (1999, pp. 154–159) offer a case study of how an Ontario, Canada, elementary school went about the process of school improvement. The process began when a new principal identified a need to raise student achievement and self-esteem. Following a two-day retreat for the entire staff and meetings back at the school, a design for change was developed and an implementation plan drafted. The design called for a code of conduct for students, a faculty-wide focus on instructional improvement, better classroom management, and increased use of technology. Everyone involved realized that school improvement efforts would take more than a few months to implement.

The centerpiece of the implementation plan was a program of ongoing staff development. In the first year, workshops on learning styles were provided for teachers. The

(continued)

CONTINUED

principal, who was well-versed in the subject, conducted several of these sessions. Over the ensuing two years, additional workshops addressed peer coaching, classroom management, the use of computers, and cooperative learning. In some cases, outside experts were hired to provide staff development. In other instances, staff members were sent for training and given the responsibility of sharing their expertise with colleagues. The school district language consultant worked on a regular basis with every grade-level team to develop model lessons using effective teaching strategies.

An additional source of staff development was professional literature. The principal, along with faculty members, shared useful readings related to effective schools research and intellectual development. Funds were provided so that teachers could be released periodically from regular duties in order to discuss what they were learning and develop practical applications of their knowledge.

As a result of several years of sustained staff development, teachers felt that their repertoire of instructional strategies had expanded and that they were spending more time attending to the learning needs of individual students—both goals of the school improvement effort. Teachers also noted that staff relationships had benefited from learning together and that teachers were more likely than in the past to share ideas and information.

The case study describes several widely used mechanisms for staff development—workshops devoted to skill development in specific areas of professional practice and reading and discussion of professional literature. Other approaches that have proven helpful include inservice courses, mentoring, coaching, videotaping, visits to demonstration sites, modeling, and clinical supervision. To assist local school systems with large-scale staff development, many states have created special centers and formed consortia of educators and schools. Virginia, for example, initiated regional Best Practices Centers to provide the training necessary to implement its comprehensive accountability initiative. These centers identified teachers whose students were doing well on state tests and provided opportunities for them to share their professional expertise with other teachers.

A growing body of research has begun to identify keys to effective staff development. In studying the National Writing Project, one of the most highly regarded teacher development programs in the United States, Lieberman and Wood (2002) found that certain distinctive social practices characterized local Writing Project sites. These practices were described as follows:

- Treat every colleague as a potentially valuable contributor.
- Teach other teachers.
- Share, discuss, and critique in public forums.

- Turn ownership of learning over to the learners.
- Situate learning in practice and relationships.
- Provide multiple entry points into learning communities.
- Reflect on teaching by reflecting on learning.
- Share leadership.
- Adopt a stance of inquiry.
- Rethink professional identity and link it to the professional community.

When a research team conducted a large-scale study of more than one thousand mathematics and science teachers who had participated in professional development activities supported by the Eisenhower Professional Development Program (Title II of the Elementary and Secondary Education Act), they discovered several "best practices":

> Our results indicate that sustained and intensive professional development is more likely to have an impact, as reported by teachers, than is shorter professional development. Our results also indicate that professional development that focuses on academic subject matter (content), gives teachers opportunities for "hands-on" work (active learning), and is integrated into the daily life of the school (coherence), is more likely to produce enhanced knowledge and skills. (Garet et al., 2001, p. 935)

In a derivative study of the preceding one that addressed the effects of staff development on 207 mathematics and science teachers in different schools and school systems, Desimone, Porter, Garet, Yoon, and Birman (2002) identified additional keys to success. The three-year study is noteworthy because it began with data collection prior to the advent of staff development, continued during teacher training, and followed up during the year after training. Researchers found training in the use of instructional technology benefits when teachers in the same school, department, or grade level collectively participate. Furthermore, teachers are more likely to improve their instructional practice when staff development provides opportunities for active learning and focuses on a particular teaching practice.

No single approach to staff development works best in every situation, and all are capable of failing if conditions are not conducive to teacher growth. Still, decades of research and experience suggest several guidelines for those planning to build staff development into their implementation plans.

Don't assume that a single exposure to new knowledge is sufficient. In the past, advocates of educational change believed that teachers would gain enough information from a single workshop or class to be able to change practices developed over a number of years. Experience has taught the folly of such reasoning. While there are always a few "quick studies" and highly motivated individuals for whom one exposure to new knowledge is sufficient, most people need more time in order to reflect on and test new ideas and practices. Effective staff development may require prolonged reflection and discussion, multiple classes, or a series of workshops interspersed with opportunities for teachers to apply and assess what they are learning.

To appreciate the value of patience when planning for changes in teachers' skills and understandings, it is instructive to read the following excerpt from a reflective essay by one of my students. Asked to consider how she had evolved as an educator, Denny Berry, a veteran teacher in Fairfax County, Virginia, wrote the following:

> When I began my career as a public educator, I spoke of learning almost exclusively in terms of teaching. The questions I asked reflected my understanding. How do you get kids to do homework or to study? How should I teach a novel or the persuasive essay or vocabulary? How can I get their attention? What activities work with bored seniors? Teaching was something I did, and learning was something my students did (or were supposed to do). While I knew I wanted my students to learn, I simply did not think much about their learning at all.
>
> Fourteen years later I have changed in my understanding of learning—a change so deep and irreversible that I struggled to think back to provide the illustrative questions above. Today I speak of teaching almost exclusively in terms of learning. The questions I ask reflect this change in understanding. Why should the kids do this homework and study for this test—what will they learn? What enduring knowledge or essential skill will my students learn if we read this novel or write this persuasive essay or study this vocabulary? What engages my students and what things stand in the way of their learning? Teaching for me today is something my students do to me easily as much as I do to them, and learning is something we all do in different ways. Learning is the essence of change itself, a collaborative, recursive and evolving process. I cannot NOT think about my students' learning now. . . .
>
> I believe I made the change from teacher-centered to student-centered, and associated changes in understandings of constructivist learning, over a period of time. The change occurred in fits and starts in a variety of different settings and contexts over more than a decade.

The message of Berry's reflections is crystal clear—meaningful teacher growth is not an overnight affair. Impatience can be an enemy of effective staff development.

Don't assume that new knowledge automatically displaces old knowledge. Beliefs and behaviors that have taken years to develop are not easily dislodged. Sarason (1982, pp. 47–60) speculated that one reason the New Math initiative failed in the sixties was the belief by proponents that teachers could spend a few weeks being trained in the summer and then enter their classrooms in September and approach mathematics instruction in a completely new way. Sarason argued that New Math advocates mis-read their first challenge. As he put it, "No one formulated the [staff development] problem as one requiring teachers to *unlearn and learn*—to give up highly overlearned ways of thinking at the same time that they were required to learn new procedures and new ways of conceptualizing" (p. 53). This oversight led staff developers to expect teachers to integrate New Math concepts and practices quickly. They failed to build in sufficient time for teachers first to examine, critique, and reject old ways of thinking about mathematics. When teachers must change established patterns of thinking and behavior, implementation plans should reflect the need for time to unlearn as well as opportunities to acquire new ideas and practices.

Don't assume that people change without feedback. Adults often become private learners. They read material on their own and decide whether or not to alter their beliefs and behavior. They sit in a class or an audience and listen to a lecture, privately determining what knowledge is worth retaining. Research, however, finds that learning without feedback is unlikely to produce substantive change (Joyce and Showers, 1980; Senge, 1990, pp. 68–92; Tennant and Pogson, 1995, p. 32). Feedback generates cognitive dissonance, alerts individuals to the quality and consequences of their actions, and reveals how thinking and skills can be refined. Feedback is both a source of correction and reinforcement. Who hasn't been spurred on to improve because of a well-timed encouraging word? The best feedback is usually the most immediate. Coaching has become a popular model for staff development because coaches observe what teachers are doing and provide immediate feedback. Mastering new instructional and classroom management techniques may require an ongoing process of practice and feedback.

Don't assume that the source of feedback is unimportant. In a perfect world, it might not matter who provides feedback. The fact is, however, that individuals react differently to feedback, depending on who offers it. Important attributes for those who supervise teachers and promote instructional improvement include skill in communicating, credibility, a thorough knowledge of teaching, trust, and patience (Duke, 1987, pp. 143–148). Teachers sometimes fail to take seriously feedback offered by individuals who have never taught or have not taught recently. Feedback also may be difficult to accept when it is regarded as a judgment or comes from persons who are not perceived to have teachers' best interests in mind.

Don't assume that novices and veterans learn in identical ways. In planning staff development, it is tempting to provide the same training for new teachers and veterans alike. Research on adult development suggests, however, that these two groups may benefit from different kinds of staff development (Evans, 1996, pp. 91–118; Levine, 1989). New teachers, for example, are less likely than their senior colleagues to feel threatened by change. Veterans may require feedback to be delivered in private and in a way that does not imply they have spent years mis-educating their students. They also may need to see new practices in action before they are willing to try them. Demonstration lessons and site visits can be particularly important aspects of staff development for more experienced teachers.

Change Key

Advice for staff development planning:

- Don't assume that a single exposure to new knowledge is sufficient.
- Don't assume that new knowledge automatically displaces old knowledge.
- Don't assume that people change without feedback.
- Don't assume that the source of feedback is unimportant.
- Don't assume that novices and veterans learn in identical ways.

CONCLUSION

Educational designs rarely jump directly from the drawing board to the school or classroom. Teachers and administrators typically have other responsibilities besides initiating change. They occupy a world characterized by complexity, time pressures, conflicting preferences, and scarce resources. Implementing a design for educational change consequently requires planning. Chapter 5 describes the key elements of the Development Phase of the change process, during which educators choose an implementation strategy and create an implementation plan. These actions should not be taken, however, until an effort has been made to assess the level of readiness for change.

Change requires readiness on the part of individuals, schools, school systems, and communities. Teachers, for example, may resist reform for various reasons, such as an unwillingness to risk failure, or a commitment to the status quo. Schools and school systems may lack the organizational capacity to support change. Resources are needed, as are an organizational structure and culture that facilitate the implementation of new programs, practices, and policies. The third component of readiness concerns the community. The history of educational change is littered with reforms that failed because local support was absent or insufficient.

Once an assessment of readiness has been completed, educators are ready to choose an implementation strategy. Chapter 5 described various options, including postponement, delayed consequences, sequenced implementation, piloting, voluntary participation, and scaling up. The final focus of the Development Phase involves creating an implementation plan to guide the change process. A list of ten important elements of an implementation plan was presented. The most critical of these elements typically is the plan for staff development. Change almost always calls for the acquisition of new skills and knowledge. Chapter 5 concluded with several guidelines for individuals charged with the responsibility of planning staff development.

■ ■ ■ ■ ■ ▬▬▬▬▬▬▬▬▬▬▬▬▬▬▬▬▬▬▬▬▬▬▬▬

APPLYING WHAT YOU KNOW

PLANNING TO ADOPT THE COMER MODEL

Imagine that you are the principal of an elementary school serving a large number of students who qualify for free or reduced-cost lunch. Your superintendent visited several elementary schools that had implemented the comprehensive set of reforms developed by Yale professor James P. Comer. He was so impressed with what he saw that he has directed you to adopt the Comer model. He is convinced that the Comer model can address the academic and social needs of low-income students. Since students at your school consistently score below their peers in more affluent neighborhoods and since they must deal with a variety of problems outside of school, you are supportive of the superintendent's directive.

The first step is to learn as much as you can about the Comer model. You discover that the heart of the model is the integration of family support services and a comprehensive school improvement program that addresses curriculum, school organization, and school management. James Comer believes that education cannot be separated from its community context. Parents play a central role in the model, helping to identify and solve school problems and serving as classroom volunteers. Besides providing for improved school–community relations, the model calls for preschool programs, before- and after-school child care, vacation care, home visitation, and help for parents in areas such as infant stimulation and academic assistance.

The Comer model reaches beyond academic development to address all phases of a young person's life, including physical, social, and emotional growth. A young person's learning cannot be separated from his nutrition, homelife, and mental health. A Comer school also becomes a community center, open during evenings as well as throughout the day. Opportunities for parent education are regularly available. Most of the decisions regarding the operation of the school are made by the teachers and parents, not by officials far removed from the school. The structure of a Comer school is based on three teams: a Parent Team, a Student and Staff Support Team, and a School Planning and Management Team. The School Planning and Management Team includes the principal and representatives of teachers, support staff, and parents. It is responsible for coordinating all school activities. The Student and Staff Support Team is made up of child development specialists and responsible for managing individual student cases. The Parent Team provides a forum for identifying parent concerns and ensuring that they are addressed.

Most of the changes called for by the Comer model concern the organization of schooling and related services. Classroom instruction tends to be relatively traditional and highly structured; although an effort is made to involve students in project-based learning whenever possible. Language development is the primary focus of academic work. Children learn best, the model holds, when they are able to form meaningful relationships with adults and peers. Educators who adopt the Comer model must believe that all children are capable of learning. Consensus and collaboration are crucial aspects of the operation of a Comer school, as is the "no fault" principle which calls for a focus on helping needy young people rather than searching for people to blame for their circumstances.

Having become familiar with the basic elements of the Comer model, it is time for you to anticipate what will be needed to implement the model successfully. Reflecting on the discussion of implementation planning in Chapter 5, how would you answer the following questions:

1. What aspects of the Comer model might generate resistance from teachers? What would you do, as principal, to reduce or address such resistance?
2. What aspects of the Comer model are likely to require special training? How would you describe the training that is needed? Who should receive this training?
3. Parent involvement in school decision making is central to the Comer model. Are there any decisions in which parents should not be involved?
4. It is difficult to implement a complex change like the Comer model all at once. Based on what you read about the reform initiative, where would you begin the implementation process?
5. How would you determine whether the Comer model was working? What criteria would you use as a basis for evaluating the initiative?

REFERENCES

Barth, Roland S. "Restructuring Schools: Some Questions for Teachers and Principals," *Phi Delta Kappan,* Vol. 73, no. 2 (October 1991), pp. 123–128.

Bodilly, Susan. "Lessons Learned." In Sam Stringfield, Steven Ross, and Cara Smith (eds.), *Bold Plans for School Restructuring.* Mahwah, NJ: Erlbaum, 1996, pp. 289–324.

Bullard, Pamela and Taylor, Barbara O. *Making School Reform Happen.* Needham Heights, MA: Allyn and Bacon, 1993.

Coleman, James S. "Social Capital in the Creation of Human Capital." *American Journal of Sociology,* Vol. 94 (1988), pp. 95–120.

Desimone, Laura M.; Porter, Andrew C.; Garet, Michael S.; Yoon, Kwang Suk; and Birman, Beatrice F. "Effects of Professional Development on Teachers' Instruction: Results from a Three-year Longitudinal Study," *Educational Evaluation and Policy Analysis,* Vol. 24, no. 2 (Summer 2002), pp. 81–112.

Duke, Daniel L. "Removing Barriers to Professional Growth," *Phi Delta Kappan,* Vol. 74, no. 9 (May 1993), pp. 702–704, 710–712.

Duke, Daniel L. *School Leadership and Instructional Improvement.* New York: Random House, 1987.

Duke, Daniel L.; Grogan, Margaret; Tucker, Pamela; and Heinecke, Walter. *Educational Leadership in an Age of Accountability.* Albany: State University of New York Press, 2003.

Duke, Daniel L.; Hall, Arcella; Hargadine, Diane; Randall, Ann; Rose, Debbie; Russell, Jim; Steinburg, Pat; Struthers, Dave; and Yoshida, Jessie. *Journeys of Discovery.* Federal Way, Washington: Washington Education Association, 1994.

Evans, Robert. *The Human Side of School Change.* San Francisco: Jossey-Bass, 1996.

Firestone, William A. "Using Reform: Conceptualizing District Initiative," *Educational Evaluation and Policy Analysis,* Vol. 11, no. 2 (Summer, 1989), pp. 151–164.

Fullan, Michael G. *The New Meaning of Educational Change,* 2nd edition. New York: Teachers College Press, 1991.

Garet, Michael S.; Porter, Andrew C.; Desimone, Laura; Birman, Beatrice F.; and Yoon, Kwang Suk. "What Makes Professional Development Effective? Results from a Na-

tional Sample of Teachers," *American Educational Research Journal,* Vol. 38, no. 4 (Winter 2001), pp. 915–945.

Hall, Gene E. and Hord, Shirley M. *Implementing Change.* Boston: Allyn and Bacon, 2001.

Hill, Paul T.; Campbell, Christine; and Harvey, James. *It Takes a City: Getting Serious about Urban School Reform.* Washington, DC: Brookings Institution Press, 2000.

Hopkins, David. *School Improvement for Real.* London: Routledge/Falmer, 2001.

Hoy, Wayne K. and Sweetland, Scott R. "Designing Better Schools: The Meaning and Measure of Enabling School Structures," *Educational Administration Quarterly,* Vol. 37, no. 3 (August 2001), pp. 296–321.

Joyce, Bruce R. and Showers, Beverly. "Improving Inservice Training: The Message of Research," *Educational Leadership,* Vol. 37, no. 4 (December 1980), pp. 379–385.

Kahne, Joseph; O'Brien, James; Brown, Andrea; and Quinn, Therese. "Leveraging Social Capital and School Improvement: The Case of a School Network and a Comprehensive Community Initiative in Chicago," *Educational Administration Quarterly,* Vol. 37, no. 4 (October 2001), pp. 429–461.

Kanter, Rosabeth Moss. "Managing the Human Side of Change." In David A. Kolb, Irwin M. Rubin, and Joyce S. Orland (eds.), *The Organizational Behavior Reader,* 5th edition. Englewood Cliffs, NJ: Prentice-Hall, 1991, pp. 674–682.

Kanter, Rosabeth Moss; Stein, Barry A.; and Jick, Todd D. *The Challenge of Organizational Change.* New York: The Free Press, 1992.

Kottler, Jeffrey A. *Making Changes Last.* London: Brunner-Routledge, 2001.

Leithwood, Kenneth. "Cognitive Perspectives in School Leadership," *Journal of School Leadership,* Vol. 5, no. 2 (1995), pp. 115–135.

Leithwood, Kenneth; Jantzi, Doris; and Steinbach, Rosanne. *Changing Leadership for Changing Times.* Buckingham, UK: Open University Press, 1999.

Leithwood, Kenneth; Steinbach, Rosanne; and Ryan, S. "Leadership and Team Learning in Secondary Schools," *School Leadership and Management,* Vol. 17, no. 3 (1997), pp. 303–325.

Levine, Sarah L. *Promoting Adult Growth in Schools.* Boston: Allyn and Bacon, 1989.

Lewin, Kurt. *Field Theory in Social Science.* New York: Harper, 1951.

Lieberman, Ann and Wood, Diane R. "The National Writing Project," *Educational Leadership,* Vol. 59, no. 6 (March 2002), pp. 40–43.

Louis, Karen Seashore; Toole, James; and Hargreaves, Andy. "Rethinking School Improvement." In Joseph Murphy and Karen Seashore Lewis (eds.), *Handbook of Research on Educational Administration,* 2nd edition. San Francisco: Jossey-Bass, 1999, pp. 251–276.

Marshall, Ray and Tucker, Marc. *Thinking for a Living.* New York: Basic Books, 1992.

McLaughlin, Milbrey W. "The Rand Change Agent Study Revisited: Macro perspectives and Micro Realities," *Educational Researcher,* Vol. 19, no. 9 (December 1990), pp. 11–15.

Mitman, Alexis L. and Lambert, Vicki. "Implementing Instructional Reform at the Middle Grades: Case Studies of Seventeen California Schools," *The Elementary School Journal,* Vol. 93, no. 5 (May 1993), pp. 495–517.

Monk, David H. and Plecki, Margaret L. "Generating and Managing Resources for School Improvement." In Joseph Murphy and Karen Seashore Louis (eds.), *Handbook of Research on Educational Administration,* 2nd edition. San Francisco: Jossey-Bass, 1999, pp. 491–509.

Pasmore, William A. and Fagans, Mary R. "Participation, Individual Development, and Organizational Change: A Review and Synthesis," *Journal of Management,* Vol. 18, no. 2 (1992), pp. 375–397.

Quinn, Robert E.; Faerman, Sue R.; Thompson, Michael P.; and McGrath, Michael R. *Becoming a Master Manager,* 2nd edition. New York: Wiley, 1996.

Rogers, Everett M. *Diffusion of Innovations,* 4th edition. New York: Free Press, 1995.

Rossman, Gretchen B.; Corbett, H. Dickson; and Firestone, William A. *Change and Effectiveness in Schools.* Albany: State University of New York Press, 1988.

Sarason, Seymour B. *The Culture of the School and the Problem of Change,* 2nd edition. Boston: Allyn and Bacon, 1982.

Schlechty, Philip C. "Assessing District Capacity." In *The Jossey-Bass Reader on School Reform.* San Francisco: Jossey-Bass, 2001, pp. 361–381.

Scott, W. Richard. *Organizations,* 3rd edition. Englewood Cliffs, NJ: Prentice-Hall, 1992.

Senge, Peter M. *The Fifth Discipline.* New York: Doubleday Currency, 1990.

Solomon, Pearl Gold. *No Small Feat!* Thousand Oaks, CA: Corwin Press, 1995.

Stringfield, Sam; Ross, Steve; and Smith, Lana. *Bold Plans for School Restructuring.* Mahwah, NJ: Erlbaum, 1996.

Tennant, Mark and Pogson, Philip. *Learning and Change in the Adult Years.* San Francisco: Jossey-Bass, 1995.

Viadero, Debra. "Whole-School Projects Show Mixed Results," *Education Week* (November 7, 2001), p. 1, pp. 24–25.

Wideen, M. F. *The Struggle for Change.* London: Falmer, 1994.

Zaltman, Gerald and Duncan, Robert. *Strategies for Planned Change.* New York: Wiley, 1977.

ACHIEVING
EDUCATIONAL CHANGE

If Part II was devoted to the "blueprint" phase of the change process, Part III addresses actual construction. This phase typically is referred to as *implementation*. According to McLaughlin (1987, p. 171), the term was popularized by policy analysts in the early 1970s "when ambitious, sweeping federal reform efforts cast 'implementation problems' in bold relief." These experts realized that large-scale educational, social, and economic change entailed more than promulgating new policies and engaging in careful planning. Political mandates and good intentions were no match for the complexities of daily life in schools, neighborhoods, and communities.

Chapter 6 addresses the challenges associated with converting plans into programs and practices. Drawing on a substantial body of research, the chapter tries to capture the experience of implementing educational change and some of the major hurdles that stand between educators and new designs for schools and classrooms. The message is clear—no implementation plan is likely to anticipate all the possible problems that can arise to slow or arrest the change process. Keys to sustaining educational change beyond initial implementation are discussed at the end of Chapter 6.

Although many factors ultimately contribute to successful educational change, one factor merits particular attention. Leadership, the focus of Chapter 7, is noted by virtually every expert on educational change as the critical ingredient in the change process. From providing direction to overcoming resistance to inspiring commitment, leaders at all levels of educational organizations are responsible for seeing that change is taken seriously.

QUESTIONS TO CONSIDER BEFORE READING PART III

1. If you have participated in an effort to implement a new program, practice, or policy, reflect on the experience. Was the implementation process smooth and trouble-free? If not, what kinds of difficulties were encountered?
2. "Expect the unexpected" might be a good slogan for those engaged in implementing educational change. Can you think of change initiatives that produced unanticipated outcomes? Why do you think that it is so difficult to achieve educational change?

3. The world does not stand still while educators go about the business of implementing change. Imagine that you are trying to implement a new reading program in your school. The process will take two years. What kinds of changes inside and outside the school could affect the success of your implementation efforts?

4. Successful educational change is not only a matter of competence. People must be committed to the change. If you were an educational leader, what could you do to inspire commitment to a new initiative such as a service learning requirement for graduation or the elimination of tracking?

5. Implementing a new program, policy, or practice is one thing; seeing that it is sustained over time quite another. What are some keys to sustaining educational change? Can you think of examples of educational innovations that have stood the test of time?

REFERENCES

McLaughlin, Milbrey Wallin. "Learning from Experience: Lessons from Policy Implementation," *Educational Evaluation and Policy Analysis,* Vol. 9, no. 2 (Summer 1987), pp. 171–178.

■ ■ ■ ■ ■ ▬▬▬▬▬▬▬▬▬▬▬▬▬▬▬▬▬▬▬▬▬▬▬

CHAPTER 6

IMPLEMENTING EDUCATIONAL CHANGE

MAJOR IDEAS

- Implementation is characterized by unanticipated developments that may require alterations in original designs for change.

- The experience of implementing change may be characterized by accomplishment, disappointment, uncertainty, conflict, and surprise.

- The success of implementation often depends on continuing staff development, talent diversity, collaborative culture, flexibility, and stability.

- Sustaining educational change may require special efforts above and beyond those needed for implementation.

- The long-term prospects for educational change are associated with the mobilization of support, continuing emphasis on the benefits of change, a facilitative infrastructure, secure funding, judicious recruitment, and ongoing monitoring of progress.

There comes a time in the change process when it is necessary to shift from preparing to change to changing. Kanter (1983, p. 229) calls this the *action phase* of the change process. A more common term is the **implementation** phase. No sooner did researchers begin to study implementation than they became aware of the *implementation problem* (McLaughlin, 1998, p. 70). Bluntly put, implementers did not always implement what they were supposed to implement. In some cases, Sarason (1971, p. 219–221) observed, implementers failed to implement anything at all!

The discovery of the implementation problem occurred in the late 1960s and early 1970s, at a time when many politicians and policy makers sought to correct major social and educational problems through top-down change initiatives. Policies flowed from Washington, D.C., to localities across the United States, where educators and other civil servants often responded in ways that were more a reflection of local culture and personal preferences than legislative intent. Overnight the study of change became a central focus of concern for legions of researchers. What needed to be done, they asked, to ensure that intended change was actually achieved?

The more that the change process was studied, the more researchers realized that the implementation problem was not the final obstacle to be overcome. Implementation of a new design did not ensure that it would survive. Sustaining change thus became an additional challenge that received scholarly attention. The term **institutionalization** often is used to refer to change that has been fully integrated into existing operations.

Key Terms

Implementation   The process of achieving intended change.

Institutionalization   The condition that is attained when an implemented change is fully integrated into normal operations.

Chapter 6 opens with an overview of the implementation experience, one that often is characterized by unpredictability and unforeseen problems. The second part of the chapter explores some of these problems in greater depth, along with ways to reduce their impact. Keys to sustaining educational change over the long haul are the central concern of the concluding part.

EXPERIENCING IMPLEMENTATION

It would be difficult to find an individual who has not experienced the implementation of educational change in some form. As students in elementary and secondary schools, we presumably were the beneficiaries of changes in curriculum, instructional practice, scheduling, and grouping. At times, however, we may have felt more like victims. As taxpayers, we were asked to support new programs and policies requiring additional resources. As voters, we were called upon to endorse candidates promoting particular change agendas. As educators, we became involved directly in the process of implementing new policies, programs, and practices. How implementation is experienced and what meaning is ascribed to the experience, of course, depends on various factors, including our status, role, values, level of understanding, and investment in the change at hand. A review of the literature suggests that the experience of implementing educational change may be characterized by accomplishment, disappointment, uncertainty, conflict, and surprise. Let us briefly examine each.

Accomplishment

Many studies of educational change concentrate on the problems involved, but implementation can be a matter of triumph as well as travail. Readers of the literature on educational change should be careful not to conclude that achieving what one sets out to accomplish is impossible. Just because a reform is modified in order to fit a particular context or is eventually supplanted by another reform does not mean that change has failed.

The sense of accomplishment that comes from implementing new educational designs is frequently found in accounts where educators have taken the initiative to create their own schools, programs, and instructional approaches. Louis and Miles (1990, pp. 55–97) provide a detailed account of successful implementation of a school improvement process in two high schools. Teachers in these schools took pride in raising expectations for students, collaborating to improve instruction, and eliminating divisiveness among the faculty. The story of Central Park East (Bensman, 2000; Meier, 1995) chronicles the efforts of a dedicated group of New York City educators to develop a unique and highly effective learning environment for urban students. Brosnan (1997) recounts the inspiring story of the Urban Collaborative, an independent public middle school for teenagers at risk of dropping out. In each case, teachers and administrators demonstrated that brilliant ideas need not be doomed to die on the drawing board.

■ ■ ■ ■ ■ ■

CASE STUDY
THE GIFT OF CONTINUING GROWTH

Cognitively Guided Instruction (CGI) is an instructional approach that requires teachers to understand how children develop mathematical thinking. Instead of dictating a particular way to teach or providing ready-made instructional materials, CGI calls for teachers to design their own practices and materials after observing and listening to students as they struggle to grasp new mathematics concepts. In a unique study, researchers (Franke, Carpenter, Levi, and Fennema, 2001) interviewed and observed twenty-two teachers four years after they had received training in CGI. All twenty-two teachers continued to focus on children's mathematical thinking when they planned lessons and delivered instruction. Ten of the teachers showed evidence of ongoing growth, as they refined their use of the CGI approach and collaborated with colleagues.

The teachers who benefited the most from CGI training were those who met regularly with colleagues. Two grade-level groups of teachers were particularly successful. They met daily to plan, share articles, and discuss their students' mathematical thinking. Overall, the researchers concluded that student thinking can serve as an excellent stimulus for sustained professional development. Teachers, it appears, find it meaningful to become students of their students.

When teachers succeed in implementing change, they are likely to experience a heightened sense of individual and collective efficacy and feel that they are more in control of their professional destiny. These feelings may continue to pay dividends when teachers confront new challenges associated with educational change. There is no substitute for confidence when the agenda involves implementing change.

Disappointment

Experts on educational change note that it is "emotional work" that can affect relationships between and among teachers, students, and parents (Hargreaves, Earl, Moore, and Manning, 2001, p. 136). One emotion associated with many efforts to reform education is disappointment. Expectations get pumped up during the preparatory phases of the change process as proponents hold out the promise of improvement. When the actual experience of implementing change falls short of these expectations, the result can be frustration, discouragement, and cynicism regarding future change efforts. Some veteran educators learn to protect themselves against disappointment by resisting or discounting change.

When Muncey and McQuillan (1996) reviewed case studies of five schools involved in implementing programs based on the principles of the Coalition of Essential Schools, they found that faculty dynamics sometimes fostered frustration and disappointment. Teachers who took the lead in school improvement were subjected to criticism by their less ambitious colleagues. Initial implementation successes were chalked up to preferential treatment by disgruntled opponents of change. The researchers offered the following conclusion:

> In sum, teachers cited three factors as reasons for backing away from CES reform work in their classrooms and schoolwide: the cumulative effects of the increased workload associated with implementing reform; the disillusionment they experienced when students did not respond or when teaming with other teachers proved problematic; and the emotional drain they experienced as they dealt with their colleagues' opposition. (Muncey and McQuillan, 1996, p. 268)

Evans (1996, pp. 58–63) characterizes implementation as a journey from loss to commitment. In other words, individuals must let go of current beliefs and practices before they can fully embrace new ones. Understandably, it is not easy traveling, and some people do not complete the journey. As Evans (p. 60) writes, the change process "involves a period—often lengthy—of distress and ambivalence as people try to grasp the full extent of what is being lost and modify their pattern of meaning to incorporate the new." Imagine, then, how disconcerting it can be to finally accept a particular reform after a prolonged period of internal struggle, only to discover that it is no better than what existed previously, and perhaps much less so.

Uncertainty

The early days of a change initiative frequently are marked not only by high hopes, but by a substantial degree of certainty on the part of proponents of change. One would hardly be inclined to support a change that even its advocates questioned. Once implementation commences, however, doubts can begin popping up like weeds in a newly fertilized lawn.

Smith and Keith (1971, pp. 398–399) described the uncertainty that marked the opening of Kensington Elementary School. This state-of-the-art facility was designed to challenge many sacred assumptions about how schooling should be organized (see Chapter 4). With innovation, however, came confusion about new roles and new ways of working together. Educational leaders failed to see a growing need for direction on the part of the young and relatively inexperienced staff. The authors captured the prevailing atmosphere thusly:

> The lack of experience with decision situations in elementary schools, much less an innovative one, the egalitarianism with initial deemphasis on procedures and rules, the high degree of interdependence, the coordination by mutual adjustment, the dimension of true belief and its correlates, the multiplicity of sentiments generated by various procedures, and the façade with its accompanying aspirations and aggrandizement all interacted to increase the level of uncertainty and the number of unintended outcomes. (pp. 398–399)

Another source of uncertainty involves not knowing what the ultimate impact of change will be. When Canadian researchers investigated how educators felt about new government accountability policies, they found that most teachers worried about what reforms would mean for students (Leithwood, Steinbach, and Jantzi, 2002, p. 108). Teachers also wondered whether they would be ready, given short preparation time, to implement the new policies.

■ ■ ■ ■ ■

CASE STUDY
THE APEX TEAM CONFRONTS AMBIGUITY

When a private boarding school for disadvantaged adolescents attempted to restructure by shifting from subject-specific to interdisciplinary teaching, two researchers decided to investigate the process (Nolan and Meister, 2000). Additional changes designed to facilitate the shift included reorganization of departments into interdisciplinary teams and adoption of block scheduling. The research team focused on how one team of five teachers, the Apex Team, representing different subjects, experienced the first year of implementation.

When Nolan and Meister analyzed their data, they discovered that a major theme of restructuring for all five teachers was uncertainty. Teachers felt that the lack of administrative guidance and feedback left them feeling abandoned and insecure. As the researchers put it, "the teachers often floundered throughout the implementation, always questioning and wondering if their method of implementing the initiative was effective, or as they often pondered aloud, 'Are we doing it right?' "

Much of the teachers' feeling of ambiguity derived from the lack of a written interdisciplinary curriculum. Pleas for help from the administration were unproductive and left the Apex Team believing that administrators did not understand the restructuring initiative and did not care whether it succeeded or failed. Uncertainty was amplified by the teachers' discovery that there were no national models of interdisciplinary curriculum and that so-called experts disagreed among themselves about what was entailed in an interdisciplinary curriculum.

The case study of the Apex Team clearly indicates that uncertainty can result from lack of administrative leadership. The role of leadership in the process of educational change will be explored in greater depth in Chapter 7. Interestingly, the five teachers forged tighter professional bonds in order to moderate the negative effects of ambiguity. Their doubts about the nature of the changes they were expected to implement, in other words, were mitigated somewhat by greater assurance of each other's support. It is important to remember that adversity on occasion can yield unexpected benefits.

Conflict

The point already has been made—educational change is highly political. The Discovery, Design, and Development Phases all are characterized by the give-and-take and contentiousness that surrounds any process with the potential to produce winners and losers. It should come as no surprise, therefore, that conflict also is part of the implementation experience. Fullan (1991, p. 106) offers the following advice to educators engaged in change:

> Assume that conflict and disagreement are not only inevitable but fundamental to successful change. Since any group of people possess multiple realities, any collective change attempt will necessarily involve conflict.

Many recent reforms have called for greater involvement of rank-and-file educators, parents, and other citizens in educational decision making. Any time the number of decision makers is increased, the potential for conflict grows. Anyone who doubts this axiom need look no further than the reform of Chicago Public Schools. When the Chicago School Reform Act authorized Local School Councils for each of Chicago's 542 schools and gave each of them control over school budgets, school improvement plans, and key personnel decisions, it ensured that the locus of political activity would shift downward from the city to the neighborhood (Hess, 1991, pp. 162–191). Reform not only pitted parents against parents, but provoked the Chicago Principals Association (CPA) to file a lawsuit in order to protect its interests (Hess, 1991, p. 187). The CPA was prompted to act by anger over loss of tenure and diminished authority. The suit was quickly dismissed by the Cook County Circuit Court.

When Louis and Miles (1990, p. 7) surveyed 178 schools that were in the process of implementing improvements, they found that many of them experienced problems related to "adult–student tensions, conflict with special interest groups, political pressures or tensions, conflicts with the district office, and problems reaching agreement among the staff over the desirability of the reform effort's goals." Conflict often begins during the pre-implementation period, and it does not always abate once a design for change has been adopted and implementation commences. In fact, implementation may only serve to intensify conflict, as individuals and groups that feel threatened by change harden their positions.

That conflict can characterize the implementation experience should come as no surprise to anyone familiar with public education. Fundamental tensions always have marked efforts to educate the nation's young people. Brouillette (1996) documented how these tensions surfaced in one school district during efforts to introduce shared decision making. Although some individuals argued that each school, like each child, was unique and deserved distinctive treatment, others maintained that standardized policies which could be applied equally to all schools were the only way to ensure public accountability. The debate among well-intentioned people regarding whether it is best to focus on how schools and students *actually are* different or on how they *should be* similar is unlikely to be resolved in the near future.

Surprise

Veterans of educational change advise newcomers to expect the unexpected. They have learned that no implementation strategy or plan can anticipate every pothole, curve, or detour in the road to reform. For those who have experienced the change process, perhaps the greatest surprise would be for the implementation to unfold exactly as planned!

One of the most frequently noted surprises during implementation is the increased amount of work that must be done. Teachers and administrators who expected meetings to abate when planning stopped and implementation commenced discover that they continue to spend excessive amounts of time in conferences, troubleshooting sessions, coordination groups, and staff development workshops. Change invariably occasions misunderstandings and unforeseen problems that require additional time and energy. That the promise of educational change is often characterized as greater efficiency and less wasted effort only heightens educators' shock and frustration over increased time demands.

In their account of the opening of innovative Kensington Elementary School, Smith and Keith (1971, p. 86) capture some of the unexpected time demands that confronted teachers:

> Other than the time spent in instruction and contact with the children during the day, there were numerous meetings, many of which were both long and frequent. There were team, subteam, and total staff meetings. All of them were in addition to the regular teacher–pupil responsibilities, and they were not during school hours. It was not unusual for a team meeting to last three-and-one-half hours to four hours. Parent meetings, the parent–school organization, and the Curriculum Committee sessions also were attended in some cases by all staff members and in the latter two instances by a part of the faculty.

One reason that surprise is a constant companion of change is that the context of change is restless. The conditions that marked the Discovery, Design, and Development Phases of the change process may shift by the time implementation begins or midway through the Implementation Phase. A leader departs, creating an opportunity for a new leader, one who may have little investment in her predecessor's initiatives, to take the helm. An economic downturn results in counted-on resources disappearing. Premature evaluation of reforms produces alarm and leads to mass defections. A crisis causes supporters of change to shift their attention elsewhere, leaving new programs and policies to suffer benign neglect.

Anticipating all the possible surprises that can derail, delay, or distract attention from implementation efforts is impossible. Still, those engaged in educational change can benefit from research on the implementation of new programs, practices, and policies. This research has identified various problems that arise during the Implementation Phase. By becoming familiar with these problems, educators can reduce the likelihood of being caught off-guard during implementation.

THE PITFALLS AND POSSIBILITIES OF IMPLEMENTATION

Experts on the implementation of educational change have divided their attention between isolating the causes of failed efforts and pinpointing the keys to successful change (Bird, 1986, p. 48). Because overcoming implementation problems does not necessarily ensure success, it is important to understand both sets of findings. In this section, we shall first examine some of the most common implementation problems and then consider the essentials of successful implementation.

Implementation Problems

The problems that plague efforts to implement educational change are of two basic kinds—deficiencies that originate in the pre-implementation phases of change, and problems that emerge once implementation begins. The former include errors in judgment, oversights, and miscalculations from the Discovery, Design, and Development Phases that return to haunt implementation. The latter encompass challenges that can arise during implementation, despite careful preparation and planning.

Inherited Problems.   The seeds for implementation problems may be sown as early as the initial phase of the change process, during which a need for change is identified and endorsed. Perhaps educators fail to characterize a need for change correctly. What they see as a need for tighter discipline in order to increase student time-on-task may turn out to be a need for more differentiated instruction. The real reason that students are inattentive and, at times, disruptive in class turns out to be teachers' failure to accommodate students' varied learning needs.

Muncey and McQuillan (1996, pp. 158–159) found that lack of consensus regarding the need for change may never be overcome during subsequent phases of the change process. Many teachers and administrators in their study of schools involved in implementing the "Essential Schools" model insisted that the problems facing their schools required changes in society, not in educational programs, policies, and practices. Others believed that they already were doing a reasonably good job educating their students. Change, from their vantage point, threatened to jeopardize success, not increase its likelihood.

Problems also may stem from decisions during the Design Phase, when specific changes to address particular needs are selected. In their investigation of educational changes prompted by federal Experimental Schools grants, Gross and Herriott (1979, pp. 364–365) discovered cases where designs for change failed to reflect compelling needs for change. The designs instead represented the preferences of superintendents or popular innovations that officials felt had to be implemented to "keep up with the Joneses." Designs also can be so complicated that implementers become confused and lose sight of the original reason for change. Mitman and Lambert (1993, pp. 515–516) found that different types of designs spawned different types of implementation problems. Introducing students to "thinking skills" caused teachers to curtail their coverage of other important subject matter, while implementing heterogeneous grouping evoked strong negative reactions from parents of more able students.

Decisions made during the Development Phase may adversely affect implementation too. Sarason (1982, pp. 78–79) warns about the problems that can result when implementation plans fail to allow sufficient time for educators to adjust to the idea of reform and acquire the training needed to proceed. One of the most frequently mentioned implementation problems—failure to involve enough stakeholders—can occur during the Development Phase, when implementation strategies and plans are being determined, as well as during the two preceding phases.

Teachers—typically the individuals on whose shoulders implementation must be borne—often feel that their input either has not been solicited or it has been sought and then ignored (Datnow, 2000, p. 367; Muncey and McQuillan, 1996, p. 154; Nolan and Meister, 2000, p. 209; Whitaker, 1998, p. 520). Resentment at being left out of important decisions regarding change can fester and grow during the pre-implementation period. By the time educational leaders are actually ready to launch a new initiative, many teachers are intent on pulling the plug. Maeroff (1994, p. 19) captured these feelings in his account of the life of an "ordinary" teacher in New Jersey:

> Romano feels he's not leaving [teaching] soon enough so far as this [new] program is concerned. . . . Many students are struggling with the [mathematics] program, unable to cope with terminology that is too difficult for them and unable to maintain the pace that the district has demanded of teachers. . . .
>
> Longevity in the public schools inevitably means exposure to many innovations of this sort, one panacea after another that is reputed to be the vaunted breakthrough that will forever improve education. Lou believes he knows better. And he thinks he understands, too, why some ideas that may be perfectly good do not work.
>
> Too often, the failure is in the implementation, he says. Teachers are not consulted. Teachers are not even led through the paces so that they can carry out the innovation properly.

Maeroff goes on to describe how Lou Romano resented the fact that his school district imported teachers from another system to train his colleagues and himself. What the "higher ups" should have realized was that these teachers came from an affluent district where students were very different from those in Lou's school. Lou and his fellow teachers felt that the training did not relate to their needs. To make matters worse, no provision was made to pilot test the new math program. Such an implementation strategy, according to Lou, would have allowed teachers to finetune and adapt the imported program.

■ ■ ■ ■ ■

CASE STUDY

SCHOOL IMPROVEMENT AT HULL
JUNIOR-SENIOR HIGH SCHOOL

Faced with problems ranging from declining student achievement to inadequate funding, the new superintendent of the Hull, Massachusetts, school system decided to create an advisory committee in 1988 to map out a strategy for school improvement. By early 1989, a bold initiative had been designed. To save money on administrative staffing, the junior high school was eliminated and seventh and eighth graders were sent to the high school. District-wide curriculum coordinators replaced department chairs, allowing for further consolidation of administrative positions. A high school dropout prevention program, based on outdoor and experiential education, was launched. Provisions were made to involve teachers and parents in school decision making and grant writing. Teachers endorsed plans to initiate interdisciplinary studies throughout the school system.

These changes were not always greeted with approval. Some teachers complained that advisory committees had been packed with the superintendent's favorites. Others pointed to flaws in the process for implementing reforms. A case study focusing on the efforts to implement team planning, interdisciplinary studies, and thinking skills in the ninth grade identified three critical implementation problems (Wagner, 1994, p. 48):

> First, there was a lack of clarity and consensus around a few clearly stated educational goals or outcomes. Second, there were no core values that might create more of a sense of community, as well as address students' emotional needs and inappropriate behaviors. Finally, most faculty were not committed to collaboration and change.

The problems that undermined reform at Hull Junior-Senior High School were derived, according to Wagner, from mistakes and oversights during the pre-implementation phases of the change process. It was during this period that district leadership failed to foster the feeling among teachers that they were an integral part of the improvement process. Compounding lack of commitment was confusion over the purpose of reform and the impression that too many changes were being undertaken simultaneously. Wagner (p. 52) concluded, "Without clear goals, there is no clear focus for change, no way to measure results, and no criteria for selecting curricula, teaching strategies, other schools to observe, or training options for teachers."

Material for this case study was taken from Tony Wagner, *How Schools Change* (Boston: Beacon Press, 1994).

New Problems.   Not all problems that threaten the success of change efforts are inherited from the pre-implementation period. Some problems develop without warning once implementation has commenced, while others simply "go with the territory." One of this latter type of problem is the *implementation dip*.

Fullan (2001, p. 40) characterizes the implementation dip as a literal drop "in performance and confidence as one encounters an innovation that requires new skills and new understanding." Change challenges people's carefully developed routines and makes them feel off-balance. They realize that what they have been doing is no longer acceptable, but they do not yet feel comfortable with new programs, practices, and policies. When these feelings of uneasiness are multiplied by the number of individuals expected to implement change, it is easy to see why the implementation dip can stall reform.

A variety of other problems can surface once the Implementation Phase of educational change has begun. The following case study describes several of these problems.

CASE STUDY

BARRIERS TO REFORM AT GRANDLAKE HIGH SCHOOL

Whitaker (1998) studied efforts to implement the principles of the Coalition of Essential Schools at Grandlake High School, a high school of approximately 1,100 students and 60 full-time teachers. The principles included an intellectual focus for school work and greater personalization of the school experience. Whitaker pinpointed five challenges that the initiative posed for the Grandlake staff.

The first involved staff development. Prior to implementation, teachers and administrators received considerable training related to the nine principles. During implementation, however, budget constraints resulted in a severe decrease in staff training activities. As a consequence, momentum was lost and commitment to reforms flagged.

Communication became another problem. When staff members went off to receive training, they often failed to share what they had learned upon their return. The principal, who initially devoted considerable time to talking with teachers about the importance of the nine principles, became caught up in political problems and spent less time cheerleading for reform.

Lack of leadership was identified as a third implementation problem. The leadership team at Grandlake was divided regarding the new program. As change proceeded, opposition was voiced by certain board members, teachers, and community members. Teachers charged that the principal, with backing from the superintendent, tried to intimidate resistant teachers into supporting change. The high school began to fragment into opposing camps.

Fragmentation was exacerbated when, three years into reform, a school-within-a-school (SWAS) was created at Grandlake. The SWAS represented the principal's judgment that it would be easier to implement the nine principles in a smaller setting, thereby creating a model for other teachers to follow. Instead, SWAS became a focus for contention and jealousy, as non-SWAS teachers accused their colleagues of monopolizing publicity and resources.

As a result of these problems, the political environment in and around Grandlake eroded during implementation. Divisions formed among the faculty, between teachers and administrators, and between staff and school board members. Opponents of the reforms were accused of favoring a back-to-basics approach to education. They, in turn, derided the nine principles as "outcomes-based education."

The implementation problems highlighted by Whitaker in her account of Grandlake High School echo those found by other researchers. Many of the problems can be traced to poor judgment on the part of leaders. So central to effective change is the issue of leadership, in fact, that it serves as the sole focus of the next chapter. Of the other implementation problems that have been identified by Whitaker and other experts on educational change, four merit further discussion: inadequate staff development, faculty divisiveness, time constraints, and organizational complexity.

There is a tendency among those who develop implementation plans to front-load staff development. Training often begins, in fact, during the pre-implementation phases. As implementation gathers momentum, training frequently tapers off, in part because teachers' energies are re-focused on putting changes into place and in part because educators sometimes assume that staff development is primarily a preparatory enterprise. As it turns out, the need for staff development actually may increase with the advent of implementation. The optimal time to acquire new skills and understandings may be when teachers are in the midst of reform rather than during a pre-implementation workshop when they can only speculate about the impact of change.

The timing of staff development is not the only potential training problem during implementation. Bird (1986, pp. 56–59) has shown that teachers respond differently to different types of training activities. Some teachers, for example, are less likely than others to embrace peer coaching or the development of a common vocabulary for discussing instructional practice. Finding ways to customize staff development during the Implementation Phase can be an important ingredient in successful educational change.

Another implementation problem concerns faculty divisiveness. Teachers may seem to be in general agreement about the necessity of reform during the early phases of the change process. Most educators probably have no desire to be known as change resisters and opponents of improvement. Only when implementation actually commences do doubts, concerns, and jealousies rise to the surface. Reforms come to be perceived, as they were in the preceding case study, as benefiting some individuals more than others. Those who are fully engaged in implementation grow to resent colleagues who stand on the sidelines and criticize. "Free riders" who, despite their wait-and-see attitude, reap the benefits of successful change are held in particularly low regard by their more industrious peers.

To encourage constructive faculty interactions during the Implementation Phase, plans frequently call for teacher teams and other configurations involving groups of educators. When Nolan and Meister (2000, p. 210) studied reform in a private boarding school (see earlier case study), however, they discovered that "creating teams of people to implement a restructuring initiative caused conflict between groups and alienated teachers from their nonteam colleagues." The researchers concluded (p. 218) that any effort to build change on a foundation of teacher teams must be coupled with a "coherent whole-school vision" in order to avoid faculty fragmentation and alienation.

If time is at a premium during the preparatory phases of change, it becomes absolutely precious during implementation. A number of implementation problems have been traced to the lack of sufficient time. Even educators who are careful to set aside adequate time to identify needs for change, create sound designs, and develop good implementation plans sometimes neglect to provide enough time for ongoing staff development, formative evaluation, and sharing of progress once the Implementation Phase has started. Implementing change is rarely the only responsibility for teachers and administrators. These individuals struggle to accommodate reforms while managing their regular workloads. If educators are not relieved of some duties or reimbursed for additional time to implement change, they can become overwhelmed and resentful. When Muncey and McQuillan (1996, pp. 161–162) reflected on impediments to effective implementation at Coalition of Essential Schools sites, they found time to be a major constraint:

> At each of our study sites time was a scarce commodity. Schools often relied on teachers and administrators who were willing to volunteer their time to design and implement Coalition programs. After programs were in place, teachers needed time to assess and refine their teaching techniques and program structure. But in many schools experienced Coalition teachers had little time to enhance their understanding of Coalition philosophy.

The fourth implementation problem involves increased organizational complexity. In many cases where the goal is school restructuring or comprehensive reform, changes may be so extensive that they actually constitute a new organizational structure, one that parallels the existing configuration of school programs and committees. These parallel structures include distinct academic and co-curricular programs, separate teams and committees, and special budgets. Teachers and administrators can become confused about lines of authority and accountability. They may wonder, for example, whether the new School Improvement Committee or School-within-a-School team of teachers enjoys a privileged status or must fit into the conventional school authority structure. Questions sometimes are raised regarding the criteria that are used to evaluate new programs in contrast to regular programs. Complaints about double standards are not unusual. Until these issues are resolved, the status of reforms may remain tenuous.

The implementation problems that so far have been identified are associated primarily with changes in individual schools. Additional problems can arise when entire school systems embark on a course of improvement. In one of the most extensive studies of reform in large urban school systems, Hill, Campbell, and Harvey (2000) investigated comprehensive change in Boston, Memphis, New York City District 2, San Antonio, San Francisco, and Seattle. Among the implementation problems that undermined improvement efforts in these localities were superintendent turnover and subsequent succession difficulties, erosion of school board support, organized teacher resistance, failure to sustain expected funding, and temporizing through delays, half measures, and the introduction of competing reforms (p. 38). The researchers suggest that those involved in district-wide change should anticipate such challenges and plan accordingly:

> A local strategy that has not been designed to nail down indispensable funding or survive a superintendent's departure or buttress a superintendent's support against political challenges from school staff members who resent performance pressures is unlikely to last long enough to succeed.

Mutual Adaptation

According to the Rand Change Agent Study (McLaughlin, 1990), the kinds of implementation problems described in the preceding paragraphs can be addressed effectively through *mutual adaptation*. This interaction between change initiatives and their contexts causes original designs for change to be modified to reflect local concerns, beliefs, and commitments. Educators like to point out that every school and every school system is unique. Whether this popular perception actually is valid hardly matters. It leads educators to *expect* adjustments and accommodations to be made in designs for change. Mutual adaptation, as Bird (1986, pp. 46–47) notes, is a politically attractive concept. Americans regard local control of education, including educational change, with reverence.

There are reasons, however, for questioning the benefits of mutual adaptation. When local pressures lead to tinkering with designs for educational change, the likelihood increases that the design's potency will diminish. If the design fails, it is difficult to determine whether the problem derives from the original design or its local adaptation. In studying local efforts to adapt the Delinquency Prevention Research and Development Program (DPRD), an initiative aimed at reducing tracking in school, Bird (1986, p. 47) found reason to reconsider the value of mutual adaptation:

> Presumably, program designs require some minimum of integrity to produce their intended effects. They rely on assumptions. Their propositions are related. They combine parts. If their characteristics are not sufficiently realized, there is no reason to expect a program design to produce the intended result. . . . In current school-improvement programs, an eroded version of an initially weak program design is the most likely condition.

Determining when efforts to adapt an imported design so alter the design that it is unlikely to achieve intended results requires courage, insight, and good judgment. Under certain circumstances, it may be better to develop a local design from scratch or postpone change than to extensively modify an externally derived design.

Implementation Essentials

Over the years, students of organizational and educational change have identified a number of essential elements of successful implementation. The most frequently mentioned of these elements is leadership (see Chapter 7). Other key aspects of successful change include continuing staff development, talent diversity, collaborative culture, flexibility, and stability.

Continuing Staff Development. Given the complexity of the education process and the challenges of educational change, it is unlikely that the skills needed to implement many new designs will be easily mastered. For example, learning how to differentiate instruction or hold the interest of students in a block schedule when classes are length-

> **Change Key**
>
> Successful implementation of change is likely to depend on—
>
> - Leadership
> - Continuing staff development
> - Talent diversity
> - Collaborative culture
> - Flexibility
> - Stability

ened to well over an hour requires continuous practice, reflection, feedback, and fine-tuning. Fullan (1991, p. 85) observes,

> Failure to realize that there is a need for in-service work *during implementation* is a common problem. No matter how much advance staff development occurs, it is when people actually try to implement new approaches and reforms that they have the most specific concerns and doubts. It is thus extremely important that people obtain some support at the early stages of attempted implementation.

A key to the success of the National Writing Project, one of the most lauded efforts to change the way teachers provide instruction in writing, is the fact that professional development is ongoing (Lieberman and Wood, 2002). Instead of hit and run workshops, teachers create learning communities in which they regularly meet to share best lessons and strategies, participate in small writing groups, and receive peer feedback. Writing project teachers make use of study groups, summer programs, and online book groups to maintain their focus on improving writing instruction.

Over time, of course, some teachers who are engaged in implementing change may require less ongoing training than others. Staff development, therefore, should be sufficiently differentiated to allow individuals to have access to the type and amount of training that are best suited to their needs. Provisions also should be made for offering staff development to teachers who are hired after implementation has commenced.

Talent Diversity.   Another key to successful implementation is a diverse pool of talent. If the goal is comprehensive or large-scale change, it is unlikely that one individual will possess all the skills and knowledge necessary to achieve it. Teams and other school-based groups can be critical elements of the change process. While it may be important for group members to share certain beliefs and expectations, groups should include individuals with an array of skills and expertise.

When Rand (Bodilly, 1996, p. 318) studied teams involved in planning and implementing New American Schools designs, researchers found that success depended on a combination of talents:

> . . . a conglomeration of visionaries to drive the design toward ambitious undertakings; expertise in development in many elements, such as standards assessment and curriculum development to ensure a quality product; "people" people who can interact with

school staff and train them; communicators who can write documents designed to convey visionary and concrete changes to be made; political negotiators for those designs that take on changes in the system governed outside of the school; and strong administrators who can count the beans. . . .

Implementation teams are likely to require expertise in planning, staff development, data collection and analysis, evaluation, public relations, project management, and budgeting, to mention only the most obvious skill areas. As the Rand study noted, it also may be crucial to have individuals who are adept at dealing with personal concerns regarding change as well as those who can write clearly and persuasively. By drawing on and acknowledging the expertise of various people, those in charge of change are more likely to increase commitment to the initiative.

Collaborative Culture.   Diversity of talent is of little benefit if people are not inclined to work together productively to bring about effective change. It would be wonderful if we could assume that all educators worked in settings characterized by close and cooperative peer relationships. Unfortunately, many schools are structured in ways that reduce the likelihood of cooperation by isolating teachers, scheduling them in ways that minimize professional interactions, and holding individuals rather than groups accountable for outcomes. In other cases, personal differences and rivalries interfere with joint ventures. A vital ingredient in successful implementation is a collaborative culture.

So central is collaboration to contemporary educational change that Hargreaves (1994, pp. 244–245) characterizes it as a *metaparadigm*—"an articulating and integrating principle of action, planning, culture, development, organization and research." He goes on to point out that collaboration is particularly important in a "world in which problems are unpredictable, solutions are unclear, and demands and expectations are intensifying." Unfortunately, the unpredictability of the world to which Hargreaves refers also means that collaboration cannot be counted on. Developing school cultures that recognize and reward people for cooperating becomes, under the circumstances, the best insurance policy against self-interest and organizational entropy.

The kind of school culture that is most likely to support educational change is one that embodies the five elements of a professional community identified by Louis, Marks, and Kruse (1996). These elements include shared norms and values, a focus on student learning, reflective dialogue, deprivatization of practice, and collaboration. When researchers from the University of Missouri (Scribner et al., 1999) conducted a two-year study of three rural middle schools to determine whether such a professional community would result from school improvement efforts, they found that success depended on four factors—principal leadership, school history, organizational priorities, and the organization of teacher work. Regarding the last factor, two of the three schools were more successful because their team structure fostered cultures in which information was freely shared and discussed. The third school also had teacher teams, but they lacked formal planning and teaming time during the school day. Opportunities to develop and maintain a professional community consequently were scarce.

Flexibility.   My first teaching assignment involved teaching African American history to high school students in a suburb of Philadelphia. Since African American history had never been taught as a separate course prior to my being hired, I was asked to develop a curriculum over the summer. I plunged into my assignment with vigor and commitment, drawing on my experience in Africa and my graduate work in Afro-American Studies. The curriculum that I developed provided students with an in-depth analysis of sub-Saharan African civilizations, a detailed investigation of the economics of slavery, and a comprehensive review of the politics of the Civil Rights Movement. Equipped with my curriculum and lesson plans, I met my classes in early September, only to realize almost immediately that my course design was far too ambitious for ninth and tenth graders. Because I had invested so much effort in developing the course and was so proud of the results, I insisted on implementing *my* curriculum. Only after three weeks of frustration on the part of my students and myself did I back off and begin making the adjustments necessary for the ages and abilities of my students.

My experience illustrates the importance of flexibility in implementing change. Despite our best intentions, designs for educational change may not always fit the circumstances at hand. In some cases, the problem may be an inadequate assessment of local conditions. At other times, the need for flexibility derives from changes in conditions that could not have been foreseen. The surest way to undermine implementation is to persist in implementing a design as originally drafted when it no longer matches the situation. In some cases, it even may be prudent to cancel reform entirely, given changing conditions. Educators' time is too precious to squander on reforms that stand little chance of achieving their aims.

John Dewey recognized the importance of flexibility when he developed his Laboratory School at the University of Chicago. According to Tyler (1991, p. 5),

> In his school, he developed plans and initiated activities based on the information he was gaining in studying the students' learning; but as he sought to implement these plans, he found unexpected difficulties and potentials not previously recognized. He realized that information being gained in implementing a plan usually suggested modification of the plan for it to be effective, modification even in the aims as the potentials and problems were identified. He reported that planning should be a continuing process and not to develop a firm outline of aims and operations.

Stability.   Having just noted the value of flexibility, it may seem odd also to stress the importance of stability. The two, in some ways, seem contradictory. Still, one of the ironies of research on implementation is that successful change frequently depends on a certain degree of stability.

Stability may take several forms. For Kanter (1988, p. 195), stability represents "continuity of people." Nothing can undermine the implementation of change any faster than personnel turnover, especially if the individuals occupy key positions. Another threat to stability can be an overly ambitious change agenda. When Elmore, Peterson, and McCarthey (1996, p. 237) investigated the impact of school-wide restructuring on classrooms in three elementary schools, they discovered that "attention to structural change often distracts from the more fundamental problem of changing teaching practice." The school where teachers were engaged in the fewest efforts to alter school organization and decision making processes was the school where instruction and classroom operations changed the most. If our goal is instructional improvement, the greatest favor we can do for teachers may be to free them from too much schoolwide change.

The Challenge of Sustaining Educational Change

Implementing educational change, as we have seen, can be a challenge. Achieving implementation, however, does not mean an end to the challenges of educational change. Implementation would hardly be worth the effort if change could not be sustained for a reasonable period of time. Sustaining change requires that reforms be integrated into the regular operations of the classroom, school, or school system. Some experts refer to such integration as *institutionalization* or *continuation*.

By studying reforms that have taken root and grown, researchers have been able to identify a number of keys to sustaining educational change beyond the initial period of implementation. These vital factors include the mobilization of broad-based support, continuing emphasis on the benefits of change, maintenance of a facilitative organizational structure, secure funding, judicious recruitment, and ongoing monitoring of progress. Let us briefly examine each of these contributors to the long-term success of educational change.

Change Key

Sustaining educational change requires—

- Mobilization of broad-based support
- Continuing emphasis on the benefits of change
- Maintenance of a facilitative organizational structure
- Secure funding
- Judicious recruitment
- Ongoing monitoring of progress

Broad-Based Support.   Educators should not assume that those who initially supported change will continue to do so or that new stakeholders will share their predecessors' enthusiasm for change. Priorities shift, resources evaporate, initial results disappoint, and yesterday's new ideas are displaced by tomorrow's.

Berman and McLaughlin (1978) were among the first researchers to link the long-term fate of educational reform to the mobilization of support. In their study of programs initially financed by federal funds, it was the willingness of school district leaders to intensify efforts to secure support for change *after* federal funds dried up that made the difference between sustained and stillborn reform. Brouillette (1996,

p. 214), in her history of educational change in Cottonwood School District, vividly captures the effort required to ensure continuing support:

> Cottonwood administrators involved in the restructuring effort repeatedly mentioned frustrations arising out of the continuing need to explain to new groups of parents the rationale behind building- and district-level policies that had been extensively discussed with stakeholders before they were adopted. The mobility of families, the continual arrival of new cohorts of students at each grade level, the number of parents who paid attention to communications from the schools only when emotion-laden issues were involved, meant that site-based decisions and policies had to be continually reexplained.

The value of a stable constituency can be seen in the enduring support for special education, Title I, and vocational education programs. Even when evaluation results are less than glowing and competing demands for education funds arise, these programs can count on loyalists to lobby actively on their behalf. To ensure that this support continues, stakeholders have organized themselves into special interest groups. These groups share information on potential threats to programs, monitor legislation, and assess needs for additional resources. Any educational leader, board member, or legislator who considers axing or reducing a program knows that she is likely to receive phone calls, formal protests, and possibly embarrassing publicity. Such expectations cause many public officials to think twice before recommending cuts.

Special interest groups, of course, are not all equally effective. If the educators responsible for initiating a change, for example, are the only ones to stand up for it when the change is attacked, the chances for survival are relatively slim. The reforms that educators alone champion frequently are perceived by noneducators as self-serving. As Muncey and McQuillan (1996, p. 279) found in their study of Coalition of Essential Schools projects, support for sustained change is most likely to succeed when inclusive coalitions of parents, community members, and educators are formed.

A Focus on Benefits.   The likelihood that educational change will be sustained is greatest when the change continues to be perceived as meaningful and important. Such perceptions, in fact, can be keys to mobilizing and maintaining stable coalitions that are ready at a moment's notice to defend reforms against attackers. Although the determination of what is meaningful is likely to vary considerably among individuals, it has been suggested that educators derive a sense of importance from two general sources—commitment to causes greater than their own self-interest and opportunities to grow professionally (Duke, 1994, p. 271). When reforms are perceived to involve *both* contributions to others and the chance for professional development, the prospects of continued support, at least by educators, increase greatly.

Franke, Carpenter, Levi, and Fennema (2001) conducted a follow-up study of teachers who had participated in a professional development program dealing with students' mathematical thinking. They found abundant evidence of *generative change*—change in which individuals continued to add to their understanding after the initial training period (pp. 655–656). The researchers reasoned that a focus on how students think about mathematics was sufficiently meaningful to teachers to sustain interest in continued reflection and growth:

> We propose that it is the engagement with student thinking that allowed teachers to develop understanding and connect ideas. As teachers engage with student thinking, they think about their daily work, about substance, content, and process, and about their own students. They come to see that they can learn through working with their own students in their own classrooms; they receive continual feedback as children discuss their thinking.

When educational change is perceived to benefit students by assisting teachers to be better teachers, the likelihood of lasting change is substantial. Reforms that do not touch the lives of students and teachers in direct ways, that appear to be designed for personal and political rather than educational purposes, and that fail to produce actual improvements in teaching and learning are reforms that can be expected to vanish soon after implementation, if they are implemented at all. There are simply too many important things to do in education to waste time and energy on marginal and meaningless activities.

A Facilitative Structure.   The point already has been made—educational change typically occurs in an organizational context. This context—characterized by various structural features—can help or hinder efforts to sustain change. Imagine, for example, that the focus of reform is instructional adjustments for students who are not experiencing success. Teachers receive training in how to modify their teaching methods for particular students who are not benefiting from whole class didactic instruction. If the system by which teachers are supervised and evaluated—an integral part of school structure—is not modified to reflect the expectation that teachers will make instructional adjustments for struggling students, then the probability of substantive changes in teaching is diminished. When teachers know that a change in teaching practice is sufficiently important to be reflected in the criteria by which they are evaluated, they are more apt to take the change seriously.

School structure—including the hierarchy of authority, rules and regulations, division of labor, and schedules and calendars—is created to enable educators to achieve their mission. The development of a structure that facilitates educational change was noted in Chapter 5 as a key ingredient of organizational capacity. In concert with individual readiness and community support, organizational capacity enables change efforts to get off the ground. Maintaining a facilitative structure allows them to stay aloft long enough to reach their final destination.

Over time, however, structure can become an end in itself. Proposals for structural change may be perceived as attacks on tradition and values, rather than efforts to improve teaching and learning. When Hargreaves, Earl, Moore, and Manning (2001, p. 161) studied how twenty-nine middle school teachers grappled with educational changes, including integrated curriculum and alternative forms of assessment, they discovered that the teachers tried "to squeeze new projects and initiatives into old, unsympathetic structures rather than transforming the structures so that they accommodate and support the new purposes and practices." Such structural elements as the traditional school schedule and the organization of departments by academic discipline ultimately ensured that promising reforms were distilled or neutralized.

Facilitative structures ensure that organizational units, policies, staffing, schedules, spatial arrangements, and evaluation procedures support and sustain change. Hargreaves, Earl, Moore, and Manning (2001, p. 164) warn, however, that a facilitative structure cannot be created overnight. Too much structural change at one time can destabilize a school or school system. Educators are advised to make adjustments in structural elements gradually.

Secure Funding.   Adequate resources have become a familiar theme in this book. They are needed to support both pre-implementation and implementation activities. Not surprisingly, resources also are needed to sustain educational change (Berman and McLaughlin, 1978; Knapp, 1997). Although the need for additional funds may diminish as implementation is completed, it does not disappear entirely. Staff development should continue in many cases, particularly for newly hired personnel. External evaluations of progress may be required. Equipment and instructional materials must be updated or replaced. Feedback on the initial period of implementation sometimes reveals a need for modifications to school facilities or the school schedule. If sustaining a change is important enough, it may even merit a line item in the annual budget. Budget visibility, however, also can make funds in support of reforms an easier target during periods of retrenchment.

Judicious Recruitment.   Personnel turnover is a fact of life for schools and school systems. Educators are promoted, retire, and take jobs elsewhere. Newcomers do not always share their predecessors' enthusiasm for particular reforms (Hargreaves, Earl, Moore, and Manning, 2001, p. 159). To sustain a change, it is important to recruit individuals who are committed to the change. Screening out applicants who are likely to resist or resent particular reforms can prolong the life of reforms and preserve school cultures that support innovation and improvement.

Ongoing Evaluation.   When educators are uncertain that new policies, programs, and practices make a difference, they are less likely to continue to support them. Hargreaves, Earl, Moore, and Manning (2001, p. 118) maintain that teachers "need time, encouragement, and support to reflect on how the change is proceeding, monitor its progress, ensure that its purposes are being met while not also pushing other purposes in the curriculum to one side, and make adjustments as they learn from their attempts to innovate." Access to sound evaluation data, as we shall see in Chapter 8, is critical to this reflection process. The potentially threatening nature of evaluation can be mitigated somewhat by making it a routine occurrence. When educators expect evaluation data to be collected and shared on a regular basis, and when their school culture reinforces continuous improvement, they are more likely to accept the findings and learn from them. Ignorance of the impact of change is not an appropriate basis for sustainability.

A Closing Cautionary Note

The preceding discussion fosters the impression that sustaining change is always desirable. Under certain circumstances, of course, it may be unwise to expend additional time and energy to preserve reforms. If reforms fail to achieve their goals after a reasonable period of time or if, in achieving their goals, they also produce unintended negative byproducts, it may be best to scrap them. Changes often beget other changes, as educators discover new and better ideas during the implementation process. Remaining loyal to a particular reform despite awareness of a more promising approach is hard to justify, especially when educators are expected to be stewards of the next generation. Fullan (1991, p. 90) warns educators to avoid thinking of change as an end in itself. Change must always be regarded as a means for ensuring continuous improvement. It should be expected that reforms give way to other reforms as research, reflection, and ingenuity reveal more desirable ways to teach and learn.

CONCLUSION

The Implementation Phase of the educational change process is a time for testing the validity of identified needs for change, the appropriateness of designs for change, and the effectiveness of plans for implementing change. Ideally, all the hard work of the pre-implementation period bears fruit during this time. The Implementation Phase provides no respite from hard work, however. The success of implementation depends on the ability of educators to cope with emotional highs and lows and a variety of unforeseen as well as predictable problems.

Although implementing change can yield great satisfaction and feelings of pride and accomplishment, it also may involve disappointment, uncertainty, conflict, and surprise. Educators must be prepared to address problems derived from mistakes made during the pre-implementation period as well as new problems, including the implementation dip—a predictable drop in performance and confidence following the introduction of change. Other implementation problems may include faculty divisiveness, insufficient time, increased complexity, and lack of adequate staff development. The ability of schools and school systems to overcome these problems depends on leadership, talent diversity, collaborative culture, flexibility, and stability.

Chapter 6 concludes by addressing the ultimate challenge of educational change—how to sustain change beyond the initial period of implementation. Among the keys to sustainability are the mobilization of broad-based support for change, a continuing emphasis on the benefits of change, the maintenance of a facilitative organizational structure, secure funding, judicious recruitment, and ongoing monitoring of progress. Educators need to realize, however, that sustaining change cannot be allowed to become an end in itself. A particular change should be regarded as a means for improvement, one that itself is eventually subject to change.

APPLYING WHAT YOU KNOW
IMPLEMENTING TEACHER EVALUATION REFORM

Teachers and administrators in South Randall School District agreed that the teacher evaluation system needed to be changed. The system required every teacher, from the first-year novice to the thirty-year veteran, to be observed three times a year, once in fall, once in winter, and once in spring. Based on these observations, school administrators prepared a written evaluation for every teacher. Teachers complained that the process had become a meaningless ritual. The written evaluations tended to say the same things year after year, and there were few concrete suggestions for improved practice. Administrators voiced concern that they spent so much time observing teachers who did not require monitoring that they had little time left over to focus on new teachers and a handful of veteran teachers who needed intensive assistance.

In response to these concerns, the superintendent of South Randall created a committee to design a new teacher evaluation system. Made up of teachers and administrators, the committee designed an innovative three-track system. The first track, called Professional Accountability, resembled the conventional arrangement, with teachers being observed several times and evaluated. Evaluations would be based on a set of performance standards linked to research on good teaching. All probationary teachers (teachers without tenure) had to participate in the Professional Accountability track, as did tenured teachers once every five years. By eliminating annual evaluation of competent tenured teachers, the new system promised to free administrators to focus their attention on teachers in need of assistance while creating opportunities for the vast majority to engage in structured professional growth activities. The second track, called Professional Growth, represented a four-year commitment by each qualified teacher to pursue an ambitious professional development goal. After completing the four-year project, these teachers return to the Professional Accountability track for one year. Participation in the Professional Growth track was voluntary, but the committee was convinced that most teachers would opt to work on a meaningful growth goal instead of electing to continue being observed and evaluated in the conventional way. The third track of the new evaluation system—the Professional Assistance track—was reserved for marginal teachers in need of intensive help. Failure to correct deficiencies could lead to employment termination for teachers in the Professional Assistance track.

The new evaluation system was implemented amidst a show of great solidarity among teachers and administrators in South Randall. The school board appropriated a significant amount of money to support teachers in their efforts to achieve challenging growth goals. Nearly every eligible tenured teacher opted to enter the Professional Growth track and work on an ambitious goal related to instructional improvement.

After five years of the new evaluation system, however, concerns began to be expressed by many teachers and administrators. Teachers who believed that the new Professional Growth track would provide an opportunity to undertake meaningful projects complained that administrators steered them toward their own pet goals. Administrators worried that some teachers in the Professional Growth track really belonged in the Professional Accountability track. Both groups noted that the new system required just as much, if not more, work than the old system. Some teachers began to opt for Professional Accountability, rather than return to the Professional Growth track. The superintendent expressed disappointment with the routine nature of many teachers' professional growth goals. Instead of ambitious goals, as had characterized the first years of the new system, many

(continued)

CONTINUED

teachers resorted to writing modest goals or goals that they already had accomplished. The school board demanded evidence that its investment in teachers' professional development was paying off.

1. If you were asked to advise the superintendent on whether to continue the new teacher evaluation system, what information would you want to obtain before formulating a recommendation? How would you gather this information?
2. Can you identify some reasons why such an initially promising reform might have lost momentum? How would you address these concerns?
3. Sometimes implementation problems can be traced back to the original design for change. Were there any possible flaws in the three-track design for the new teacher evaluation system?
4. Do you believe that teacher evaluation can lead to improved instruction and genuine professional growth? If so, under what conditions would teacher evaluation be most likely to yield these desirable outcomes?
5. Assuming that the initial complaints of teachers (teacher evaluation had become a meaningless annual ritual) and administrators (too much time was spent observing good teachers, leaving little time to help marginal teachers) were legitimate, how would you have addressed them?

REFERENCES

Bensman, David. *Central Park East and Its Graduates.* New York: Teachers College Press, 2000.

Berman, Paul and McLaughlin, Milbrey. *Federal Programs Supporting Educational Change: Vol. VIII, Implementing and Sustaining Innovations.* Santa Monica, CA: Rand Corporation, 1978.

Bird, Tom. "Mutual Adaptation and Mutual Accomplishment: Images of Change in a Field Experiment." In Ann Lieberman (ed.), *Rethinking School Improvement.* New York: Teachers College Press, 1986, pp. 45–60.

Bodilly, Susan. "Lessons Learned." In Sam Stringfield, Steven Ross, and Lana Smith (eds.), *Bold Plans for School Restructuring.* Mahwah, NJ: Erlbaum, 1996, pp. 289–324.

Brosnan, Michael. *Against the Current.* Portsmouth, NH: Heinemann, 1997.

Brouillette, Liane. *A Geology of School Reform.* Albany: State University of New York Press, 1996.

Datnow, Amanda. "Power and Politics in the Adoption of School Reform Models," *Educational Evaluation and Policy Analysis,* Vol. 22, no. 4 (Winter 2000), pp. 357–374.

Duke, Daniel L. "Drift, Detachment, and the Need for Teacher Leadership." In Donovan R. Walling (ed.), *Teachers As Leaders.* Bloomington, IN: Phi Delta Kappa Educational Foundation, 1994, pp. 255–274.

Elmore, Richard F.; Peterson, Penelope L.; and McCarthey, Sarah J. *Restructuring in the Classroom.* San Francisco: Jossey-Bass, 1996.

Evans, Robert. *The Human Side of School Change.* San Francisco: Jossey-Bass, 1996.

Franke, Megan Loef; Carpenter, Thomas P.; Levi, Linda; and Fennema, Elizabeth. "Capturing Teachers' Generative Change: A Follow-up Study of Professional Development in Mathematics," *American Educational Research Journal,* Vol. 38, no. 3 (Fall 2001), pp. 653–689.

Fullan, Michael. *Leading in a Culture of Change.* San Francisco: Jossey-Bass, 2001.

Fullan, Michael G. *The New Meaning of Educational Change,* 2nd edition. New York: Teachers College Press, 1991.

Gross, Neal and Herriott, Robert E. "Theoretical and Practical Implications." In Robert E. Herriott and Neal Gross (eds.), *The Dynamics of Planned Educational Change.* Berkeley: McCutchan, 1979, pp. 353–379.

Hargreaves, Andy. *Changing Teachers, Changing Times.* New York: Teachers College Press, 1994.

Hargreaves, Andy; Earl, Loma; Moore, Shawn; and Manning, Susan. *Learning to Change.* San Francisco: Jossey-Bass, 2001.

Hess, G. Alfred, Jr. *School Restructuring, Chicago Style.* Newbury Park, CA: Corwin Press, 1991.

Hill, Paul T.; Campbell, Christine; and Harvey, James. *It Takes a City: Getting Serious about Urban School Reform.* Washington, DC: Brookings Institution Press, 2000.

Kanter, Rosabeth Moss. *The Change Masters.* New York: Simon & Schuster, 1983.

Kanter, Rosabeth Moss. "When a Thousand Flowers Bloom: Structural, Collective, and Social Conditions for Innovation in Organization." In Barry M. Staw and L. L. Cummings (eds.), *Research in Organizational Behavior,* Vol. 10. Greenwich, CT: JAI Press, 1988, pp. 169–211.

Knapp, Michael S. "Between Systemic Reforms and the Mathematics and Science Classroom: The Dynamics of Innovation, Implementation, and Professional Learning," *Review of Educational Research,* Vol. 67, no. 2 (Summer 1997), pp. 227–266.

Leithwood, Kenneth; Steinbach, Rosanne; and Jantzi, Doris. "School Leadership and Teachers' Motivation to Implement Accountability Policies," *Educational Administration Quarterly,* Vol. 38, no. 1 (February 2002), pp. 94–119.

Lieberman, Ann and Wood, Diane R. "The National Writing Project," *Educational Leadership,* Vol. 59, no. 7 (March 2002), pp. 49–43.

Louis, Karen Seashore; Marks, H. J.; and Kruse, S. "Teachers' Professional Community in Restructuring Schools," *American Educational Research Journal,* Vol. 33, no. 4 (1996), pp. 757–798.

Louis, Karen Seashore and Miles, Matthew B. *Improving the Urban High School.* New York: Teachers College Press, 1990.

Maeroff, Gene I. "My Ordinary Career," *Education Week* (April 27, 1994), pp. 17–20.

McLaughlin, Milbrey W. "Listening and Learning from the Field: Tales of Policy Implementation and Situated Practice." In Andy Hargreaves, Ann Lieberman, Michael Fullan, and David Hopkins (eds.), *International Handbook of Educational Change.* Dordrecht, The Netherlands: Kluwer, 1998, pp. 70–84.

McLaughlin, Milbrey W. "The Rand Change Agent Study Revisited: Macro Perspectives and Micro Realities," *Educational Researcher,* Vol. 19, no. 9 (December 1990), pp. 11–15.

Meier, Deborah. *The Power of Their Ideas.* Boston: Beacon Press, 1995.

Mitman, Alexis L. and Lambert, Vicki. "Implementing Instructional Reform at the Middle Grades: Case Studies of Seventeen California Schools," *The Elementary School Journal,* Vol. 93, no. 5 (May 1993), pp. 495–517.

Muncey, Donna E. and McQuillan, Patrick J. *Reform and Resistance in Schools and Classrooms.* New Haven: Yale University Press, 1996.

Nolan, James and Meister, Denise G. *Teachers and Educational Change.* Albany: State University of New York Press, 2000.

Sarason, Seymour B. *The Culture of the School and the Problem of Change.* Boston: Allyn and Bacon, 1971.

Scribner, Jay Paredes; Cockrell, Karen Sunday; Cockrell, Dan H.; and Valentine, Jerry W. "Creating Professional Communities in Schools through Organizational Learning: An Evaluation of a School Improvement Process," *Educational Administration Quarterly,* Vol. 35, no. 1 (February 1999), pp. 130–160.

Smith, Louis M. and Keith, Pat M. *Anatomy of Educational Innovation.* New York: Wiley, 1971.

Tyler, Ralph W. "The Long-term Impact of the Dewey School." Paper presented at the meeting of the John Dewey Society, San Francisco, 1991.

Wagner, Tony. *How Schools Change.* Boston: Beacon Press, 1994.

Whitaker, Kathryn S. "Implementation Processes, Structures, and Barriers to High School Restructuring: A Case Study," *Journal of School Leadership,* Vol. 8 (November 1998), pp. 504–532.

CHAPTER 7

LEADERS, LEADERSHIP, AND EDUCATIONAL CHANGE

MAJOR IDEAS

■ Successful educational change depends on individual leaders and the quality of their leadership.

■ Leadership for change may be needed at all levels, not just at the top.

■ No single style of leadership has been found to work best under all conditions of change. Change leadership may need to vary with the situation.

■ Predictable challenges of change that leaders must address include combating complacency, overcoming resistance, inspiring commitment, and providing direction.

■ Leaders interested in authentic change must be prepared to challenge popular beliefs and assumptions.

■ When schools and school systems experience high turnover among leaders, sustained educational change becomes more difficult.

Do individuals shape society, or are they shaped by it? This issue has occupied the thoughts of legions of social scientists and philosophers over the years. In a democratic society, a certain uneasiness can arise when too much credit is given to individual leaders. The ultimate source of authority, after all, is presumably the will of the people. When Dwyer and Smith (1987, p. 176) analyzed the four principals who led Kensington Elementary School from its innovative beginnings through its "return to the fold" fifteen years later, they concluded that the influence of individual leaders is most pronounced when investigated over a brief period of time. They went on to observe that "any notion of strong, effective leadership erodes when a larger, longer perspective is taken. Kensington's leaders led within the limits defined by their contexts. None affected his larger context; instead, each was swept along by it."

There is no disputing the fact that leaders are products of their times and their contexts. Still, considerable evidence exists that these times and contexts can be shaped to varying degrees by ambitious and inspired individuals. Chapter 7 examines research on the key role of *leaders* and *leadership* in the process of educational change.

Why the distinction between leaders and leadership? Despite the fact that many people use the two terms synonymously, they represent different things (Duke, 1986). *Leader* refers to an assigned, ascribed, or assumed role occupied by an individual. *Leadership,* on the other hand, is an attribute or a perception. Some individuals who occupy roles as leaders may be perceived to manifest leadership, at least on certain occasions, whereas other leaders are not so perceived. Leadership may be attributed to those who do not occupy the role of leader as well as those who do. Successful educational change has been linked to both individual leaders and the phenomenon of leadership. Leadership has been attributed to individuals and groups at every level of education.

Education leaders and leadership may be viewed in various ways. Depending on the circumstances, leaders can be the target of change or the instrument of change. Leadership can be an antecedent to or a consequence of change. Educational leaders are called upon to respond to change as well as to initiate change. In some cases, they must initiate change *in order to* respond to change. One analysis of contemporary pressures for organizational change found that leaders in both education and business faced an array of new challenges, including the need for greater market sensitivity, demands for greater involvement in decision making by employees and other stakeholders, rejection of traditional reliance on control and compliance, and increased complexity of relationships (Duke, 1996, p. 849). Leaders who deal with such challenges successfully are likely to be perceived as manifesting leadership.

Chapter 7 begins with several propositions concerning the relationship between leadership and educational change. The discussion then addresses four predictable challenges of change for educational leaders—combating complacency, overcoming resistance to change, inspiring commitment to change, and providing direction during the change process. The chapter concludes with a review of key aspects of leadership for educational change.

THE NATURE OF LEADERSHIP AND CHANGE

As we have seen, the concept of change is extraordinarily complex. So, too, is the phenomenon of leadership. To make the task of understanding the relationship between these two complicated ideas a little easier, four research-based propositions are presented and discussed.

FOUR PROPOSITIONS REGARDING LEADERSHIP AND EDUCATIONAL CHANGE

Proposition 1   Educational change requires both leadership and management.

Proposition 2   No single type or style of leadership is best for every situation involving educational change.

Proposition 3   Leadership may be required during every phase of the educational change process.

Proposition 4   Leadership may be required at every level of educational organization by those in designated leader roles as well as others.

Leading and Managing Change

This chapter's emphasis on leading change does not deny the importance of managing change. Although some experts try to diminish the value of management, others recognize that it is an essential component of successful change. Northouse (1997, p. 8) concludes that leadership and management are similar in many respects:

> Leadership involves influence, as does management. Leadership requires working with people, which management requires as well. Leadership is concerned with effective goal accomplishment and so is management.

Where a distinction often is drawn between leadership and management, interestingly, is the matter of change. Barr and Bizar (2001, p. 229), for example, conceptualize leadership as "the risk-taking force leading to new forms of schooling" and management as "the conservative force maintaining what has proven effective in existing school culture." Kotter (1990, pp. 3–8) argues that the purpose of leadership is to produce change and movement, whereas the purpose of management is to produce order and consistency. Kotter overlooks the fact that the success of change actually may depend on a certain degree of order and consistency. As already has been noted, stability is not the enemy of change, but a worthy ally.

Instead of regarding leading and managing as polar opposites, it makes more sense to think of them as distinct, but compatible, processes. Fullan (1991, pp. 175–158) recognizes this symbiotic relationship when he notes:

> Leadership relates to mission, direction, inspiration. Management involves designing and carrying out plans, getting things done, working effectively with people.

Both sets of functions are crucial to the success of educational change. What's more, leaders do not always lead and managers do not always manage. Under certain circumstances, leaders must manage and managers must lead.

The Situated Nature of Leadership

The second proposition holds that no single type or style of leading is best for every situation involving educational change. Another way to express this idea is to say that leading change is *situated*. Research on the relationship between leadership style and organizational effectiveness has a long history and is reflected in the development of situational leadership theory and contingency theory (Bolman and Deal, 1997; Northouse, 1997). The kind of leadership that is suited to reducing the negative impact of budget cuts in poor rural school systems may be quite different from the kind of leadership required to transform a mediocre high school in an affluent suburban community. Although researchers do not know enough at this point to predict which type or style of leadership will be most effective in a particular situation, they acknowledge that certain types or styles are a better match for certain circumstances than other types or styles.

That leadership experts recognize variations in leading can be seen in the array of adjectives they use to modify the word *leadership*. Among the most widely used modifiers are charismatic, servant, shared, symbolic, transactional, and transformational. In the field of education, terms such as democratic, instructional, moral, and visionary have been used to modify leadership. Each term implies a relatively distinct set of assumptions regarding the purpose and practice of leading. The notion of leadership types or styles also suggests that leaders are capable of some degree of behavioral consistency over time.

Opinions vary regarding the capacity of particular leaders to vary their leadership style when facing particular situations. Goleman (2000) reports on research with an international sample of corporate executives that revealed six distinctive leadership styles: coercive, authoritative, affiliative, democratic, pacesetting, and coaching. Each style was found to influence organizational climate and productivity. Rather than specializing in a particular style, Goleman (p. 87) urges leaders to master at least four leadership styles. Drawing on his own investigations, he cites examples of business leaders who were adept at varying their style to fit the circumstances:

> Such leaders don't mechanically match their style to fit a checklist of situations—they are far more fluid. They are exquisitely sensitive to the impact they are having on others and seamlessly adjust their style to get the best results.

With regard to educational change and leadership styles, the work of Hall and Hord (2001) is especially noteworthy. They stumbled onto the idea of variation in *change facilitator style* while conducting a multisite study of the implementation of a new science curriculum. Despite similar training and comparable students, teachers in different schools had different experiences with implementation. These differences eventually were traced to variations in school leadership. In some schools, principals actively supported teachers as they implemented the new science curriculum. In other schools, principals did not press teachers to go beyond the minimum expectations for implementation. Principals in a third group of schools "talked a good game," but did nothing to help teachers.

Based on this study and subsequent investigations, Hall and Hord developed the concept of change facilitator style. The concept recognizes that principals and other individuals in a position to lead change are likely to vary in terms of their priorities and how they view their role in the change process. At this point in their inquiries, Hall and Hord have identified three change facilitator styles, which they refer to as the *initiator,* the *manager,* and the *responder* (pp. 131–134). Initiators possess a clear image of what changes are needed and why they are needed. They are willing to push people to implement the changes and provide whatever assistance and guidance are necessary. Managers see themselves as intermediaries, not initiators, in the change process. They offer support to those who are expected to implement change, but they also take it upon themselves to protect individuals from excessive demands of change. Managers rarely encourage people to go beyond the basic requirements of change. Responders see their role as making certain schools run smoothly while others take the lead in implementing change. They are concerned that everyone has a voice in the change process, a tendency that reflects their desire to please others. Responders typically display little passion for change.

To some it may seem that the initiator style is preferable to the other two when change is on the agenda. Hall and Hord (2001, p. 131) point out, in this regard, that initiators sometimes push people too hard, making them feel anxious and resentful toward reform. This style consequently may not be well suited to situations in which teachers already feel overwhelmed and stressed.

While Goleman believes that leaders can master and manifest many leadership styles, Hall and Hord (2001, pp. 141–142) contend that change facilitator style is relatively stable. In other words, leaders are unlikely to be able to switch styles easily, depending on the nature of the change and the particular circumstances.

A Continuing Need for Leadership

Proposition 3 indicates that leadership may be required during every phase of the educational change process. Each step along the path, from identifying a need for change to ensuring that the change is fully integrated into regular operations, poses predictable challenges. These challenges, in most cases, are best addressed at the time they arise, rather than being passed along. In many instances, however, participants in various phases of the change process have a variety of other commitments and responsibilities. They may be unable or unwilling to take charge of handling the problem.

Consider the initial or Discovery Phase of the educational change process. The crucial task at this point is to determine whether a legitimate need for change exists. When researchers (Gross and Herriott, 1978, p. 368) studied five Experimental Schools projects in the seventies, they found that leadership had been lacking at each site during the Discovery Phase. Anxious to secure federal funds, local education officials neglected to do a thorough investigation of the need for new programs:

> Officials of the central administration in each of the five school districts uncritically accepted innovations without regard to their quality or relevance to the basic problems of their school systems. They did not raise questions about these matters or the assumptions underlying the innovations. One of the major consequences of their abdication of leadership responsibilities was that most of the innovations introduced to their school systems did not appear to be relevant to their basic problems.

During the Design Phase, the central challenge is to adopt, adapt, or create a design that stands a reasonable chance of addressing the previously identified need for change. Once again, leadership can be important, this time for ensuring that "sacred" assumptions about existing programs and practices are interrogated and that a variety of options are considered. Failed change frequently can be traced to premature commitment to a particular design or failure to evaluate design options carefully. When Datnow and Castellano (2001, p. 243) examined principals' roles in introducing the Success for All program, they found that principals closely monitored teachers' efforts to make modifications in the highly structured reform model. When adapting an imported design, leaders must prevent overmodifying the design to the point that it no longer is likely to make a difference.

The Development and Implementation Phases pose additional problems requiring effective leadership. Leaders must guard against planning that is hurried and that fails to involve those upon whom implementation ultimately depends. During implementation, leaders should see that necessary training and resources are available and that momentum is maintained. Since many reforms quietly disappear following implementation, leaders also need to ensure that worthy changes are sustained.

Distributed Leadership

Traditional views of leadership focused exclusively on the head of the organization. Experts today realize that ambitious goals are unlikely to be achieved unless leadership emerges at various levels of the organization. This phenomenon is sometimes referred to as *distributed leadership* (Spillane, Halverson, and Diamond, 2001). Proposition 4 states that leadership may be required at every level of educational organization by those in designated leader roles as well as others.

Hall and Hord (2001, pp. 148–156) were among the first researchers to recognize the key role of teacher leaders in the change process. Whenever they discovered a change-oriented principal, they also tended to find another person who was actively involved in promoting innovation and reform. Dubbed the *second change facilitator* or *consigliere,* this individual—typically a veteran teacher—was trusted by the principal and fellow teachers. The consigliere played a key role in proposing adjustments to designs for change, assisting colleagues in implementing change, and monitoring the effects of change. Hall and Hord found instances where second change facilitators occupied roles specifically associated with new initiatives as well as situations where their leadership emerged in unofficial ways. Change facilitators were found outside, as well as within, schools. Depending on the situation, they could be based in district offices, intermediate units, regional labs, or universities.

■ ■ ■ ■ ■ ▬▬▬▬▬▬▬▬▬▬▬▬▬▬▬▬▬▬▬▬▬▬▬▬▬▬▬▬▬▬▬

CASE STUDY

A SCHOOL WITH MANY LEADERS

When Barr and Bizar (2001, pp. 232–238) studied the reform of Chicago schools, they found that principals were not alone in the vanguard of improvement efforts. One school in particular, Best Practice High School, was characterized by a high degree of distributed leadership (Zemelman, 2001). The success of this enterprise has been traced, in large measure, to the proliferation of teacher leaders and external change facilitators.

Located in a multiplex facility with two other small high schools, Best Practice High School (BPHS) serves a student body that is largely poor and nonwhite. Designed by veteran teachers, parents, community members, and faculty from National-Louis University, BPHS opened its doors in 1996. Intentionally small, the 400-student high school embodies

(continued)

CONTINUED

a state-of-the-art curriculum, flexible schedule, and teacher–student advisory system. Students benefit from the school's many partnerships with local businesses and agencies.

BPHS was able to avoid many of the problems experienced by other downsized Chicago schools because effective leaders emerged at various levels to guide the fledgling undertaking. Important work regarding resource acquisition and district-school relations was undertaken by the multiplex principal. Teacher leaders handled the day-to-day administration of school affairs as well as guiding the implementation and finetuning of various changes once the school was up and running. Teacher teams were responsible for making decisions regarding each grade level and special programs. University-based consultants directed much of the initial planning and staff development and then stuck around to help secure additional funds, track the school's progress, and direct special projects such as the development of student portfolios. Students exercised leadership by speaking up about aspects of the school program that required adjustment and participating in the selection of faculty. Parents and community members played leadership roles through their involvement in the Local School Council, which was authorized to make budget decisions and hire the multiplex principal.

Given the traditional focus on the solitary leader at the top, such as a principal or a superintendent, concern in the past naturally centered on what that individual knew and could do. Now that awareness has grown of the presence of multiple leaders, concern is shifting to what these people can accomplish together. Knowledge and skill are of little value if they are withheld or used to enhance individual influence rather than improve teaching and learning. An ongoing study of distributed leadership in 13 Chicago elementary schools is finding various examples of the successful pooling of leaders' talents and expertise (Spillane, Halverson, and Diamond, 2001, p. 25). In one instance, the tasks of analyzing and interpreting student test results and identifying instructional needs and priorities based on this data analysis were undertaken by the principal, assistant principal, and counselor. Each brought different knowledge and experience to the endeavor. In the words of the researchers,

> Working together, these leaders study the "item analysis" for each grade level, identifying language arts and mathematics skills students have difficulty with, and crafting a professional development program designed to help teachers revise their practice and address these needs. The leadership tasks in this example are co-enacted by the three leaders. (p. 25)

The message of this and other studies is clear—educational change requires many leaders and multiple talents. Reforms that depend on the leadership of one key individual frequently unravel when the person shifts focus to a new priority, burns out, or departs for another job. Capable leaders may be able to do many of the individual tasks of change, but they are unlikely to be able to do them all simultaneously and equally well.

FOUR PREDICTABLE LEADERSHIP CHALLENGES

Change poses a variety of challenges for educational leaders. Although some challenges are unique, others are likely to arise regardless of the circumstances. Four predictable leadership challenges of change include combating complacency, overcoming resistance, inspiring commitment, and providing direction. Although individual leaders who face change may have to deal with each of these challenges, *how* they deal with them is likely to vary considerably, depending on the particular situation, their expertise, and the resources available. This part of Chapter 7 examines these challenges and how educational leaders can address them.

Combating Complacency

We have found that some measure of organizational stability can facilitate successful change. Not so with complacency. Complacency results in individual and organizational inertia, a reluctance to entertain even the possibility that change is needed. If a compelling sense of urgency is the accelerator for change, complacency is the brake.

Complacency derives from various sources and manifests itself in different ways. Kotter (1996, pp. 38–42) identifies nine organizational sources of complacency, including an overabundance of resources, the absence of a major crisis, and low performance expectations. Several individual sources of complacency were presented in Chapter 5's discussion of readiness for change. One example involves professional and personal routines. We expect and encourage new teachers to develop routines for handling predictable classroom tasks. Over time, however, these routines can become impediments to change. When we speak of educators who have not taught for twenty years, but who have taught one year twenty times, we are making fun of the tendency of some teachers to settle quickly into patterns of behavior. Altering these patterns can be a daunting challenge for leaders, especially when they seem to be producing desired results.

Perception plays a central role in the etiology of complacency. When teachers perceive that they are doing a good job or the best job they are capable of doing, they are more likely to become set in their ways. Even when they realize that they are not meeting desired goals, teachers can grow complacent because they perceive that the reasons for their lack of success are due to factors beyond their control. The belief that students from poor or single parent families are unlikely to be high achievers, for instance, may lead some teachers to stop searching for new and better ways to provide instruction for these students. Other teachers believe that there is little they can do to reach every student when class sizes are perceived to be too large. As a consequence, they lose interest in research on teaching effectiveness and advances in instructional practice that can offset the impact of large classes.

Concern over complacency is captured in the adage, "Nothing fails like success." The Swiss watch industry serves as a vivid illustration of its validity. Because of their preeminent position as watch producers for the world, the Swiss did not take seriously the possibilities of digital technology. They allowed the Japanese to corner the market on inexpensive digital watches because they failed to see beyond their existing level of success. Such myopia can be found in some high-performing school districts. With the advent of educational standards, many states have established criteria that schools must meet in order to be fully accredited. Some educators fear that high-performing schools that easily meet these criteria will grow complacent, thereby sowing the seeds for eventual decline.

The campaign to combat complacency begins at the top. Argyris (1991, p. 106) urges leaders first to examine their own beliefs and practices. They may appear to be resistant to self-improvement, even though they urge others to improve. When leaders model the willingness to change the way *they* do business, they send a powerful message to those they supervise. Kotter (1996, pp. 38–42) notes that complacency can result from "too much happy talk from senior management." It is difficult to generate support for change when leaders mislead employees and other stakeholders by always putting a positive spin on negative performance data. Like the boy who cried "Wolf!" too often, they discover that people may not believe them when the situation finally deteriorates so much that change is the only option.

Guarding against complacency is a continuous process that requires welcoming feedback concerning performance problems and potential trouble spots. Savvy leaders recognize and reward those closest to problems for disclosing them. Ineffective leaders, on the other hand, tend to discourage people from sharing bad news and from whistle blowing. Like ostriches, they operate on the belief that ignoring problems will make them disappear. In reality, such conduct is more likely to result in the *leaders'* disappearance!

Educational leaders who are committed to keeping complacency at bay insist on sharing, analyzing, and evaluating performance data on a regular basis. They expect teachers and other staff members to talk with dissatisfied students and parents. They create information management systems to monitor complaints and track what is done to address them. They encourage people to visit the competition and learn why certain students are withdrawing from some schools and enrolling in others. They seek advice from advisory groups, student cabinets, and focus groups. They invite evaluations of their own performance as leaders. In other words, leaders spread the word that they want to know when things can be done better, including how they are leading.

Change Keys

In order to combat complacency, educational leaders should—

- Model a positive orientation to change.
- Avoid concealing bad news or putting a "positive spin" on negative data.
- Recognize and reward people for sharing information on performance problems.
- Establish mechanisms for monitoring complaints, concerns, and competitors.
- Conduct regular evaluations of organizational progress.

Overcoming Resistance

In the preceding discussion, we learned that educational leaders may need to confront complacency in order to get people to entertain the possibility of change. Entertaining the possibility of change does not mean that people *embrace* change, however. In many cases, the immediate consequence of considering a need for change may be denial or open resistance. Chapter 5 noted that there are many reasons why people resist change. These reasons include commitment to the status quo, lack of awareness of a need for change, heightened anxiety resulting from the prospect of change, the potential for disruption and discomfort, the risk of failure, the potential for negative impacts on personal life, increased work, threats to job security, and work-related alienation. Resistance can arise during every phase of the change process and from a variety of predictable and sometimes unpredictable sources. Only a naive leader would anticipate no resistance when undertaking educational change.

In order to overcome resistance to change, leaders must begin by doing two things—(1) determine who is resisting change and their reasons for resistance and (2) convert this information into useful knowledge.

Identifying which individuals and groups oppose change is not always easy to do. People may fear reprisals if they openly resist change. Janis (1972) urges leaders to avoid committing to a particular change or course of action until they have heard from all the relevant advisors or stakeholders. In this way leaders are more likely to obtain open and honest feedback concerning proposals for change. People who distrust leaders and who lack confidence that their concerns will be heard also may be reluctant to make their feelings public. Leaders must convince these individuals that what they have to say is important and valued.

Even if leaders are able to identify resisters, they may have trouble pinpointing the real reasons for resistance. Some reasons are perceived to be more socially acceptable or politically correct than others. Resisting change because it threatens one's job security may seem to be too self-serving. Those who fear job loss therefore may express other reasons for opposing change. A key goal for every educational leader should be to create a climate in which people feel sufficiently safe to express their real reasons for resisting change.

Information regarding who is resisting change and their reasons for resistance must be analyzed, interpreted, and evaluated before leaders can put it to practical use. Finding beneficial knowledge in data regarding resistance may not come naturally to some leaders. These are the individuals who treat resistance as a personal attack and who prefer to pretend that everyone supports their reforms. "No news is good news" is their motto. Wise leaders, on the other hand, are able to *redefine resistance*. This expression, offered by Fullan (2001, pp. 41–43), reflects the fact that resisters have important information to offer those engaged in leading change. Instead of resisting resistance, leaders should view it as an opportunity to acquire insights concerning various aspects of proposed change. What, for example, seems to be the real focus of people's concern—the identified need for which change is justified, the particular design intended to address the need, the timetable for implementing change, the source of the change proposal, or the criteria to be used to determine whether change has succeeded? Does resistance derive from issues of preference and convenience or matters of conscience? Resistance based on personal dislike of who proposed a reform probably needs to be addressed quite differently from resistance based on a design for change that is judged to be fundamentally flawed.

The source or sources of resistance also are important information on which to reflect. It is one thing for a few teachers to register their opposition and quite another for most of the faculty to line up against change. Educational leaders should not proceed with plans for change until they have consulted all stakeholder groups, from school board members to students. Ultimately, leaders must identify who supports and who opposes change, evaluate their reasons, estimate the depth of their support and opposition, and make a judgment as to whether to accommodate concerns, abandon change, or move forward while making an effort to overcome resistance.

Manuals on leading change suggest various strategies for overcoming resistance. Calabrese (2002, p. 67), for example, believes that leaders should acknowledge that change occurs in stages and seek to move individuals, based on their level of readiness, from one stage to the next. The particular stage theory that Calabrese (pp. 74–79) uses is an adaptation of Elisabeth Kübler-Ross's stages of grieving. He contends that change involves loss and that people affected by change may have to go through denial, anger, bargaining, and depression before they come to accept change.

Hall and Hord (2001) provide a different, though not unrelated, set of stages. Like Calabrese, they believe that the best way to overcome resistance is for leaders to focus on moving individuals from one stage to the next (p. 192). They warn that "Tarzan leaps" from nonacceptance to complete acceptance of change are unrealistic. Depending on the next stage in their Concerns-Based Adoption Model, a leader may need to provide more information about change, encourage experimentation without negative consequences, or create opportunities for collaboration. The message from both the work of Calabrese and Hall and Hord is that leaders need to handle resistance to change by employing customized and incremental strategies.

Another approach to overcoming resistance to change involves maintaining a focus on why change is needed. Unlike the preceding example, this strategy does not zero in on individuals. Resistance is met, instead, by gentle confrontation around the need for change. Leaders strive to gain agreement that current performance is failing to meet identified needs. Resisters who reject this position are asked to provide evidence that current performance is adequate. The more public are these interactions over the perceived need for change, the better. Acceptance of the fact that change is needed is an important first step to overcoming resistance, and it avoids putting particular resisters on the spot.

Of all the possible strategies for dealing with resistance, only one is almost universally inappropriate, and that is *ignoring* resistance. Confrontation and conflict may not be relished by educational leaders, but they should not respond by trying to avoid resisters. As Evans (1996, p. 273) puts it,

Authentic leaders acknowledge and address opposition to their priorities, trying to surface the sources of conflict and foster an open, substantive debate on their merits. . . . When these sincere efforts at resolution fail, they confront directly those who continue to resist, especially when this resistance becomes exceptional—that is, when it violates the school's essential purposes or basic norms.

Change Keys

In order to overcome resistance to change, educational leaders should—

- Refrain from ignoring resistance.
- Determine who is resisting change and the reasons why they are resisting change.
- Analyze and evaluate data on resistance.
- Consider addressing the concerns of individual resisters.
- Maintain a focus on why change is needed in the first place.

Inspiring Commitment

Overcoming resistance to change is not equivalent to inspiring commitment to change. Resisters whose concerns have been addressed do not necessarily become enthusiastic supporters of reform. They, instead, can linger in limbo between resistance and support, waiting for events to unfold. If change fares badly at first, these individuals may slip back into the resisters' camp. Supporters, of course, also can change their mind regarding change, but they are more likely to be patient and give reform a fair chance to succeed. One of the most critical aspects of leading change, therefore, involves inspiring commitment to change.

Apathy, not hate, it is said, represents the antithesis of love. Love and hate both involve strong feelings and deep emotions. Apathy, on the other hand, is marked by the absence of strong feelings and deep emotions. Similarly, detachment, rather than resistance, should be regarded as the opposite of commitment. In an essay on teacher leadership, detachment was characterized by "situations from which individuals withdraw psychologically while remaining physically present" (Duke, 1994, p. 258). People appear to be going through the motions, their activity failing to engage them emotionally or intellectually.

Evans (1996, p. 70) maintains that there are three levels of commitment to change: "Make it happen, help it happen, and let it happen." When educators are committed to making or helping change happen, leaders need not rely on control and compliance strategies, strategies which may only generate greater resistance to change as well as diminish personal support for leaders. Few people, especially highly trained professionals, appreciate being told that they must implement reforms. Inducements and extrinsic motivation also become less necessary when commitment is high.

Experienced educational leaders realize that there is no magic formula for inspiring commitment. Like virtually everything else about the educational change process, what is needed to fully engage educators in implementing change is likely to vary with the situation. Nonetheless, one generalization does apply to the challenge of inspiring commitment—commitment is a matter of meaning. Educators are likely to be committed to that which they find meaningful. Evans (1996, p. 17) observes that implementation "depends crucially on the meaning the change has to those who must implement it." Causes greater than one's self-interest and opportunities to grow professionally are two powerful wellsprings of meaning for educators (Duke, 1994). So close is the connection between leadership and meaning that the former can be defined in terms of the latter. My aesthetic theory of leadership (Duke, 1989, p. 351), for example, regards leadership as that which "helps bring meaning to the relationships between individuals and greater entities—communities, organizations, nations."

Meaning, and consequently commitment, are closely associated with individuals' deeply held values, beliefs, and aspirations. It is difficult to imagine an educational leader inspiring commitment without knowing something about the values, beliefs, and aspirations of those expected to effect change. When Mitman and Lambert (1993, p. 500) studied middle school reform in California, they discovered that commitment by some teachers was contingent on perceived changes in student performance and behavior. Until those students who teachers considered "low achievers" achieved more, participated more, and seemed more motivated, the teachers withheld their complete support for particular reforms.

One of the difficulties associated with recent efforts to implement accountability systems in public school systems across the United States concerns the fact that many teachers harbor serious reservations about the value of standards and standardized tests as the primary basis for judging student achievement. Teachers sense that the real impetus behind these reforms has more to do with politics than professional judgment regarding the best interests of young people. When educators are skeptical of the motives behind change, they are likely to withhold their whole-hearted commitment. Ohanian (1999, p. 149) captures the doubts about standards and standardized tests held by many of her fellow educators:

> What worries me is that the Standardisto requirements are accepted as a given; there is no talk of what good these requirements do for students . . . We hear lots of talk of world-class standards leading students into world-class jobs with world-class paychecks, but there is no talk of our improved education system educating citizens for the common ground of a democracy, no talk of the standards that will help our children build better lives, build a better world.

When Leithwood, Jantzi, and Steinbach (1999, p. 143–147) investigated what research had to say about the conditions that fostered teacher commitment, they found a variety of factors related to leadership. The abilities of leaders to identify and articulate a vision, enhance teachers' beliefs about their own capacities, and draw teachers' attention to gaps between current and desired practice were all linked to the generation of commitment to change. Leithwood, Jantzi, and Steinbach regarded teachers' commitment to change as a function of their individual goals for improvement (p. 147). The implication is that an important way to generate commitment involves helping teachers to create meaningful goals for themselves. Too much emphasis on organizational goals, instead of individual goals, actually may be counterproductive when it comes to building commitment.

Still, it would be a mistake to assume that teachers do not respond well to schoolwide goals, assuming they regard the goals as meaningful and they have sufficient time and support to achieve them. In her study of New American Schools projects, Bodilly (1996, p. 320) found that the creation of teams dedicated to accomplishing common reform goals was a powerful spur to commitment:

> The experiences of the schools we sampled indicated that initial buy-in to a design was fleeting. Long-term commitment by teachers was developed over time in a working relationship where a team and a school staff interacted with each other toward common goals. Strong assistance toward change, concrete models, coaching, and time produced change and, therefore, more commitment.

CHALLENGE OF CHANGE

Controlling Overcommitment

As important as commitment can be to successful change, overcommitment can lead to problems. Overcommitment causes people to ignore warning signals and make excuses when particular reforms fail to yield desired results. Fanatical devotion to change is not the answer to our need for school improvement. The stability and flexibility so essential to effective implementation can be undermined by single-minded zealots who are either overly committed to eliminating what they don't want or to implementing what they do want. Leaders must be careful to avoid whipping up too much enthusiasm for particular reforms, lest they invite problems when it eventually becomes clear that adjustments are needed in the original design for change.

Overcommitment on the part of those expected to implement change is not the only potential problem related to commitment. Leaders themselves must walk a tightrope where commitment is concerned. They obviously should be supportive of change, but there is considerable evidence to indicate that leaders subvert their efforts when they are too passionate in their commitment to a particular change or course of action (Janis, 1972). Teachers, for example, may withhold their commitment when they feel a principal or superintendent is steering them toward a pet reform. Professionals do not usually appreciate being asked to participate in the drama of educational change when the last scene already has been written. Fullan (1991, p. 95) points out that "strong commitment to a particular change may be a barrier to setting up an effective process of change." Evans (1996, pp. 16–17) offers wise counsel to educational leaders:

> Being heavily committed makes one less likely to establish the lengthy procedures vital to implementation, less amenable to modifications, and less tolerant of the unavoidable

delays and setbacks that ensue as others struggle to adopt the change. It is not that innovators should not have deep convictions but rather that they must be open to the realities of others, to the necessary modification their ideas will undergo as others encounter them—and to the delays this will surely cause.

Change Keys

In order to inspire commitment to change, educational leaders should—

- Identify the values, beliefs, and aspirations of those expected to implement change.
- Connect proposed changes to that which people find meaningful.
- Articulate a vision of educational improvements that can result from successful change.
- Help teachers develop meaningful individual and shared goals related to change.
- Avoid becoming overcommitted to a particular reform or design for change.

Providing Direction

Leaders experienced in the change process realize that commitment is necessary, but not sufficient, to effect change. Direction is critical if people are to stay the course through implementation and eventual integration of reforms. What is *direction?* It is not simply the giving of instructions, though direction typically involves guidance. Direction is best understood from the vantage point of staff members rather than the perspective of leaders. In my essay on the aesthetics of leadership, I regard direction as a basic property of perceived leadership (Duke, 1989, p. 353):

> In the presence of leadership the individual senses direction. Direction is more than a course to follow. It is a path *together* with a reason for traveling it. Direction presumes meaning. Furthermore, with direction the elements of uncertainty and surprise are minimized.

Under normal operating conditions, educators may be clear about what they need to do and why. If they also are committed to doing it, the need for leadership is relatively low. Change, however, can blur direction and undermine commitment. Teachers, students, and parents question why change is necessary and whether the need for change is a reflection on their own inadequacies. Forging ahead with reforms, the ultimate consequences of which are unknown, generates anxiety and uncertainty. Those charged with implementing change wonder if they are doing it right. If the perceived need for leadership is variable, it is during times of change that the need is likely to be seen as greatest.

It is hard to pinpoint one phase of the educational change process when direction is more essential than other phases. McCaskey (1982, pp. 1–8) claims that ambiguity is ubiquitous during the change process. At any given time some individuals may be uncertain about the goals of change, the nature of intended change, the training and resources needed to implement change, who is responsible for implementing change, and how the success of change will be measured. Odiorne (1981, p. 15) cautioned leaders to be alert to *the activity trap:*

> It is the abysmal situation people find themselves in when they start out for what once was an important and clear, perhaps even noble, objective, but in an amazingly short time become so enmeshed in the activity of getting there that they forget where they are going.

In the last chapter we encountered the implementation dip, a predictable decline in performance and confidence following the commencement of implementation (Fullan, 2001, pp. 40–41). Even at this relatively late stage, when a need for change has been agreed upon and a design for change has been accepted, the need for direction persists. "Leaders who understand the implementation dip," according to Fullan (p. 41), "know that people are experiencing two kinds of problems when they are in the dip—the social-psychological fear of change, and the lack of technical know-how or skills to make the change work." To address these concerns, leaders must encourage people to develop the expertise required to implement change and remind them of the benefits successful change is likely to bring.

■ ■ ■ ■ ■ ▬▬▬▬▬▬▬▬▬▬▬▬▬▬▬▬▬▬▬▬▬▬▬▬▬▬▬▬▬▬▬

CASE STUDY

KEEPING ALL EYES ON THE PRIZE

When Eric J. Smith became Superintendent of the Charlotte-Mecklenburg school district, there was no doubt about the direction in which he wanted the large school system to head. Closing the gap between the achievement of African American and white students was goal number one. How to accomplish this goal that had eluded so many of Smith's counterparts in other large school systems became the focus of his attention.

Smith was convinced that student achievement data held the key to a design for change. He soon discovered that white students in middle school advanced classes outnumbered African American students at a rate of nearly three to one. Dropping behind in middle school almost ensured that African American students would remain behind their white peers in high school. Smith decided that the first step in the change process was to tear up the schedules of 8,000 middle school students and reassign them. African American students were placed in advanced classes.

Many teachers and parents protested this radical move. Smith, however, continually reminded people that test scores demonstrated that African American students were capable of doing the work required in advanced classes. The function of a public school system was not to sort and select students, but to enable each student to achieve their full potential.

Eventually Smith initiated other changes to narrow the gap. During his six years at the helm, the number of students taking college-level courses was tripled and test scores

(continued)

CONTINUED

were raised 20 percentage points. A prekindergarten program that placed poor students on the same academic footings as more advantaged students was started. Advanced Placement and International Baccalaureate programs were introduced in all 16 Charlotte-Mecklenburg high schools. Most importantly, the number of African American students taking college-level courses climbed 450 percent. Charlotte-Mecklenburg educators were able to narrow the gap because Smith made certain that no one forgot what they were expected to accomplish.

Material for this case was drawn primarily from Darragh Johnson, "School Chief Works Fast, Furious," *Washington Post* (May 5, 2002), p. C5.

The case study of Eric Smith's leadership reveals what single-mindedness of purpose can accomplish. At no stage of his tenure as superintendent were educators in the Charlotte-Mecklenburg school system uncertain about their central mission.

Research suggests that direction can be provided in a variety of ways. Leithwood, Jantzi, and Steinbach (1999, pp. 55–70), for example, maintain that three important bases for direction-setting are (1) building a shared vision, (2) developing consensus about goals, and (3) creating high performance expectations. When they investigated direction-setting in a large Canadian comprehensive school, the researchers found that a sense of direction for school improvement gradually evolved from an informal and somewhat vague notion into an increasingly more explicit and formal understanding of what needed to be done. The gradual emergence of an official vision to guide teachers through the change process meant that people had a chance to get to know and trust the new principal and appreciate his dreams and desires for the school. Once the vision had been formalized, it served as a continuing reference point when resources had to be allocated and priorities determined.

The development of a sense of direction entails several risks for which educational leaders should be prepared. Put simply, these risks involve too much control and too little control. When Datnow and Castellano (2001) studied leaders involved in implementing the Success for All program, they found that principals were often seen as too controlling because they were expected to make sure teachers implemented the Success for All curriculum exactly as prescribed. This particular reform package discourages any deviation from program guidelines. As a result, implementing Success for All did little to narrow the divide between teachers and administrators.

Leaders can err on the side of insufficient direction as well as too much. Nolan and Meister's (2000, p. 209) study of a team of private school teachers (see case study of the Apex team in Chapter 6) revealed that reforms foundered when administrators refrained from playing an active and ongoing role in the change process. Administrators mistakenly assumed that teachers desired to be left alone to implement an interdisciplinary curriculum and new schedule (p. 209):

> The administrators tried to be supportive by providing for material needs such as release time and money. They then decided to leave the teachers alone so that the teachers would not feel pressured by constant administrative surveillance. The teachers who needed and wanted emotional and technical support felt abandoned, not empowered, by being left alone.

How much direction to provide and how best to provide it are likely to vary with the situation, including the particular design for change, the perceived justification for change, the experience and expertise of teachers, and the relationship between leaders and staff members. In general, however, direction probably is more likely to be effective when it is provided by leaders who are not regarded as remote, overly ambitious, and insensitive to the challenges of change.

Change Keys

In order to provide direction for change, educational leaders should—

- Recognize the potential for individuals to lose track of the reason for change and the steps needed to achieve it.
- Develop a coherent vision of what the completed change should look like.
- Be sensitive to the possibility of coming across as overly controlling as well as insufficiently involved in the change process.

KEY ASPECTS OF LEADERSHIP FOR CHANGE

During the past three decades, states and school districts have increasingly formalized expectations for educational leaders. States have developed standards to guide the certification of principals and other administrative personnel. School districts have identified competencies on which to base the evaluation of administrators. Many of these sets of standards and competencies include items related to educational change. Connecticut's "Standards for School Leaders" (1999), for example, contains a school improvement standard that states, "The school leader works with staff to improve the quality of school programs by reviewing the impact of current practices on student learning, considering promising alternatives, and implementing program changes that are designed to improve learning for all students."

Space does not permit a discussion of all the knowledge, skills dispositions, and performances that leaders should possess and demonstrate in order to effect educational change. A number of these aspects of leadership for change have been alluded to in the preceding chapters. They include identifying the educational needs of students; assessing the extent to which current programs, policies, and practices are meeting students' needs; designing ways to address unmet needs; developing plans to implement designs; and mobilizing support for change. The following discussion looks at some aspects of leadership for change that so far have not received much attention. They include openness to change, desire to challenge assumptions, good judgment, the capacity to earn trust, balance, and willingness to stay the course.

Openness to Change

It may seem almost too obvious to mention, but leadership for change depends, at least initially, on leaders' openness to new ideas and change (Leithwood, Jantzi, and Steinback, 1999, p. 216). The likelihood of successful reform and improvement is reduced dramatically when leaders resist change, defend the status quo, and insist that everything is fine as it is. Understandably, leaders who have occupied their positions for a long time may interpret change as a negative reflection on their own leadership. If they have been doing a competent job, why should change be necessary? Fragile egos do not tend to be associated with openness to change.

Openness to change need not imply a blind devotion to change for the sake of change. Such an extreme orientation to change, in fact, may actually reduce the chances for change by fostering burnout, stress, and cynicism in those who must implement change. Openness to change also does not mean overly enthusiastic endorsement for a particular reform. Such selective zeal, as already has been noted, may foster resistance and raise questions about a leader's objectivity. Openness to change simply implies a receptivity to the possibility that there might be better ways to promote learning and achieve the educational mission of the school or school system.

When Berman and McLaughlin (1977, p. 124) studied innovation in nearly 300 school districts, they found that the *active* support of principals was a key to project success. Active support depends on what educational leaders do, not just on what they say. If they are truly open to change, they are willing to examine their own practice as well as that of others. What leaders who are open to change should value most is not change, but improvement. When change is unlikely to foster educational improvement, it is unwelcome.

Desire to Challenge Assumptions

Change can occur without challenging basic assumptions or beliefs. This kind of change sometimes is referred to as *first-order* change (see Chapter 1). First-order change often fosters the illusion of change, while allowing underlying patterns of thought and behavior to go unaltered. As a result, meaningful improvement is minimized. The likelihood of genuine improvement may be greatest when change challenges basic assumptions regarding the why, what, when, where, and how of education. This kind of change is known as *second-order* change.

Educational leaders who are fearful of challenging assumptions or who are unaware of the underlying beliefs that guide their actions and the actions of those around them may make ineffective change leaders. One of the dispositions associated with Connecticut's School Improvement Standard for school leaders recognized the importance of examining assumptions:

> The school leader believes that there are no "sacred cows," and is willing to examine all assumptions, beliefs, and practices regarding school programs. (Connecticut State Board of Education, 1999)

In Chapter 4, we learned that a key element of the Design Phase of the educational change process involved identifying and challenging assumptions, including leaders' own assumptions about change and schools. When problems persist for long periods of time, despite efforts by educators to address them, it may be an indication that basic beliefs and assumptions have been left untouched. This includes beliefs and assumptions about leaders and leadership. How many promising reforms have run aground because teachers believed that they were passengers on a course for change and it was the principal's job alone to get them there?

In a fascinating study of how educational leaders learn and grow, Jentz and Wofford (1979) followed five principals as they reflected on their work and on themselves as human beings. True growth required them to interrogate their assumptions about what it meant to be a leader. One principal, Lew, realized that he believed true leaders must be liked, right, in control, invulnerable, and rational (pp. 123–170). When he started to question these beliefs, he acknowledged that leading was not a popularity contest, that he did not have to possess the correct answer whenever an issue arose, that he needed to take responsibility for himself but not try to control others' feelings, that it was all right to show caring, and that sharing information was more important than being rational. Revelations of these kinds lie at the heart of individual development and change. Without such individual growth, it is unlikely that educational change will produce substantive improvements.

Good Judgment

The educational change process probably will never be reduced to a recipe that leaders simply can follow in order to achieve desirable results. During each phase of the change process, judgments are required. The Discovery Phase, for example, requires leaders to determine whether a need for change exists. Sometimes multiple needs are discovered. Should every identified need for change be addressed, or should they be prioritized? Which needs for change should be addressed first? How should the existence of high priority needs be explained to the public and to those who are expected to implement changes that address these needs? No manual has been written that instructs leaders on the appropriate judgments to make regarding these questions. Appropriateness varies with local conditions, available resources, and competing concerns.

Another set of judgments is required during the Design Phase. Typically, a need for educational change can be addressed in a variety of ways. If reading performance is low, principals can choose from a variety of commercial reading programs. They can decide to adopt or adapt one of these existing programs or create a unique program. Other options include expanding the amount of time that reading instruction is provided, grouping students based on reading level, and supplementing existing staff with reading specialists. Some designs for change are more likely to challenge sacred assumptions than others. Leaders must weigh the potential benefits of radical designs against the possibility that they will generate substantial resistance, resistance that might ultimately undermine the design's effectiveness.

The need for good judgment does not end with the selection of a design to address identified educational needs. During the Development Phase, leaders have to make a variety of judgments regarding an implementation plan. How much time should be allotted for implementation? What strategies, such as pilot tests and initial reliance on volunteers, are most likely to facilitate implementation? What resources and staff development are required to launch implementation?

The adage about best-laid plans pertains to the process of educational change. No matter how carefully crafted is the implementation plan, the advent of actual implementation occasions additional judgments. Circumstances can change between the Development Phase and the Implementation Phase. New needs emerge unexpectedly. Resources disappear. Personnel come and go. New mandates are received from state and local authorities. Leaders must make judgments regarding modifications in original designs, timelines, and implementation strategies. In some cases, resistance to change necessitates judgments about whether or not to continue the change process. Some of the toughest judgments concern how to deal with staff members who are either unwilling or unable to implement change successfully.

Although it is pointless to predict in advance which judgments must be made in a particular situation, it is generally the case that sound judgments are based on good information derived from as many sources as possible. To increase the likelihood of getting good information, Janis (1972, pp. 207–224) urges leaders to keep their opinions to themselves until they have heard from all involved parties. Furthermore, he recommends assigning one staff member the role of devil's advocate. This individual is expected to challenge prevailing sentiment in the hopes of identifying underlying issues and weaknesses in initial judgments.

Leaders make judgments every day about various matters. In the final analysis, what makes a judgment good is whether it is made with the best interests of those served in mind. Schools exist to serve the educational needs of young people. When judgments about change, or anything else concerning schooling, can be traced back to this fundamental mission, they are likely to be the right judgments.

The Capacity to Earn Trust

Trust cannot be declared; it can only be conferred. For most people, trust takes time to build. It results from consistency and predictability. Unfortunately, years of developing trust can be lost in a split second if leaders make a poor judgment. Experts recognize that trust is a crucial aspect of change leadership. It only stands to reason that asking people to alter established practices and abandon familiar programs would require a measure of trust in those making such requests. Change invariably brings the possibility of failure as well as the promise of success. Until educators trust their leaders, they are unlikely to wholeheartedly embrace change, and without such total commitment, the prognosis for effective change is limited.

■ ■ ■ ■ ■ ▬▬▬▬▬▬▬▬▬▬▬▬▬▬▬▬▬▬▬▬▬▬▬▬▬▬▬▬▬

CASE STUDY
THE MISSING INGREDIENT AT JACKSON ELEMENTARY

Located in a low-income Chicago neighborhood, Jackson Elementary School enrolled more than 600 students and employed thirty-five faculty when a new principal, Ms. Morgan, was assigned in 1989 to transform the low-achieving school. Jackson's problems ranged from inadequate facilities and discipline problems to lack of a coherent instructional program and ineffective leadership.

Ms. Morgan did what she could to address these concerns, including initiating a student recognition program, establishing partnerships with local businesses, and ending the practice of departmentalization. This last measure was accomplished, however, over the strong objections of faculty members. Although Morgan accomplished much that was useful, she failed to win the trust of many faculty members. As Bizar (2001, p. 39) notes in her case study of Jackson under Morgan's leadership,

> The process of shared decision making is based on respect and trust, and at Jackson respect and trust were major problems. The principal acted in ways that indicated to the entire school community that she did not trust them to make good decisions. She did not hold faculty meetings; instead, she tended to communicate in written form or give directives over the PA (public address) system. She seemed to be uncomfortable with open meetings. There was always the notion of "keeping a lid on it."

Without trust, Morgan was unable to cultivate a shared vision of what Jackson was or could be. Teachers refused to accept responsibility for low student achievement, preferring to attribute academic problems to the impact of poverty and poor parenting. When called upon to draft a school improvement plan, teachers went through the motions, but never addressed fundamental issues related to instructional practice and teacher beliefs. Teachers insisted on maintaining a classroom perspective, rather than looking at change from a schoolwide viewpoint.

The lack of successful change at Jackson suggests that the fate of reform may hinge on reciprocal trust. The faculty did not trust Morgan, and Morgan did not trust the faculty. Under such circumstances, excuse-making and finger pointing substituted for substantive movement toward needed reform.

Material for this case was drawn from Marilyn Bizar, "Reform at Jackson Elementary: Transition to Site-Based Management." In Marilyn Bizar and Rebecca Barr (eds.), *School Leadership in Times of Urban Reform*. Mahwah, NJ: Erlbaum, 2001, p. 23–45.

Whether Morgan could ever have earned the trust of the Jackson faculty is debatable. Her charge was to go in and clean up the school, hardly a mission likely to win the allegiance of a veteran group of teachers. Perhaps the only hope under these circumstances would have been to strike a balance between top-down direction and grassroots initiation of change. Morgan's style revealed a discomfort with such an accommodation. Leadership for change, however, often depends on just such a balancing act.

Balance

The change process can cause people to feel off balance. They bid goodbye to the familiar without knowing the exact nature of its replacement. Some are unclear about why change is necessary, while others fret about the unanticipated consequences of change. Anyone who has experienced the change process realizes that things can get worse as well as better. To address the disequilibrium that attends change, educational leaders should strive for a *balanced* approach to reform.

Students of change have noted the value of various kinds of balance. When Muncey and McQuillan (1996, p. 271) studied Coalition of Essential Schools projects, for example, they discovered that schools where reforms were sustained had principals who were able to "strike a balance between top-down decision making and grassroots change." Achieving such balance can be especially challenging, however, when reforms originate at the state or school district level. In such cases, principals may be expected to function more as supervisors of implementation than solicitors of teacher opinion (Barr and Bizar, 2001, p. 232). Teachers value the opportunity to be involved in making certain decisions that relate to their areas of expertise and concern, but they also expect principals to take the initiative during occasions when teachers are anxious to stop deliberating and get about the business of implementing change.

Leaders of educational change often need to balance reliance on commitment and willingness to control. In an ideal world, those who are expected to implement change can be counted on to support it and to make a good faith effort to carry out implementation plans. The real world, however, is characterized by individuals who sometimes allow self-interest to supersede collective commitments. Without the judicious use of control by leaders, these individuals can undermine the hard work and dedication of those who embrace the need for educational change.

One of the most difficult, but also one of the most important, balancing acts occasioned by change involves human emotions. Effective change leaders realize that they must tiptoe between overzealous support for change and disinterest. The problem with disinterest is obvious. Less obvious, perhaps, is the fact that excessive support of change by leaders can raise suspicions regarding their motives and objectivity. Not only must leaders balance their own emotions, but they must monitor the emotions of those they supervise and serve (Leithwood, Jantzi, and Steinbach, 1999, pp. 189–203). Leaders who allow teachers to become too excited about a particular reform eventually may confront teachers' disappointment and disillusionment when implementation fails to produce anticipated results. Although no one appreciates a wet blanket, the interests of change are well served by reasonable expectations. When educators, students, parents, and community members are cautioned against developing illusions concerning change, they are less likely to grow disillusioned when the pace of improvement slows and the initial pay-off of change is modest.

The fate of educational reform ultimately may depend on the ability of leaders to balance change and stability. As had been noted earlier in the book, everything cannot change at once. If teachers are expected to alter classroom practice, it may be unwise to weigh them down with schoolwide projects. Comprehensive change need not require multiple simultaneous changes. Achieving change requires individuals to focus their attention and energy. They are more likely to do so if they do not have to worry about surprises and multiple reform projects that compete for their time.

Leaders must not only guard against excessive change, but against excessive stability. Hargreaves, Earl, Moore, and Manning (2001, p. 175) point out, for instance, that principals typically are under great pressure to maintain stability in their schools. With hardly enough time to take care of daily routines and issues, they easily can come to regard change as an unwelcome addition to an already packed agenda. Balance, therefore, requires that leaders value the importance of continuous improvement as well as stability.

Willingness to Stay the Course

Inspiring commitment to change was noted earlier as a key challenge facing educational leaders. Successful change depends, however, on more than winning over those who are affected by and who must implement change. Leaders themselves must manifest commitment to change, and they can do this by refusing to abandon initiatives prematurely or moving on to a new job before changes have been fully integrated. Leader turnover frequently is linked to the demise of educational reform (Muncey and McQuillan, 1996, p. 272). Ironically, it is often their advocacy of change and their initial success in launching new programs and practices that increases the visibility of leaders and produces invitations for them to assume new positions.

When I think about the importance of leaders staying the course, I reflect on my own high school principal, William Brock. Brock served as principal of Thomas Jefferson High School in Richmond, Virginia, from 1958 to 1976. These years were glory days for the school, but they also included the advent of desegregation and court-ordered busing. It would have been easy for Brock to retire from public service in 1970, when the educational world of Thomas Jefferson and of Richmond Public Schools was turned upside down as a result of court-ordered busing and racial balancing of faculty. Many of Brock's premier teachers and teacher leaders were transferred to other schools or opted for early retirement. As I note in my history of Thomas Jefferson High School, however, Brock was not the kind of leader to abandon a school in distress (Duke, 1995).

Brock knew that the fate of a desegregated Thomas Jefferson depended on balancing the preservation of traditional programs, such as the vaunted Honor System and Advanced Placement courses, and the introduction of changes that would address the needs of newly arriving African American students, many of whom were performing below grade level. He realized that the tide of white flight would only be stemmed by ensuring the safety and welfare of all students. In the aftermath of court-ordered busing, Brock rallied his faculty to ensure a smooth transition by asking his most talented senior teachers to assume responsibility for teaching some classes of low-achieving students and by requesting that all teachers begin tutoring weaker students during their planning periods. Mathematics and language arts learning centers were created as an alternative to study hall for students in need of focused assistance, and Project Read, a special ninth grade transition program for poor readers, was initiated. When Brock finally stepped down, he could look back with pride on a peaceful and productive adjustment to desegregation.

Leaders are many things, including symbols. We all understand the symbolism of a captain being the first to depart a sinking ship. The refusal of educational leaders to be lured away in the midst of change sends a powerful message to teachers, students, and parents. When leaders demonstrate by their actions that they believe in change, the commitment of others is much more likely to be won and held.

CONCLUSION

Leaders and leadership have come to be so closely associated with reform and improvement that it is difficult to conceive of constructive change occurring without them. Chapter 7 explored the complex relationship between leaders, leadership, and change, noting that successful change may depend on leadership at various levels, not just the top, and during every phase of the educational change process, not just the beginning. Leaders lead in various ways, and there is little evidence at this point that one form or style of leading works best in all situations involving change. One thing is clear, however—educational change calls for good management as well as leadership.

Educational leaders who deal with change are likely to confront predictable challenges. Overcoming complacency often is the first of these, for teachers and other staff members can grow comfortable over time with their routines and established ways of dealing with problems. Failure to rouse educators to the need for change usually dooms reform initiatives. Once the change process has gotten under way, overcoming resistance and inspiring commitment become primary concerns for leaders. It is important to realize that eliminating opposition to change is not equivalent to winning support for change. Leaders can forge ahead once resistance has been addressed adequately, but true progress may not be experienced until the "hearts and minds" of those who must implement change have been won. A fourth challenge of change entails providing direction. Even committed educators can lose their way once the complicated process of change has begun. Guidance and reminders of why change is necessary may be required at each stage, and especially during implementation.

The last part of the chapter considered some of the keys to effective change leadership. It goes without saying that leaders should be open to new ideas and improvement if change stands a chance of proceeding beyond exploratory discussions. In addition, it is important that leaders exercise good judgment and demonstrate a willingness to challenge prevailing beliefs and assumptions. True change, in fact, may be difficult to achieve unless and until the things people take for granted are placed under the microscope. Other aspects of leadership that experts have found to be important include the capacity to earn trust, maintain a sense of organizational and personal balance, and stay the course until changes have been fully implemented. Leaders and leadership alone may not account for successful change, but they clearly are crucial ingredients in the change process.

■ ■ ■ ■ ■ ▬▬▬▬▬▬▬▬▬▬▬▬▬▬▬▬▬

APPLYING WHAT YOU KNOW

A PRINCIPAL RESPONDS TO THE CHALLENGE OF STATE TESTING

As principal of Coolidge High School, Greta Grogan had much about which to feel proud. The school's top students could compete for academic honors with any students in the state. The school boasted a high graduation rate and sent a substantial number of students to prestigious colleges. Parents were actively involved in the school, and the faculty was the best that Grogan had ever led.

In her third year as Coolidge's principal, Grogan was surprised to discover that students had not fared as well as expected on the new state subject-matter tests. State accreditation standards required that a minimum of 70 percent of students (not counting special education and ESL students) pass state tests in 11 subjects. Coolidge students achieved 70 percent passing rates on six of the 11 tests—excellent results relative to other high schools in the state, but not good enough to satisfy Coolidge parents. The day after the test results appeared in the local newspaper, Grogan began receiving phone calls and emails from concerned parents. Students who failed the tests were at risk of not graduating. Passing rates on the tests in Algebra I and Algebra II were a particularly disappointing 26 and 30 percent.

Realizing that parents expected action to be taken, Grogan convened her leadership team, which consisted of two assistant principals, the director of special education, the director of counseling, and various department heads. She acknowledged that something had to be done to raise achievement in the five areas where students had not achieved 70 percent passing rates, but she also noted that they must avoid taking any action that would slow the progress of Coolidge's brightest students. Several parents already expressed fear that so much attention would be devoted to helping struggling students pass state tests that high-achieving students would suffer. Department chairs were asked to go back to their departments, meet with their teachers, review how well their students performed on the state tests, identify areas of low performance, and develop a tentative plan to address deficiencies.

Two weeks later the leadership team again met, this time to review each department's plan. Consensus emerged that courses that failed to support the core academic program—courses such as Gourmet Cooking and Technical Drawing—should be dropped. Several new courses to expose low-achieving students to more rigorous content were approved. Recognizing that Algebra was a trouble spot, the team urged that weaker students be given an

(continued)

CONTINUED

additional dose of the subject by blocking together Introduction to Algebra and Algebra I. In addition, a two-week Algebra prep workshop in August could provide these students with a running start. Grogan accepted the proposals.

Everyone on the leadership team agreed that poor reading skills often were responsible for low test performance. Coolidge already had a full-time reading teacher, but her case load was too great to permit additional responsibilities. Other teachers would have to assume responsibility for helping students become better readers. Considerable staff development would be required, but Grogan felt that some of her veteran staff members were capable of providing the necessary training. If they needed occasional outside assistance, she agreed to find the funds.

Grogan decided that Coolidge's strongest teachers needed to teach the courses in which students took state tests. When she began altering teachers' assignments, some faculty members expressed concern that faculty morale might suffer. Grogan agreed that this was a possibility, but she stated that it would be unfair to students to assign new teachers and teachers with average evaluations to teach these key courses.

Grogan asked her leadership team to anticipate problems that might arise in the process of focusing energy on passing state tests. Several department chairs warned that parents would be upset if their children got good grades in their courses, but failed the state tests. They also suggested that parents should receive plenty of advance warning that their children were experiencing difficulties in courses for which they had to take a state test. Grogan recommended that interim reports be sent to parents three weeks prior to the end of each grading period. These reports should explain to parents the importance of the state tests as well as suggest what their children needed to do to improve their grades.

One of Grogan's toughest decisions concerned class size in Advanced Placement courses. Her predecessor had allowed Advanced Placement classes to have relatively low enrollments. Grogan argued that courses requiring students to take state tests needed to have low enrollments so teachers could give struggling students individual assistance. As a result, she increased the size of Advanced Placement courses. She believed that students taking Advanced Placement courses were less likely to suffer negative consequences from larger classes. Several department chairs contended that it would be Advanced Placement teachers, not students, who would be most adversely affected by the change.

To help prepare the Coolidge faculty for the new focus on achieving 70 percent passing rates on all state tests, each department chair was asked to select a senior teacher to attend a series of state-sponsored workshops related to the state's accountability initiative and ideas for instructional adjustments. Grogan told these teachers that she expected them to get as much information as possible so they could return to Coolidge and serve as mentors for their colleagues. She promised to hire substitutes so that these teacher–mentors could work with teachers during their duty-free periods. Coolidge teachers expressed appreciation for the fact that they would not be required to attend workshops after a busy school day when they were exhausted.

1. How do you feel about the measures taken by Greta Grogan to raise student performance on state tests? Do you feel she exercised adequate leadership for change?
2. The chapter noted the growing interest in distributed leadership. Do you believe Grogan valued the leadership of others in her school?

3. In reflecting on Grogan's handling of the new state accountability initiative, can you differentiate between what she did that constituted leadership for change and what she did that constituted management of change?

4. Imagine that the Coolidge plan had been implemented in your local high school. How would the plan be received? Would you anticipate any resistance and, if so, from what sources? Would you make any adjustments in the plan?

5. Imagine that you are the principal of Fillmore High School, where students failed to achieve 70 percent passing rates on *all* 11 state tests. Would you have chosen a different approach from the one used by Greta Grogan? What would you have done and why?

REFERENCES

Argyris, Chris. "Teaching Smart People How to Learn," *Harvard Business Review,* Vol. 69, no. 4 (May/June 1991), pp. 99–109.

Barr, Rebecca and Bizar, Marilyn. "Insights into Leadership during Times of Urban Reform." In Marilyn Bizar and Rebecca Barr (eds.), *School Leadership in Times of Urban Reform.* Mahwah, NJ: Erlbaum, 2001, pp. 229–252.

Berman, Paul and McLaughlin, Milbrey. *Federal Programs Supporting Educational Change: Vol. VII. Factors Affecting Implementation and Continuation.* Santa Monica, CA: Rand Corporation, 1977.

Bizar, Marilyn. "Reform at Jackson Elementary: Transition to Site-Based Management." In Marilyn Bizar and Rebecca Barr (eds.), *School Leadership in Times of Urban Reform.* Mahwah, N.J.: Erlbaum, 2001, pp. 23–45.

Bodilly, Susan. "Lessons Learned." In Sam Stringfield, Steven Ross, and Lana Smith (eds.), *Bold Plans for School Restructuring.* Mahwah, NJ: Erlbaum, 1996, pp. 289–324.

Bolman, Lee G. and Deal, Terrence E. *Reframing Organizations,* 2nd edition. San Francisco: Jossey-Bass, 1997.

Calabrese, Raymond L. *The Leadership Assignment.* Boston: Allyn and Bacon, 2002.

Connecticut State Board of Education. *Standards for School Leaders.* Hartford: author, 1999.

Datnow, Amada and Castellano, Marisa Eileen. "Managing and Guiding School Reform: Leadership in Success for All Schools," *Educational Administration Quarterly,* Vol. 37, no.2 (April 2001), pp. 219–249.

Duke, Daniel L. "The Aesthetics of Leadership." In Joel L. Burdin (ed.), *School Leadership.* Newbury Park, CA: Sage, 1989, pp. 345–365.

Duke, Daniel L. "Drift, Detachment, and the Need for Teacher Leadership." In Donovan R. Walling (ed.), *Teachers as Leaders.* Bloomington, IN: Phi Delta Kappa Educational Foundation, 1994, pp. 255–274.

Duke, Daniel L. "Perception, Prescription, and the Future of School Leadership." In Kenneth Leithwood, Judith Chapman, David Corson, Philip Hallinger, and Ann Hart (eds.), *International Handbook of Educational Leadership and Administration.* Dordrecht, The Netherlands: Kluwer, 1996, pp. 841–872.

Duke, Daniel L. *The School That Refused to Die.* Albany: State University of New York Press, 1995.

Dwyer, David C. and Smith, Louis M. "The Principal as Explanation of School Change: An Incomplete Story." In William Greenfield (ed.), *Instructional Leadership.* Boston: Allyn and Bacon, 1987, pp. 155–178.

Evans, Robert. *The Human Side of School Change.* San Francisco: Jossey-Bass. 1996.

Fullan, Michael. *Leading in a Culture of Change.* San Francisco: Jossey-Bass.

Fullan, Michael G. *The New Meaning of Educational Change,* 2nd edition. New York: Teachers College Press, 1991.

Goleman, Daniel. "Leadership That Gets Results," *Harvard Business Review,* Vol. 78, no. 3 (March/April 2000), pp. 78–90.

Gross, Neal and Herriott, Robert E. "Theoretical and Practical Implications." In Robert E.

Herriott and Neal Gross (eds.), *The Dynamics of Planned Educational Change.* Berkeley, CA: McCutchan, 1979, pp. 353–379.

Hall, Gene E. and Hord, Shirley M. *Implementing Change.* Boston: Allyn and Bacon. 2001.

Hargreaves, Andy; Earl, Lorna; Moore, Shawn: and Manning, Susan. *Learning to Change.* San Francisco: Jossey-Bass, 2001.

Janis, Irving L. *Victims of Groupthink.* Boston: Houghton Mifflin, 1972.

Jentz, Barry C. and Wofford, Joan W. *Leadership and Learning.* New York: McGraw-Hill, 1979.

Johnson, Darragh. "School Chief Works Fast, Furious," *Washington Post* (May 5, 2002), p. C-5.

Kotter, John P. *A Force for Change: How Leadership Differs from Management.* New York: Free Press, 1990.

Kotter, John P. *Leading Change.* Boston: Harvard Business School Press, 1996.

Leithwood, Kenneth; Jantzi, Doris; and Steinbach, Rosanne. *Changing Leadership for Changing Times.* Buckingham, UK: Open University Press, 1999.

McCaskey, Michael B. *The Executive Challenge.* Boston: Putnam, 1982.

Mitman, Alexis L. and Lambert, Vicki. "Implementing Instructional Reform at the Middle Grades: Case Studies of Seventeen California School, " *The Elementary School Journal,* Vol. 93, no. 5 (May 1993), pp. 495–517.

Muncey, Donna E. and McQuillan, Patrick J. *Reform and Resistance in Schools and Classrooms.* New Haven: Yale University Press, 1996.

Nolan, James and Meister, Denise G. *Teachers and Educational Change.* Albany, NY: State University of New York Press, 2000.

Northouse, Peter G. *Leadership: Theory and Practice.* Thousand Oaks, CA: Sage, 1997.

Odiorne, George S. *The Change Resisters.* Englewood Cliffs, NJ: Prentice-Hall, 1981.

Ohanian, Susan. *One Size Fits Few.* Portsmouth, NH: Heinemann, 1999.

Spillane, James P.; Halverson, Richard; and Diamond, John B. "Investigating School Leadership Practice: A Distributed Perspective," *Educational Researcher,* Vol. 30, no. 1 (April 2001), pp. 23–28.

Zemelman, Steve. "The Best Practice High School: Creating a New Small School in a Big City." In Marilyn Bizar and Rebecca Barr (eds.), *School Leadership in Times of Urban Reform.* Mahwah, NJ: Erlbaum, 2001, pp. 195–223.

■ ■ ■ ■ ■

PART 1

UNDERSTANDING EDUCATIONAL CHANGE

By now it should be clear that achieving educational change involves a variety of challenges. Many well-intentioned efforts fall short of the mark. Some leave students and educators worse off than they were prior to reforms. Other initiatives, however, succeed, and they do so, in part, because those involved in planning and implementing change understand the change process. The relationship between understanding and achieving change, at its best, is one that continues over time. Understanding change helps educators achieve change; achieving change, in turn, enables educators to better understand change. The essence of understanding lies in its constant pursuit. There is, quite simply, no end to understanding, especially where a complex subject such as educational change is involved.

Part IV addresses two activities closely associated with understanding educational change—evaluation and explanation. In Chapter 8, we consider various approaches to evaluating change and offer some principles of good evaluation practice. Then we examine some of the key questions that evaluators of educational change may want to address. These questions concern not only the consequences of change, but the extent to which intended change actually has been achieved. The chapter closes with a discussion of several evaluation issues, such as the utilization of evaluation results, that confront and confound those engaged in evaluating new educational policies, programs, and practices.

The focus of Chapter 9 is explaining educational change. A variety of models, theories, perspectives, and narratives have been used to account for educational change, why and how it occurs, and whether it succeeds. Although theorizing about change may seem far removed from schools and classrooms, the fact is that precious time, energy, and resources can be saved and the likelihood of successful improvement initiatives can be increased when educators and those who make education policy understand why and how educational change takes place.

QUESTIONS TO CONSIDER BEFORE READING SECTION IV

1. Think of several examples of educational change (for instance, a switch from a seven-period school day to an alternating day block schedule). By what criteria can you evaluate the success of each example?

211

2. Many educational reforms are evaluated in terms of their impact on student academic achievement. Can academic achievement be assessed in different ways? Think of at least five different indicators of academic achievement. Which one would you choose, if you could only select one indicator? Why?

3. Sometimes the first step in evaluating educational change involves determining whether the intended change actually has been achieved. What data should be collected to determine whether a new curriculum has been implemented? A new instructional practice?

4. Imagine that you have been invited to conduct a study of educational change. You are free to choose any topic that interests you. What would you want to investigate and why? Can you express your interest in the form of one or two research questions that need to be answered?

5. Researchers devote considerable energy to explaining why things do or do not happen. What phenomena may need to be explained when the subject is educational change?

6. What are your beliefs regarding why efforts to improve schools sometimes succeed and sometimes fail? Can you express these beliefs in the form of a *theory* or explanation of educational change? Remember, the theory needs to account for both successful *and* unsuccessful change efforts.

CHAPTER 8

EVALUATING
EDUCATIONAL CHANGE

MAJOR IDEAS

- Understanding educational change requires patience and a genuine interest in others' perceptions and experience.

- Evaluation is both a consequence of and an impetus to change.

- Evaluating educational change involves more than collecting data on student outcomes. Educators need to determine whether intended changes actually have been implemented.

- The design of evaluations of educational change involves a variety of approaches and methods.

- Evaluators of educational change need to be clear about the uses to which their evaluations will be put.

- Evaluations have the potential to disrupt, as well as enhance, the educational change process.

It is difficult to achieve what we do not understand. From time to time, people can get lucky, but, in general, understanding something about change is a prerequisite for accomplishing change. There is much to understand—the readiness of individuals to commit to and participate in change, the capacity of organizations and communities to support and sustain change, the viability of various designs for change, and so on. No individual is likely to understand everything about change, but there are ways to increase and enhance our understanding. Evaluation is one of those ways.

That evaluation *can* enhance understanding of educational change does not necessarily mean that it *does* in all cases. Most veteran educators know from experience that evaluations, on occasion, may serve political purposes, such as confirming preexisting conclusions held by influential parties or discrediting initiatives that have fallen out of favor. When particular politicians want to slash education spending, it is amazing how much evaluation data they can locate that demonstrate educational reforms are a poor investment. In a similar vein, pro-education interests never seem to be at a loss for evaluation data linking higher outcomes with greater spending on

213

schools and teachers. My hope is that these manipulations of evaluation information will not discourage those who seek greater understanding of educational change through evaluation.

Evaluating change, like most ways to improve understanding, calls for considerable patience. Educators, however, can be notoriously impatient, an *understandable* reaction to the fact that they daily address the needs of many young people and typically have more to do than time available to do it. Evaluating change also requires a genuine interest in the perceptions and experiences of others. Evaluation, in other words, is more than just collecting information on student test performance and other "objective" outcome measures. Because they spend so much time working alone with a class and they rarely observe or interact with peers, educators sometimes come to rely exclusively on their own perceptions and experiences. When educators fail to exhibit an interest in how others feel and think about change, they not only increase the likelihood of unsuccessful reform, they betray the very foundations on which the field of education is based.

Before a new drug reaches the pharmacy, it is supposed to be thoroughly tested and evaluated. Results are discussed by experts. The welfare and well-being of students demands that a comparable level of scrutiny accompany educational change initiatives. Like anything else, evaluations of educational change can be done well or poorly. Good evaluations reflect good design, thorough planning, and careful implementation.

Chapter 8 is not intended to be a how-to guide for evaluators of educational change. Plenty of helpful manuals for evaluators already are available. The objectives of this chapter are to (1) introduce some of the options that should be considered in planning an evaluation of educational change, (2) identify some principles of good evaluation, (3) review key questions that need to be addressed by evaluators, and (4) discuss several difficult issues concerning the evaluation process in general.

EVALUATION OPTIONS

Evaluating educational change at first might seem to be a relatively simple and straightforward process: Identify the intended goals of change and measure the extent to which they are achieved. Upon closer examination, however, evaluating educational change turns out to be much more complicated. Educators confront a variety of possibilities when they sit down to plan an evaluation. First they need to consider the purpose or purposes the evaluation is meant to serve. Then they must weigh various design options related to the kind of evaluation best suited to the purpose or purposes and the most appropriate methods for conducting the evaluation. The following discussion explores some of the choices involved in designing an evaluation of educational change.

A Plethora of Purposes

- A new education policy is promulgated to raise student achievement. Did the policy accomplish its purpose? Were there any undesirable side effects?

- A new program for at-risk students is developed in order to reduce dropping out of school. Did local educators implement the program as it was designed?
- Referrals to the office for misbehavior have fallen in one school for three consecutive years. What could have happened to account for this pleasant surprise?
- Three middle schools in the same school system adopt and implement a new mathematics curriculum. Test scores in mathematics climb in one school and remain the same in the other two. Why?
- In a neighboring district, three middle schools adopt and implement three different mathematics programs. Which program works best?

Questions such as these reflect some of the different purposes involved in evaluating educational change. The most obvious purpose probably concerns determining the extent to which the intended goals of change have been achieved. In order to interpret the results of such a goal-based evaluation, however, it may be important to know the extent to which a change has been faithfully implemented. Without such evaluative information, it is difficult to account for the positive or negative outcomes of attempted reforms. We sometimes detect positive or negative outcomes without being clear about what might have caused them. Evaluation can reveal possible reasons for shifts in performance. Evaluation also allows us to make comparisons across teachers, groups of students, programs, schools, school districts, and even nations. These comparisons enable educators to determine which educational changes work best and understand why particular changes fare better in some settings than others.

One way to think about the range of evaluation purposes is to consider the kinds of decisions for which evaluation data may be used. Weiss (1972, pp. 16–17) identifies six types of decisions, each of which relates in some way to educational change:

1. To continue or discontinue a program
2. To improve a program's practices and procedures
3. To add or drop specific program strategies and techniques
4. To institute similar programs elsewhere
5. To allocate resources among competing programs
6. To accept or reject a program approach or theory

Particular decisions and purposes are associated with particular groups of stakeholders. Scriven (1993, p. 20) challenges the conventional wisdom that stakeholders are only concerned about whether goals have been met:

> Most consumer or taxpayer groups have little interest in whether a program meets its goals as such, only in whether it does something that needs doing, whether the cost is reasonable, and whether it does it better than alternative ways of doing it.

School boards may request an evaluation in order to decide whether one new program is more deserving of limited resources than another. Teachers involved in a program, meanwhile, may desire an evaluation in order to improve program performance and identify areas where additional training is needed. Evaluations that address one group's purposes can be questioned or dismissed as self-serving by other groups.

The purpose of evaluation may vary depending on the phase of the change process. Lewy (1977, pp. 14–23), for example, sees different roles for evaluation during each of his six stages of curriculum development.

STAGE	ROLE OF EVALUATION
Determination of general aims	Studies on: expected changes, cultural values, present level of achievement, feasibility of programs, and so on
Planning	Examine adequacy of objectives, content, and material
Tryout	Collect evidence from students and teachers, including samples of student work
Field trial	Collect evidence on program efficiency under various conditions
Implementation	Collect evidence of quality of teacher training
Quality control	Examine quality of implementation

If we think of evaluation as a highly formalized process, it is staggering to imagine the amount of work involved in evaluating each phase of educational change. Evaluation methods, however, need not always entail comprehensive data collection and sophisticated forms of analysis. With relatively little effort and a good sampling strategy, it is possible to collect and reflect on evaluation data throughout the course of the change process. Doing so increases an understanding of change and allows educators to make the adjustments necessary to ensure successful change.

Several key terms have been used in recent years to differentiate evaluation purposes. **Formative evaluation** was introduced by Scriven (1967) to describe the process of collecting and analyzing data to improve a curriculum during its development. He contrasted formative evaluation with **summative evaluation,** which takes place *after* the curriculum has been developed. These terms now are applied to a variety of circumstances, not just curriculum development. Formative evaluation applies to evaluations that are intended to help individuals improve that which is being evaluated. Summative evaluation, on the other hand, refers to evaluations that lead to judgments of a conclusive nature, such as whether a reform has succeeded and if it should be continued.

■ ■ ■ ■ ■

CASE STUDY

FORMATIVE EVALUATION OF ESSENTIAL SCHOOLS

The Coalition of Essential Schools provides criteria for members to judge their progress in implementing the essential schools reform program. These criteria include the following:

■ Substantial agreement among those in the school that change is needed and that change should be guided by the principles of the Coalition of Essential Schools.

- Observable changes in the structure of the school.
- Engagement of all or most faculty members in some concrete essential schools activity.
- Leadership that is exercised by all members of the school in the interest of implementing the essential schools principles.

Using these criteria as benchmarks, researchers conducted a formative evaluation of four schools that were at the mid-point of a five-year restructuring effort intended to implement the complete essential schools program. The researchers maintained that it would not be worthwhile to evaluate desired student outcomes until a determination could be made of whether the essential schools program actually was in place.

Data were gathered on a longitudinal basis using "intensive open-ended interviews and follow-up focused interviews." Key respondents at each site were asked to keep reflective journals over the three-year course of the study. In addition, documentary and archival evidence was examined and observations were conducted. Data initially were compiled as case studies, and a cross-case analysis was conducted to reveal similarities and differences across the four sites.

Researchers concluded that the four schools achieved "very different degrees of success and progress as measured by the four benchmarks of change." They attributed their findings to differences in the interaction of three elements—the substance of change (the essential schools program), the process of change, and organizational understandings of the reforms.

Nona A. Prestine and Chuck Bowen, "Benchmarks of Change: Assessing Essential School Restructuring Efforts," *Educational Evaluation and Policy Analysis,* Vol. 15, no. 3 (Fall 1993), pp. 298–319.

In Scriven's (1967) pathbreaking chapter on "The Methodology of Evaluation," he also introduced two other useful terms—**intrinsic evaluation** and **pay-off evaluation.** The purpose of intrinsic evaluation is to determine if what was intended to be done actually was done according to specifications. An English department chair, for instance, may want to know to what extent all chapters of a new grammar text are being taught in line with the instructor's manual provided by the publisher. Pay-off evaluation, meanwhile, concerns outcomes. What is the impact of the new grammar text? Are students more knowledgeable about the principles of good writing? Are they able to apply these principles? Are they actually writing better? If a pay-off evaluation reveals that expected outcomes are not being achieved, one reason may be that teachers are not teaching the new text according to the guidelines provided by the publisher, a conclusion that would be drawn from an intrinsic evaluation.

We see that when educators consider the purpose or purposes for evaluating educational change, they may need to take into account the kinds of decisions that will be made with evaluation data, the stakeholders to whom evaluation data will be reported, and the phase in the change process during which the evaluation is conducted. Having settled on the purpose of the evaluation, educators next must choose a design for the evaluation. Here, again, they face a range of options.

Key Terms

Formative evaluation   Evaluation for the purpose of improvement.

Summative evaluation   Evaluation for the purpose of making a decision regarding the status of that which is being evaluated.

Intrinsic evaluation   Evaluation for the purpose of determining whether what was planned was actually implemented.

Pay-off evaluation   Evaluation for the purpose of determining the impact of what was actually implemented.

Evaluation Design Options

Imagine that a superintendent wants to evaluate a new school safety program that involves testing students on school rules and requires school uniforms. According to the *Evaluator's Handbook* (Herman, Morris, and Fitz-Gibbon, 1987, p. 10), there are at least seven possible models on which program evaluation can be based. They include *goal-oriented* evaluation, *decision-oriented* evaluation, *responsive* evaluation, *evaluation research, goal-free* evaluation, *advocacy-adversary* evaluation, and *utilization-oriented* evaluation. Each type is geared to a somewhat different purpose. Responsive evaluation, for example, seeks to "depict program processes and the value perspectives of key people." The goal of evaluation research is to "focus on explaining effects, identifying causes of effects, and generating generalizations about program effectiveness."

Choosing an evaluation model is not the final decision to be made, because evaluation questions must be selected, along with how and whom to ask. Space does not permit a detailed discussion of every evaluation design possibility. It is important, though, to note some of the key options. The choice of particular options ultimately will be based on such factors as the purpose to be served by the evaluation; whether the educational change involves a process, policy, or product; the amount of time available for conducting the evaluation; the resources available to support the evaluation; and contextual factors such as local culture and the current political climate.

Goal-Based Versus Goal-Free Evaluation.   It seems logical to evaluate educational change by identifying the intended goals of particular reforms and then collecting data to determine the extent to which these goals have been achieved. The vast majority of evaluations of educational change, in fact, are goal-based. In 1980, however, Scriven made a case for what he called *goal-free evaluation.* When conducting a goal-free evaluation, the evaluator purposely avoids identifying the intended goals of reform. Instead, he searches for all possible effects and consequences of change, unintended as well as intended. Scriven argued that goal-based evaluations put blinders on evaluators, causing them to overlook unanticipated outcomes and unexpected byproducts of change. Patton (1987, p. 36) suggests that there are four reasons for doing goal-free evaluation:

(1) to avoid the risk of narrowly studying stated program objectives and thereby missing important unanticipated outcomes; (2) to remove the negative connotations attached to the discovery of unintended effects . . . ; (3) to eliminate the perceptual biases introduced into an evaluation by knowledge of goals; and (4) to maintain evaluator objectivity and independence through goal-free conditions.

Comparative Evaluation.   Variability is ubiquitous in education. Each classroom, school, and school system is, to some extent, unique. To help educators better understand the role of local differences in the change process, new policies, programs, and practices can be evaluated simultaneously at multiple sites. Sites can be chosen in order to maximize or minimize contextual differences.

When Virginia introduced new state standards and tests as part of a comprehensive accountability initiative, a colleague and I (Duke and Tucker, 2003) decided to assess the initial impact of the initiative on high schools. We conjectured that the impact might vary, depending on how well students had performed on the first round of state tests and the level of per-pupil funding. High schools were identified that represented high achievement, high expenditure; high achievement, low expenditure; low achievement, high expenditure; and low achievement, low expenditure categories. The results of our evaluation research suggested that Virginia high schools varied in their programmatic responses to new state standards and tests. Special programs, such as after-school test preparation sessions and summer school for students who failed a state test, were found more frequently in some types of schools than in others. Resources did not appear to be an influence on the initiation of special programs, but prior performance on state tests was related to the number of new programs initiated at a given high school. Resources were linked to particular curriculum adjustments, however. Course changes, including the elimination of electives and the addition of an extra semester of Algebra for struggling students, were more likely to occur in resource-rich high schools.

Educators are sometimes suspicious of evaluations that compare classrooms, schools, and school systems, but parents and policy makers want to know where educational change is and is not working and why. Access to such data is essential if educational institutions are to be truly accountable and responsive to the needs of those they serve. Comparative evaluations can focus on how a particular policy, program, or practice is working in different settings or on how different policies, programs, and practices are working for similar problems in different settings. Comparisons also can be made across time as well as across sites. The impact of a new science program, for instance, can be compared to the impact of the science program it replaced. Eisner (2002, p. 176) cautions, however, that such comparisons can be misleading, since new programs rarely have exactly the same goals as their predecessors. Sarason (1971, pp. 29–48) illustrated Eisner's point when he noted the unfairness of using traditional measures of mathematics achievement in the late 1960s to evaluate the success of New Math curriculum initiatives.

Qualitative Methods.   Evaluations of educational change often call for the compilation of various statistics, ranging from differences in test scores before and after the implementation of reforms to numerical ratings of student and parent satisfaction with recent innovations. Statistical data are perceived by some to be more objective and convincing than other types of data. Although evaluations of educational change should rely on statistics where appropriate, educators are increasingly aware of the value of qualitative data.

In *How to Use Qualitative Methods in Evaluation,* Patton (1987, pp. 40–42) offers helpful guidelines concerning when evaluators should choose qualitative over quantitative data. He believes that the following conditions call for the collection of qualitative evaluation data:

- When a new program is expected to affect individuals in qualitatively different ways
- When decision makers want to understand how a new program actually is working
- When detailed information is needed by program sites and individuals affected by programs
- When information is needed on how well a new program has been implemented
- When detailed information is needed to finetune new programs

A good example of an evaluation employing qualitative methods for data collection and analysis involved a foundation's efforts to develop a network of schools and community organizations in Chicago (Kahne, O'Brien, Brown, and Quinn, 2001). For almost five years evaluators conducted observations and interviewed administrators, teachers, and students in order to determine the extent to which interactions between educators and community members reflected the central assumptions underlying the foundation's initiative. Their findings revealed the fact that efforts to integrate the work of schools and community organizations faced difficulties when distrust prevailed and external accountability measures threatened educators with substantial sanctions for poor performance. It is hard to imagine evaluating the complexities of school–community relations by relying solely on quantitative data.

Eisner (2002), a long-standing advocate of qualitative evaluation, argues that grades and standardized test results are poorly suited vehicles for conveying to parents what has happened to their children over the course of the school year. To get at the richness of daily life in schools, he recommends the use of *educational criticism.* This approach, borrowed from the arts, seeks to draw on actual experience in order to render a detailed and engaging picture of educational activities. Words may be supplemented by still photographs and videotape. Eisner explains the role of the educational critic thusly:

> What critics do or should try to do is not to translate what cannot be translated but rather to create a rendering of a situation, event, or object that will provide pointers to those aspects of the situation, event, or object that are in some way significant. (pp. 219–220)

Continuous Versus Episodic Evaluation.   Another decision in designing evaluations of educational change concerns the matter of timing. Some reform initiatives call for only one summative evaluation. Others require an evaluation to be conducted prior to the renewal of funding. Evaluation, however, also can be treated as an episodic activity conducted during each phase of the change process. During the Design Phase, for example, educators may need to evaluate alternative programs that address an identified need for change. Later, during the Implementation Phase, it may be important to evaluate the impact of staff development. If teachers fail to acquire new skills and knowledge, there may be little reason to expect reforms to succeed.

Neale, Bailey, and Ross (1981, p. 213) contend that the evaluation of educational change should be regarded as a *continuous* process. They maintain that structured feedback on a regular basis is the best way to ensure that new policies, programs, and practices are responsive to local needs. Educators are less likely to react defensively to constructive feedback if it is provided as a normal and regular part of the change process.

Internal Versus External Evaluation.   The last decision to be discussed involves the selection of evaluators. Evaluations of educational change may be conducted by school system employees (internal evaluators), outside consultants (external evaluators), or some combination of the two. The advantages of relying on internal evaluators include ease of access, low cost, and familiarity with local context. A major disadvantage, however, concerns credibility. Results of evaluations conducted by internal evaluators can be dismissed as subjective and self-serving. External evaluators, while costly, can provide greater assurance of nonpartisan data collection and analysis. Also, small school systems may lack individuals with high levels of evaluation expertise.

Educators sometimes find it beneficial to rely on internal evaluators for ongoing formative feedback and external evaluators for summative evaluations. In both cases, the goal is to enhance the credibility of evaluation results. Judgments of credibility vary with the audience. Because the primary audience for formative feedback typically is local educators involved in planning and implementing change, insiders may be more likely to be listened to than outsiders. Outside evaluators may have the edge, however, when it comes to summative or high-stakes evaluations designed to inform policy makers and community members.

SOME PRINCIPLES OF GOOD EVALUATION

We have seen that evaluating educational change presents educators with a variety of options. The range of design possibilities does not mean, though, that one evaluation design is necessarily as good as any other design. Evaluation experts have identified criteria for distinguishing good from mediocre evaluations. The American Evaluation Association, for example, developed "Guiding Principles for Evaluators" (Shadish,

Newman, Scheirer, and Wye, 1995) to help people who are involved in planning and conducting evaluations. Rather than review all possible criteria, several particularly important principles of good evaluation are highlighted below.

1. *Evaluations of educational change should be carefully planned and negotiated.* Busy educators may be tempted to take shortcuts when developing evaluations of educational change. Given the potential of evaluations to adversely affect the fate of new policies, programs, and practices, however, it is best that the design of evaluations be approached with the same care and concern as the design of the educational changes to be evaluated.

Designing an evaluation requires consideration of the time and resources available for data collection, analysis, and reporting. Interview and survey questions may need to be developed, field-tested, and refined. Decisions must be made regarding which individuals will be interviewed or surveyed. Designers need to determine what evidence will be used to judge whether change has been effective. Poorly designed evaluations not only produce questionable results, they increase the likelihood of contentiousness. Achieving educational change is difficult enough without the distraction of controversial evaluations.

One way to increase the likelihood that evaluation results will be accepted is to involve representatives of stakeholders in evaluation planning. An evaluation plan, according to Stecher and Davis (1987, p. 64), consists of three key elements: "(1) questions or issues to be examined by the evaluation, (2) procedures to be employed in the evaluation, and (3) resources needed to accomplish the evaluation tasks." Stakeholders can provide valuable input concerning each of these elements. They understand, for instance, the local context in which change is to be evaluated and the provisions most likely to establish the credibility of an evaluation. Planning an evaluation of educational change is best viewed as a series of negotiations between evaluators and those who are the subject of the evaluation or who are likely to be affected by the results.

2. *Evaluation purposes should be clear.* Evaluations, as noted earlier, can be intended for various purposes. For both practical and ethical reasons, the reason or reasons for conducting an evaluation should be clear from the outset to all involved in or affected by the evaluation. Clarifying evaluation purposes is essential for efficient data collection and analysis. The information needed to determine whether a new program should continue differs from that required to finetune and adjust it. If the reason for evaluating a new program is to help officials decide whether to continue it, program participants have a right to know this reason in advance. It is unethical to conceal the true purpose of an evaluation in an attempt to gather less biased data.

3. *Evaluation plans should include the collection of baseline data.* The focus of this book is educational change. Without the collection of baseline, or pre-implementation, data, it is difficult to be certain that change has occurred. Unfortunately, the decision to conduct an evaluation sometimes is an afterthought, thereby eliminating the possibility of gathering baseline data. Educators are urged to develop a plan for collecting baseline data well before the Implementation Phase of educational change. Collecting baseline data constitutes an evaluation of the status quo—that which existed prior to the onset of educational change.

4. *Evaluation plans should provide for the collection of data from multiple sources.* If efficiency was the primary concern of evaluators of educational change, they might be prompted to limit data collection to a few key informants. It is much easier to interview a school principal regarding the impact of a new science curriculum than to gather data from science teachers and students. The problem, of course, is that the principal does not work with the new science curriculum on a daily basis. Science teachers and their students are the individuals most likely to provide informed judgments regarding the new curriculum. Confidence in evaluation findings is directly related to the number of data sources. A well-designed evaluation takes into account the fact that individuals and groups may regard a new policy, program, or practice differently.

Because gathering data from different groups is time consuming and costly, evaluators often rely on random sampling. An evaluation of a new after-school academic enrichment program, for example, need not involve interviews with every student and every student's parents. If the sampling strategy is truly randomized, interviews with a subset of all students and parents should be sufficient to provide an accurate sense of people's feelings about the new program. In some cases where evaluators want to know how representatives of particular groups feel, it may be necessary to use a stratified random sample. This strategy requires arranging evaluation subjects by groups—for example, ethnic groups—and then randomly selecting participants from each group. A stratified random sample is useful when it is important to hear from certain groups with so few members that regular random sampling might miss them altogether.

5. *Evaluation plans should provide for the collection of different types of data.* Evaluation data can be gathered in four general ways—observation, interview, questionnaire, and document review. Each of these, in turn, involves various options. Interviews, for example, can be conducted on an individual basis or in focus groups. Questionnaires may require open-ended responses, numerical ratings, check marks (yes/no answers), or selections from multiple choice answers. The validity and reliability of evaluation findings can be enhanced by relying on more than one type of data. Imagine that we are evaluating a new program designed to reduce discipline problems. We could decide to distribute a questionnaire asking teachers if student behavior has improved since the implementation of the new program. Although useful, this information may not tell the whole story. To verify teachers' impressions, it would be helpful to review and analyze disciplinary referrals. Students also have important information on school discipline to share. If the results of questioning teachers and students and reviewing disciplinary referrals all suggest similar program outcomes, the likelihood that the results will be taken seriously is much greater. When results tend to vary with the source, evaluators are obliged to try to account for differences.

■ ■ ■ ■ ■

CASE STUDY

EVALUATING ONE SCHOOL'S EFFORTS TO REDUCE MISCONDUCT

In an effort to reduce disorder in a Baltimore junior high school, a three-year organizational development project was initiated. Key elements of the program included the creation of a school improvement team, extensive staff development based on two approaches to classroom management, additional training in cooperative learning techniques, a parent volunteer program, development of a coherent set of school rules and consequences for breaking them, and an extra-curricular program designed to foster school attachment and pride.

To determine whether these efforts had reduced disorder in the school, an evaluation was conducted. The design of the evaluation called for data collection at two schools—the junior high where the new program was implemented and a comparable junior high where no systematic attempt to reduce disorder had been made. The use of a comparison school was important because it enabled evaluators to determine whether factors other than the new program might be at work to reduce behavior problems in Baltimore schools.

In order to have a solid basis for detecting program effects, baseline data were collected prior to program implementation. Program goals were developed by the school improvement team, and measures were selected for each goal. Teachers were asked to complete surveys (scaled items) concerning organizational health and classroom orderliness. Students were asked to complete surveys (scaled items) concerning delinquent behavior, rebellious behavior, social integration, attachment to school, positive peer associations, and rewards. A review also was undertaken of office referrals and disciplinary actions.

Once the project was up and running, additional data related to implementation were collected. Observations of classrooms were undertaken, logs were kept by teachers, and interviews with various staff members were conducted. The school improvement team met monthly to monitor program progress. At the end of the three-year project, teachers and students again completed instruments based on desired outcomes, and disciplinary data were reviewed. Similar data were collected at the comparison school.

Evaluation results revealed some successes and some areas of continuing concern. Modest improvements were noted in social integration and rebellious behavior, but students' educational expectations declined during implementation. Suspensions for students involved in the new program fell significantly, but this was true for other students as well. Consequently, it was impossible to credit the new program alone for the drop in suspensions.

Material for this case study was taken from Denise C. Gottfredson, "An Evaluation of an Organization Development Approach to Reducing School Disorder," *Evaluation Review,* Vol. 11, no. 6 (December 1987), pp. 739–763.

The evaluation described in the case study reflects several principles of good evaluation. Members of the school improvement team were involved in planning the evaluation and identifying the program goals that would serve as the basis for data collection. Provisions were made for collecting baseline data, and students as well as teachers and administrators were questioned. Various types of data were collected, and the reforms were given a reasonable amount of time to take effect before evaluation data were gathered.

EVALUATION PRINCIPLES
- Evaluations of educational change should be carefully planned and negotiated.
- Evaluation purposes should be clear.
- Evaluation plans should include the collection of baseline data.
- Evaluation plans should provide for the collection of data from multiple sources.
- Evaluation plans should provide for the collection of different types of data.

FOCAL QUESTIONS FOR EVALUATING EDUCATIONAL CHANGE

Efforts to achieve educational change give rise to a variety of practical questions. Evaluation is a systematic approach to gathering the data needed to answer these questions. Questions range from those concerning how well a particular reform has been implemented, to the long-term effects of change. This part of the chapter examines some specific questions that may be addressed in the process of evaluating educational change.

Questions Related to Implementation

"Program evaluation," according to Bickman (1987, pp. 6–7), "has progressed in the last twenty years from applying the simple input/output, or black box, model of evaluation to moving 'inside' the box to try to understand what goes on in the program." Focusing only on the extent to which new initiatives achieved desired goals did not prove particularly helpful when it came to making program improvements and accounting for the results of reform. Educators needed information concerning the change process itself and the extent to which new policies, programs, and practices actually had been implemented.

1. *How was the new initiative implemented?* In most cases, educational change is a protracted experience involving training, trial, and tuning. The longer the implementation period lasts and the more people involved in implementing change, the greater the possibility of deviation and variation. By monitoring how a change has been implemented, evaluators can provide a valuable descriptive record that eventually may be used to account for the success or failure of the new initiative.

■ ■ ■ ■ ■

CASE STUDY

EVALUATING A SCHOOL-BASED GANG PREVENTION PROGRAM

The Gang Resistance Education and Training (G.R.E.A.T.) program is a school-based gang prevention program developed in 1991 by the Phoenix, Arizona, Police Department. The program calls for law enforcement officers to teach a nine-week curriculum on resistance skills and violence prevention to seventh graders. In 1994 the National Institute of Justice funded a national evaluation of the G.R.E.A.T. program. A key component of the evaluation

(continued)

CONTINUED

was a process evaluation focused on the training received by law enforcement officers and their subsequent delivery of instruction to seventh graders.

The first part of the evaluation called for the collection of qualitative data in the form of field observations of six 40-hour officer training sessions. Evaluators investigated the extent to which the training followed the guidelines in the G.R.E.A.T. Instructor Training Activity Book and whether all groups of officers received comparable training. Evaluators concluded that training was consistent with printed guidelines across all six sessions.

The second part of the evaluation involved monitoring the officers as they delivered instruction to seventh graders. Program developers wondered whether individual officers would deviate from the curriculum or give more emphasis to certain topics than others. In order to collect data during the nine-week school program, eighteen observers were trained. A total of eighty-seven lessons delivered by nineteen different law enforcement officers were observed. Particular lessons were observed between eight and eighteen times to provide a basis for comparison across instructors. Observers used checklists based on G.R.E.A.T. guidelines and created narratives describing each officer's performance.

Evaluators found that most of the officers followed the guidelines reasonably closely. In twelve lessons, however, material from the instructor's manual was omitted. Some officers brought up discussions of recent crimes that were not part of the curriculum. In nine cases, officers covered material in a large group, when the manual called for dividing the class into small groups. Some officers completed the curriculum in less than nine weeks. Evaluating the fidelity with which law enforcement officers delivered the G.R.E.A.T. curriculum provided a foundation for interpreting the actual results of instruction.

Christine S. Sellers, Terrence J. Taylor, and Finn-Aage Esbensen, "Reality Check: Evaluating a School-based Gang Prevention Model," *Evaluation Review,* Vol. 22, no. 5 (October 1998), pp. 590–608.

It is not enough, in many cases, to know whether a new initiative achieved its goals. If, as often is the case, the consequences of change are somewhat different from what is expected, educators should be able to reconstruct the implementation experience in order to understand why. A descriptive record of implementation is a critical part of this process. Under no circumstances should educators simply assume that implementation plans and guidelines have been faithfully followed.

2. *To what extent was the new initiative implemented?* The previous question focused on *how* implementation occurred. It is also important to know exactly *what* was implemented. The evaluation of the G.R.E.A.T. program in the preceding case study indicated that some law enforcement officers were not covering all of the topics in the gang prevention curriculum. By not fully implementing this curriculum, these individuals may have reduced the chances that program goals would be achieved.

When evaluations of educational change include an *intrinsic* evaluation component, evaluators are able to go beyond observing whether or not goals have been achieved. In the event that actual performance falls short of intentions, they can offer an explanation. Educators need to know when unsuccessful change is attributable to inadequate implementation and when change fails despite by-the-book implementation. In the case of the former, the new initiative still may have merit. When desired outcomes are not achieved in spite of faithful implementation, however, the reform itself may be at fault.

To determine the extent to which an intended change has been implemented, evaluators should not rely exclusively on indirect sources of data such as interviews and questionnaires. Conducting observations in schools and classrooms may be necessary in order to determine whether new policies, programs, and practices are being implemented as designed. Direct observation can be particularly important when the change involves new curriculum content and instructional practices. Research (Cohen and Hill, 2001, p. 11) suggests that variability is more likely than consistency to characterize the implementation of educational change.

King, Morris, and Fitz-Gibbon (1987) provide a helpful manual for designing intrinsic evaluations of new programs. In describing a new program in action, evaluators are advised to "highlight the program's most important characteristics, including a description of the context in which the program exists—its setting and participants—as well as its distinguishing activities and materials" (p. 7). This description of the program *as implemented* then can be compared with the proposed program in order to identify any discrepancies. Discrepancies may offer clues concerning the program's lack of success.

After Central Elementary School in Amherst County, Virginia, adopted the principles of the Coalition for Essential Schools, the principal wanted a status check on how implementation was going. He invited several outside observers to join him in conducting a day-long "Walkabout" assessment. To guide their observations, behavioral indicators were identified for each of the Coalition's principles. For example, because Coalition students are expected to develop as thinkers, observers looked for evidence that teachers were requiring students to defend their work. On the day the Walkabout was scheduled, each observer visited eight classrooms for a minimum of 10 minutes each. Following these visits, they conferred to determine the extent to which the Coalition's principles were actually in effect. Their findings then were shared with the faculty and used to finetune the implementation process.

Questions Related to Outcomes

Evaluations of educational change typically are conducted because people are interested in the effects of change. Effects may be either intended or unexpected. A thorough evaluation should examine both possibilities.

3. *To what extent were intended goals achieved?* In order to answer this question, evaluators need to identify the intended goal or goals associated with a particular reform. In some cases, designers and planners carefully specify the outcomes they hope will be achieved by change. In other cases, however, goals are not explicitly stated, or the explicit goals expressed at the outset of the change process are superseded by new and sometimes unwritten goals. In these instances, evaluators must devote time to identifying altered goals and implicit expectations.

The goals of educational change can be divided into short-term and long-term goals. Short-term goals often involve changes in school organization and teacher competence. Achieving short-term goals is presumed to pave the way to long-term goals, which typically involve changes in student achievement, behavior, and aspirations. The short-term goal of a new block schedule, for example, may be to reduce the number of students with whom teachers come in contact on a daily basis and thereby increase the likelihood that struggling students receive timely assistance. Accomplishing these short-term goals should lead, in turn, to fewer failing grades and higher levels of student performance on end-of-course tests.

Short-term goals of educational change frequently call for changes in teachers' knowledge, skills, and beliefs. These changes are supposed to result from staff development, coursework, coaching, and other types of inservice training. The first step in evaluating the outcomes of educational change therefore may entail determining whether teachers have acquired the knowledge, skills, and beliefs necessary to achieve long-term goals. Enhanced teacher expertise serves as an important checkpoint on the road to improved student outcomes.

Most educational change, as noted, is intended ultimately to produce changes in students. Some changes—such as improved scores on standardized tests, higher grades, and greater credit accumulation—are relatively easy to measure. Other changes, including improved attitudes toward learning and higher aspirations, pose challenges for evaluators. Many evaluators believe that what is most easily evaluated is not necessarily what is most important. Educational change may not always focus on academic achievement. Some reforms are designed to reduce absenteeism and dropping out, improve student behavior, and encourage students to become more caring and responsible.

Evaluating the effects of educational change on students presents evaluators with a variety of problems. How to analyze and present evaluation results is one such concern. It is easier in many ways to aggregate evaluation results, reducing student achievement to a single statistic such as an average score or average rate of improvement. Aggregated data, however, can conceal considerable variation in performance. Educators need to know when particular change benefits certain students, but not others.

Questions also have been raised about the volatility of year-to-year test scores for successive groups of students in the same school (Linn and Haug, 2002). The instability of changes in student achievement from one year to the next suggests that evaluators must be very cautious about drawing conclusions about the impact of particular reforms based on data from only one or two years.

■ ■ ■ ■ ■ ▬▬▬▬▬▬▬▬▬▬▬▬▬▬▬▬▬▬▬▬▬▬▬▬▬

CASE STUDY
DO HIGHER STANDARDS BENEFIT AT-RISK STUDENTS?

During the 1980s, states and school districts across the United States introduced reforms aimed at raising the level of student achievement. Graduation requirements were stiffened, and students were required to pass standardized tests aligned with curriculum standards. Critics feared that at-risk students would be adversely affected by these measures. In order to evaluate the impact of these initiatives on at-risk students, the General Accounting Office of the federal government examined student outcomes before and after reforms in four school systems.

The evaluation design called for comparing two cohorts of at-risk students—a pre-reform group and a post-reform group—in four cities on two achievement measures each (reading and mathematics). This design resulted in a total of eight comparisons of achievement scores. The results indicated that no achievement gains resulted from the reforms in five of the eight comparisons. The gains in the other three comparisons were modest.

Based on the GAO evaluation, educators should be careful about expecting raised academic standards to produce dramatic improvements in the achievement of at-risk students. At the same time, the results also indicated that at-risk students were not as adversely affected by higher standards as many critics had feared.

General Accounting Office. *Education Reform: Initial Effects in Four School Districts.* Washington, DC: Author, 1989.

Evaluating student outcomes has the potential to contribute to, as well as monitor the effects of, educational change. Stiggins (2002, p. 761) distinguishes between assessments *of* and assessments *for* learning: "If assessments *of learning* provide evidence of achievement for public reporting, then assessments *for learning* serve to help students learn more." More than formative evaluation, assessments for learning engage students in understanding how changes are expected to affect their learning and build students' confidence in themselves as learners. Students also can learn to conduct self-assessments and report on their progress to teachers and parents.

Efforts to raise student achievement sometimes entail a variety of reforms. A school improvement plan, for example, may call for closer supervision of struggling students, elimination of tracking, greater parent involvement, and training for teachers in classroom management. In evaluating the impact of the school improvement plan, evaluators may discover evidence of increased student achievement. What they are unable to do, however, is determine whether this positive outcome was due to all of the changes or a particular change. Separating the effects of multiple reforms that are simultaneously implemented is extremely difficult.

4. *Did change result in unintended consequences?* Imagine the problems that could result if the Food and Drug Administration failed to assess the possible side effects of new medicines. The possibility exists that a new medicine may achieve its intended effect and, in addition, produce undesirable consequences under certain circumstances. Educational change also has the potential to produce negative, or at least unanticipated, byproducts. A tough new discipline policy may require teachers to spend more time monitoring student conduct and, in so doing, adversely affect their instructional responsibilities. A new reading initiative may seek to raise reading achievement by doubling the time students spend on reading activities. The time taken away from other subjects, however, can lead to lower achievement in these areas.

As a precautionary measure, evaluators of educational change should always make an effort to look beyond the stated goals of a new policy, program, or practice.

Unfortunately, the practice of assessing unanticipated byproducts of change is not common. Scriven (1993, p. 24) notes,

> The monitoring of progress toward achieving program goals does not usually or necessarily involve an active search for side effects. Indeed, identification of side effects in any systematic way is often difficult because those who know the program well quickly develop tunnel vision, their attention becomes focused on what they are looking for and hoping to find.

The solution, according to Scriven, is to rely on external evaluators who may be able to investigate the impact of reforms with greater objectivity. He further advocates having at least one evaluator engage in goal-free evaluation. By remaining purposely unaware of the desired goals of reform, the goal-free evaluator is more likely to detect unexpected and possibly undesirable byproducts of change.

Evaluation-Based Judgments about Change

Evaluation is not an academic exercise. The information gathered during an evaluation is supposed to enable educators and policy makers to arrive at informed decisions regarding the fate of particular changes.

Consider the implementation questions that were discussed earlier. Data concerning implementation allows a judgment to be made concerning the extent to which an intended change actually has been achieved. If it is decided that the actual change is what was intended, then educators can turn their attention to outcomes. If, however, the desired change has not been fully implemented, a decision must be made regarding whether to continue with implementation. Before making such a decision, educators need to consider the reasons why planned changes have not been achieved, the resources needed to achieve full implementation, and the consequences of partial implementation.

In the event that a new policy, program, or practice has been fully implemented, educators can turn their attention to the extent that the desired goals of the new initiative have been achieved. If desired goals have not been achieved, a judgment must be made concerning whether to continue the initiative. It may be the case that more time is needed for the reform to take effect. Alternatively, the reform simply may lack the capacity to produce desired effects. In the latter case, educators eventually must decide whether to modify their expectations, abandon the new initiative, or modify it.

A change that produces desired effects is not assured of continuation. If it also produces unanticipated and undesirable side effects, educators will need to weigh the benefits of the change against the costs. In some cases, the benefits may be judged sufficient to accept the costs. Educators currently are debating whether an increased dropout rate is an acceptable price to pay for higher academic standards and greater student testing. Such decisions frequently result in winners and losers, regardless of which way the decision goes. It is only fair to point out, however, that deciding *not* to change also can adversely affect certain individuals.

No educational change is ever completely safe from elimination. Even if the change results in the achievement of desired goals with no negative side effects, it may be subject to displacement as a result of shifting priorities, lost resources, and other factors. Evaluation data cannot ensure that educational change will be sustained, only that decisions regarding the fate of change will be based on more than whim and guesswork.

ISSUES FOR EVALUATORS OF EDUCATIONAL CHANGE

Evaluation is an imperfect discipline practiced in settings characterized by controversy and contention. When evaluation of educational change is poorly planned and executed, it can be like adding gasoline to a fire. In this part of the chapter, we examine several potential sources of concern related to evaluating educational change.

Premature Evaluation

How long should educators wait before scheduling an evaluation of a new policy, program, or practice? The answer depends, in part, on the type of evaluation. Formative evaluations designed to provide constructive feedback to implementers so that they can finetune a reform are appropriate almost any time following the beginning of implementation. Summative evaluations that lead to decisions concerning the fate of a reform are another matter. Before conducting a summative evaluation, educators should be certain that an intended change actually has been implemented.

Accelerated Schools, a comprehensive school improvement program developed by Henry Levin, was evaluated by the Manpower Demonstration Research Corporation. Evaluators investigated eight years of test-score data for third graders in eight Accelerated Schools sites. The results suggested that students in the program begin to show significant gains after four to five years (Viadero, 2002). These findings countered some earlier evaluations that questioned the program's effectiveness. It is unfortunate when promising programs are abandoned simply because they did not have sufficient time to become fully effective.

Solomon (1995, p. 168–170) drew on Fullan's notion of the implementation dip to caution educators that indicators of success may slip somewhat until a new initiative has been implemented completely. What happened in an example that she presented, a high school that eliminated tracking in order to raise student achievement, was that initial results following the first year were very encouraging. About 55 percent of the students who previously would have taken non-Regents-level courses passed the Regents exam after being assigned to Regents-level courses. The next year, however, produced disappointing test results. Some critics of de-tracking dismissed the first year's success as a result of the Hawthorne effect and lobbied for a return to the old tracking system. Had the high school bailed out of its de-tracking initiative at this point, students never would have reaped the benefits in academic achievement that eventually began to emerge following the one-year dip.

Disruption

As important as evaluation can be, there is no denying its potential for disruption. Educators involved in implementing change may be called on to meet with evaluators, participate in interviews and focus groups, fill out surveys, and host observers. If evaluators are not careful, their demands on educators' time can constitute a disruption of the very change process that they are seeking to study.

The potential for disruption does not necessarily end when an evaluation is concluded. Evaluation findings can generate considerable controversy when they are perceived to be unfair or based on questionable data and analysis. Negative findings may lead individuals to clamor for modifications in or termination of reforms. Although I do not advocate doctoring evaluations so that they contain only positive conclusions, I agree with Weiss (1972, p. 92) when she stresses that "evaluation has to adapt itself to the program environment and disrupt operations as little as possible."

The disruptive potential of evaluation can be minimized if it is carefully planned and conducted. By involving educators in the planning process, evaluators gain insight into the most appropriate methods and times for gathering data. Providing educators with an opportunity to review and help analyze evaluation data before they are published in an official report can eliminate embarrassing misinterpretations of evaluation data and increase the likelihood that findings will be heeded. Evaluators should bear in mind at all times that evaluation is a means to improve education, not an end in itself.

Utilization

No matter how carefully evaluators conduct their work and report their findings, there is no guarantee that the findings will be used. The reasons findings may be ignored vary. In some cases, changing circumstances reduce the importance of the educational change being evaluated. In other cases, the change may be so popular that its future is secure, regardless of what evaluators discover. Other reasons for lack of utilization include questions about evaluation methodology, sampling strategy, and evaluators' competence and objectivity. Weiss (1972, pp. 110–128) notes that findings may not be disseminated to those in a position to take action or they may not be reported in a way that necessarily leads to action. Weiss goes on to observe that evaluation findings often indicate little or no positive effect of change. It is difficult for consumers of evaluation data to know how to respond to reports of modest "effects." If a new policy or program has not achieved all of its goals, should it necessarily be terminated? Should efforts be made to make adjustments? Should the reform be given more time to work? The decision-making clarity that attends highly positive and highly negative evaluation results can evaporate in the presence of findings that indicate limited progress has been made.

Preskill and Torres (2000, p. 26) contend that the likelihood that evaluation results will be put to good use is increased when planners decide how results should be used *before* the evaluation is conducted. They acknowledge that evaluations may need to be used to determine the fate of new initiatives, but they also emphasize the importance of the evaluation process as a resource for individual and organizational learning. Evaluation's potential for promoting growth suggests that evaluation can serve as an impetus for, as well as a response to, educational change.

Seeing that evaluation results are actually used is one type of utilization problem. Preventing the misuse of evaluations and the evaluation process is another. The potential for misuse exists at every stage of evaluation, from the commissioning of an evaluation to the collection and analysis of evaluation data to the handling of evaluation findings, according to Stevens and Dial (1994, pp. 6–8). Misuse can occur, claim these authors (p. 10), when pressure is brought to bear on evaluators to bias the scope of evaluation research, meet unrealistic deadlines, distort evaluation results to benefit or harm a particular party, employ evaluation results selectively, and suppress the release of an evaluation report. The more public the evaluation process and the more representatives of stakeholder groups involved in the evaluation, the lower the likelihood of misuse.

CONCLUSION

Understanding educational change depends, in part, on the availability of evaluation data. Without such information, it is difficult to know with reasonable confidence whether change has occurred and, if so, what impact it has had. Educators engaged in planning evaluations must be clear on the purpose or purposes to be served by an evaluation in order to make appropriate choices regarding evaluation design. Choices range from the methods to be used to collect and analyze data to sampling strategy, from who conducts the evaluation to who receives evaluation results. Other choices involve the timing of evaluation, the format for presenting results, and the duration of the evaluation process.

Evaluations of educational change vary considerably in quality. To help educators think about evaluation design, Chapter 8 offered several design principles. Evaluations should be carefully designed and negotiated and evaluation purposes should be clear. In addition, evaluation plans should include the collection of baseline data, provide for collecting data from multiple sources, and rely on different types of data.

Evaluations can serve as an impetus for educational change as well as a response to it. Evaluation findings point in the direction of new initiatives and suggest ways to modify and adjust reforms. Participating in the evaluation process raises educators' awareness of the context in which they work, promotes the examination of beliefs and assumptions, and encourages collaboration and the sharing of new ideas. For all the good that can result from evaluating educational change, the process also is capable of causing harm. Evaluation can disrupt the educational process and threaten promising reforms through premature conclusions and the misuse of findings.

REFERENCES

Bickman, Leonard. "The Functions of Program Theory." In Leonard Bickman (ed.), *Using Program Theory in Evaluation. New Directions for Program Evaluation,* no. 33 (Spring 1987). San Francisco: Jossey-Bass, pp. 5–18.

Cohen, David K. and Hill, Heather C. *Learning Policy.* New Haven: Yale, 2001.

Duke, Daniel L. and Tucker, Pamela. "Initial Responses of Virginia High Schools to the Accountability Plan." In Daniel L. Duke,

Margaret Grogan, Pamela Tucker, and Walter Heinecke (eds.), *Educational Leadership in an Age of Accountability*. Albany: State University of New York Press, 2003.

Eisner, Elliot W. *The Educational Imagination,* 3rd edition. Upper Saddle River, NJ: Merrill Prentice Hall, 2002.

General Accounting Office. *Education Reform: Initial Effects in Four School Districts*. Washington, DC: author, 1989.

Gottfredson, Denise C. "An Evaluation of an Organization Development Approach to Reducing School Disorder," *Evaluation Review,* Vol. 11, no. 6 (December 1987), pp. 739–763.

Herman, Joan L.; Morris, Lynn Lyons; and Fitz-Gibbon, Carol Taylor. *Evaluator's Handbook*. Newbury Park, CA: Sage, 1987.

Kahne, Joseph; O'Brien, James; Brown, Andrea; and Quinn, Therese. "Leveraging Social Capital and School Improvement: The Case of a School Network and a Comprehensive Community Initiative in Chicago," *Educational Administration Quarterly,* Vol. 37, no. 4 (October 2001), pp. 429–461.

King, Jean A.; Morris, Lynn Lyons; and Fitz-Gibbon, Carol Taylor. *How to Assess Program Implementation*. Newbury Park, CA: Sage, 1987.

Lewy, Arieh. "The Nature of Curriculum Evaluation." In Arieh Lewy (ed.), *Handbook of Curriculum Evaluation*. New York: UNESCO, 1977, pp. 3–33.

Linn, Robert L. and Haug, Carolyn. "Stability of School-building Accountability Scores and Gains," *Educational Evaluation and Policy Analysis,* Vol. 24, no. 1 (Spring 2002), pp. 29–36.

Neale, Daniel C.; Bailey, William J.; and Ross, Billy E. *Strategies for School Improvement*. Boston: Allyn and Bacon, 1981.

Patton, Michael Quinn. *How to Use Qualitative Methods in Evaluation*. Newbury Park, CA: Sage, 1987.

Preskill, Hallie and Torres, Rosalie T. "The Learning Dimension of Evaluation Use." In Valerie J. Caracelli and Hallie Preskill (eds.), *The Expanding Scope of Evaluation Use. New Directions for Program Evaluation,* no. 88

(Winter 2000). San Francisco: Jossey-Bass, pp. 25–37.

Prestine, Nona A. and Bowen, Chuck. "Benchmarks of Change: Assessing Essential School Restructuring Efforts," *Educational Evaluation and Policy Analysis,* Vol. 15, no. 3 (Fall 1993), pp. 298–319.

Sarason, Seymour B. *The Culture of the School and the Problem of Change*. Boston: Allyn and Bacon, 1971.

Scriven, Michael. *Hard-won Lessons in Program Evaluation. New Directions for Program Evaluation,* no. 58 (Summer 1993). San Francisco: Jossey-Bass.

Scriven, Michael. *The Logic of Evaluation*. Inverness, CA: Edgepress, 1980.

Scriven, Michael. "The Methodology of Evaluation." In Ralph W. Tyler, Robert M. Gagne, and Michael Scriven (eds.), *Perspectives of Curriculum Evaluation,* AERA Monograph Series on Curriculum Evaluation, Number 1. Chicago: Rand McNally, 1967, pp. 39–83.

Sellers, Christine S.; Taylor, Terrence J.; and Esbensen, Finn-Aage. "Reality Check: Evaluating a School-based Gang Prevention Model," *Evaluation Review,* Vol. 22, no. 5 (October 1998), pp. 590–608.

Shadish, William R.; Newman, Dianna L.; Scheirer, Mary Ann; and Wye, Christopher (eds.). *Guiding Principles for Evaluators*. San Francisco: Jossey-Bass, 1995.

Solomon, Pearl Gold. *No Small Feat!* Thousand Oaks, CA: Corwin Press, 1995.

Stevens, Carla J. and Dial, Micah. "What Constitutes Misuse?" In Carla J. Stevens and Micah Dial (eds.), *Preventing the Misuse of Evaluation, New Directions for Program Evaluation,* no. 64 (Winter 1994). San Francisco: Jossey-Bass, pp. 3–13.

Stiggins, Richard J. "Assessment Crisis: The Absence of Assessment for Learning," *Phi Delta Kappan,* Vol. 83, no. 10 (June 2002), pp. 758–765.

Viadero, Debra. "Study Shows Test Gains in 'Accelerated Schools'," *Education Week* (January 9, 2002), p. 6.

Weiss, Carol H. *Evaluation Research*. Englewood Cliffs, NJ: Prentice-Hall, 1972.

CHAPTER 9

EXPLAINING
EDUCATIONAL CHANGE

MAJOR IDEAS

■ Explaining educational change involves a variety of options, including different levels and forms of explanation and different perspectives on explanation.

■ Understanding educational change involves explaining the origins and causes of change, how the change process takes place, and why the change process is or is not successful.

■ Within each phase of educational change are keys to successful reform.

■ A comprehensive theory of educational change currently does not exist, but it is possible to make generalizations about educational change that ultimately could lead to such a theory.

The quest to explain change has occupied legions of historians, philosophers, and social scientists for hundreds of years. Plato associated scientific knowledge with the search for explanations (Barnes, 2000, p. 37). When it comes to explaining educational change, the focus of inquiry can vary. Some seek to account for the origins or causes of educational change. Others are concerned primarily with explaining *how* educational change occurs. Still others want to offer reasons why educational change succeeds or fails.

The relationship between achieving and explaining educational change is best regarded as reciprocal. It is questionable, for example, whether change can be explained if it never has been achieved. Attempts to account for change in the abstract typically miss the mark. At the same time, it can be argued that the likelihood of achieving change is greatly enhanced by knowledge of why and how change happens.

Chapter 9 opens with an overview of efforts to explain change in general. Variety characterizes these efforts, just as it did for the evaluation of change. Students of change may choose from different levels and forms of explanation and different perspectives on explanation. The discussion of optional approaches to explaining change is followed by an analysis of one aspect of educational change for which practitioners are especially desirous of explanations. *What factors account for successful educational change?* Answering this important question requires revisiting each of the phases of educational change—discovery, design, development, and implementation. The outcome of educational change depends, to a great extent, on how each of these phases is undertaken. The chapter concludes with some thoughts about the development of a comprehensive theory of educational change.

VARIETIES OF EXPLANATION

Seeking explanations may be a primary pursuit of researchers, but it is also a daily activity for most human beings. It is difficult to imagine a person who makes no effort to explain such practical concerns as why he has trouble losing weight or why she cannot seem to meet the right companion. Every day we speculate about why certain things happen to us. The dictionary states that explanation is "a statement made to clarify something and make it understandable" (*The Random House College Dictionary,* p. 466). Clarification often involves determining the connections and relationships between what we do and feel, on the one hand, and the world in which we live, on the other.

Explaining change may seem to be a fairly straightforward endeavor, but it can involve a complex array of approaches and methods. In this part of the chapter, we investigate some of the considerations involved in trying to explain change in general and educational change in particular.

Levels of Explanation

The "something" in the preceding definition that we seek to clarify and make understandable may vary greatly, from why my nephew failed his algebra test despite tutoring to why world peace is so elusive. In our efforts to explain change, it is therefore important to be clear about the level of explanation that we wish to undertake.

Babbie (2001, pp. 33–34) identifies two basic levels of explanation—*idiographic* and *nomothetic*. Idiographic explanation is a type of causal reasoning in which individuals try to account for things that are "unique, separate, peculiar, or distinct." Explaining the success of a new reading initiative in one inner-city elementary school is an example of idiographic explanation. Nomothetic explanation, on the other hand, involves explaining "a class of situations or events rather than a single one." Accounting for the outcomes of the same reading initiative in 100 inner-city elementary schools exemplifies nomothetic explanation.

Levels of explanation can be differentiated in another way. Individuals may focus on explaining *attempted* change, *achieved* change, or *successful* change. Explaining attempted change involves addressing the following question: *What factors contribute to or account for attempted change?* Attempted change represents any intentional effort to effect change.

Obviously not all intentional efforts to effect change result in the achievement of change. A principal can try to change the way teachers assess student performance, but ultimately fail to alter assessment practice. In other words, achieving the changes that are intended cannot be assumed. Some would argue, in fact, that achieving meaningful change is a relatively rare occurrence. When intended change is achieved, it is worthy of explanation. Explaining achieved change involves addressing the following question: *What factors contribute to or account for achieved change?*

Achieved change does not necessarily mean successful change, however. A school may implement a new schedule as intended, only to discover that it does not have the desired effect on teaching practice and student achievement. Successful change is change that accomplishes its stated purposes, or at least produces desirable outcomes. Because successful change is not automatic, it, too, is worthy of explanation. Explaining successful change involves addressing the following question: *What factors contribute to or account for successful change?*

Forms of Explanation

Explanations of change can take a variety of forms, ranging from the very formal and systematic to the very informal and anecdotal. Among the most frequently encountered forms of explanation are theories, models, and narratives.

Theories.   Babbie (2001, p. 51) describes theories as "systematic sets of interrelated statements intended to explain some aspect of social life." He goes on to contrast theories and paradigms: "Whereas a paradigm offers a way of looking, a theory aims at explaining what we see" (p. 51). According to Babbie, theories can be of two kinds—inductive and deductive (pp. 34–36). Inductive theories move from the particular to the general, while deductive theories reverse the order, going from the general to the particular. An inductive theory of change begins with observations of individual cases of change and uses these cases to identify patterns and generalizations. A deductive theory starts out with a general explanation of change and tests the explanation against specific examples.

Strauss and Corbin stress that a theory is more than a set of findings. Above all else, a theory is concerned with relationships. Their definition of theory goes as follows:

> . . . theory denotes a set of well-developed categories (e.g., themes, concepts) that are systematically interrelated through statements of relationship to form a theoretical framework that explains some relevant social, psychological, educational, nursing, or other phenomenon. The statements of relationship explain who, what, when, where, why, how, and with what consequences an event occurs. (1998, p. 22)

Strauss and Corbin (p. 23) distinguish between more and less formal theories. A theory of educational change, in their view, would be less formal than a theory of change because it would be limited to a specific area—education. More formal theories would have to apply to change in various areas of endeavor. It is not uncommon for a theory of change that is developed to explain change in one area eventually to be adapted to explaining change in another area. The following case study provides an example of such an adaptation.

■ ■ ■ ■ ■

CASE STUDY

ADAPTING A THEORY OF ADAPTATION

Darwin's theory of evolution is one of the most well known as well as one of the most controversial theories of change. His theory characterized biological change as a slow, incremental process. In recent years, however, researchers such as Stephen Jay Gould have challenged this view, contending that changes occur in sudden spurts or leaps following prolonged periods of stability (Burke, 2002, p. 64). The name given to this revision of evolution theory is *punctuated-equilibrium* theory.

In an effort to account for dramatic shifts in the area of politics and policy, some social scientists have been drawn to punctuated-equilibrium theory. True, Jones, and Baumgartner (1999, p. 97) contend that this theory was needed to account for the fact that incrementalism did not explain large-scale departures from past policy and practice. Many theories of politics and policy-making focus on explaining *either* stability or change. Punctuated-equilibrium theory does both.

Punctuated-equilibrium theory zeroes in on two elements of the policy process: issue definition and agenda setting. True, Jones, and Baumgartner (1999, pp. 97–98) provide a brief overview of how the theory works:

> As issues are defined in public discourse in different ways, and as issues rise and fall in the public agenda, existing policies can be either reinforced or questioned. Reinforcement creates great obstacles to anything but modest change, but the questioning of policies at the most fundamental levels creates opportunities for dramatic reversals in policy outcomes.

It is easy to see that, once a theory like punctuated-equilibrium theory has been applied to the general area of policy making, it can be tested as an explanation for education policy in particular. It should be noted, though, that punctuated-equilibrium theory is suited primarily to explaining how change occurs, not why change occurs or why particular changes succeed or fail. The factors that account for these phenomena must be sought from other theories.

Relatively few efforts have been made to develop original theories of educational change, and no comprehensive theory of educational change has won the widespread approval of both educators and educational researchers. The theories used to explain educational change frequently are borrowed and adapted from other fields. In other cases, Fullan argues (1999, p. 20), theories of educational change are implicit in the actions taken by educators to effect change. Fullan urges educators engaged in the change process to work at making explicit the theories of change that guide their efforts.

Models.   The distinction between models and theories is not always easy to discern. Although both offer explanations, theories are more likely to explain causes, while models tend to focus on processes. Models typically begin with descriptions of processes leading to various types of outcomes, including outcomes derived from the change process. Diagrams often are used to portray the components of these processes, with vectors indicating the relationship between and among components.

Chapter 1 presented a number of models of the change process. Rogers' model of the innovation-development process (see Figure 1.1), for example, began with a need or problem and proceeded through research, development, commercialization, diffusion, and adoption until consequences were realized. Other models included Havelock's linkage model, Kanter's innovation model, and Chambers' model of large-scale innovation. Many models of change processes are prescriptive rather than descriptive. In other words, they represent how change *should* take place rather than how change *does* take place.

Descriptive models of the change process often follow a common pattern—inputs, throughputs, and outputs. These so-called *systems* models are particularly popular in political science and policy analysis (Birkland, 2001, p. 194–229). Systems models try to explain how particular inputs are converted into particular outputs. The conversion process, referred to as throughputs, replaces what has been labeled "the black box." This term captures the vagueness of previous generations of social scientists when it came to explaining what happened between inputs and outputs. Recent years, however, have found growing interest on the part of researchers and practitioners in what goes on during the throughput phase. An example of a recent model appears in the following case study.

■ ■ ■ ■ ■ ▬▬▬▬▬▬▬

CASE STUDY

THE BURKE-LITWIN MODEL OF ORGANIZATIONAL PERFORMANCE AND CHANGE

Developed by two individuals with experience consulting on organizational change in private corporations, the Burke-Litwin model emerged inductively from field work with Citibank and British Airways (Burke, 2002, pp. 198–216). The model is an elaboration of the basic inputs–throughputs–outputs model. It is based on assumptions of the open systems perspective on organizations and organizational change.

The open systems perspective recognizes the continuous interaction between organizations and their external environments. The environment in the Burke-Litwin model is the source of all inputs. These inputs, such as resources, labor, raw materials, and demands for goods and services, are converted into outputs in the form of individual and organizational performance. This performance presumably leads to the production of goods and services that can be sold to consumers.

The Burke-Litwin model explains the conversion of inputs to outputs by identifying ten organizational components that affect the production process. These components include the following:

- Leadership
- Mission and strategy
- Organization culture
- Management practices
- Structure
- Systems (policies and procedures)

(continued)

CONTINUED

- Work unit climate
- Motivation
- Task requirements and individual skills and abilities
- Individual needs and values

The Burke-Litwin model (Burke, 2002, p. 199) proposes that these components are all interrelated, creating a complex system where changes in one component eventually affect the other components. A feedback loop in the model connects inputs (environment) and outputs (individual and organizational performance), suggesting that a reciprocal relationship exists between the two. Not only does the environment influence what is produced, but what is produced affects the environment.

The Burke-Litwin model further indicates that changes in certain components, such as leadership and organization culture, are more likely to produce particular kinds of change—episodic and revolutionary change. Changes in other components, such as structure and climate, are more likely to produce incremental and evolutionary change (Burke, 2002, p. 215).

Narratives.   Less formal than theories and models, change *narratives* are stories of a kind. Narratives can derive from experience, reflection, observations, professional judgment, and research. Change narratives constitute another way of explaining change. Although theories of change often focus on what causes change and models of change account for the processes of change, change narratives frequently provide reasons why change succeeds or fails. The appeal and power of change narratives relate, in part, to their relatively straightforward and accessible nature. Often relying on pithy characterizations and everyday language, change narratives present easy-to-understand explanations that stand in marked contrast to highly technical theories and models of change. The latter often sacrifice simplicity in order to capture complexity.

Change narratives frequently can be found on the editorial page of newspapers. When corporate scandals regarding questionable accounting practices rocked the U.S. economy in 2001–2002 and resulted in a concerted effort by Congress to rein in rogue CEOs and their minions, Robert J. Samuelson (2002) produced a change narrative in his editorial to account for moves he characterized as "reform hysteria." The economist–columnist asked the following question to launch his narrative:

> Why be surprised? We live in an era of moral exhibitionism. Every reform moment is an opportunity for public figures—politicians, TV commentators, columnists—to strut their self-righteousness. Their crusades become orgies of rhetorical self-promotion. This is why the present campaign to restore confidence in the stock market is, almost certainly, backfiring.

Unlike many theories and models, most change narratives are never held under the microscope long enough to be tested systematically. Nonetheless, they can be highly persuasive. Sarason (1971), for example, appropriated the axiom—the more things change, the more they remain the same—and crafted it into a compelling narrative to explain the persistence of certain educational practices. Many educators, educational researchers, and reformers have taken his words to heart. The essence of Sarason's narrative is that educational reforms rarely challenge behavioral and programmatic "regularities." Who would think of proposing that schools stay open on Sunday? Or that teachers refrain from asking questions? Or that the curriculum need not include physical education? By leaving such regularities untouched, advocates of change, according to Sarason, ensure that the essential features of schooling survive the merry-go-round of change initiatives to which many schools are subjected.

Cohen (1988) has added to the narrative that explains why the more things change in education, the more they remain the same. He contends that change was not much of an issue in American education until John Dewey held out the prospect of a type of schooling vastly different from that which prevailed across the United States. Prior to Dewey, the primary change in education was expansion of school systems to accommodate larger numbers of young people. When schools failed to adopt Dewey's progressive ideas regarding curriculum, instruction, and school organization, reasons were needed to account for the lack of substantive change.

Four primary narratives, according to Cohen (1988, pp. 32–39), have been advanced to explain why Dewey's ideas failed to take root. The first narrative maintains that schools were so decentralized that teachers were able to function with relative autonomy. If they so desired (which apparently they did), they could choose not to follow the advice of education leaders to adopt new ideas and methods. Another narrative holds that the conditions of teachers' work were antagonistic to change. So tightly scheduled and busy were most teachers that they had precious little time to devote to improvements in practice. A third narrative contends that reforms based on Dewey's ideas were flawed in important ways. They failed, for example, to include adequate resources and personnel to support meaningful change. Lack of sufficient incentives for educators to change is the heart of the fourth narrative. Public schools, so the argument goes, do not need to adopt new ideas in order to attract students. They are assured of getting students and, hence, funds, regardless of their policies, programs, and practices.

It is interesting to revisit Cohen's quartet of explanations in light of recent events. With the advent of greater school choice, state-monitored accountability programs, and more funding for educational change, some of his narratives no longer may be defensible. Change narratives, like virtually everything else we have discussed, are themselves subject to change.

Perspectives on Explaining Change

Theories, models, and change narratives can be organized into categories based on the *perspective* they represent. Perspectives frequently reflect the assumptions and concerns of academic disciplines. Historians, psychologists, social psychologists, sociologists, and other scholars have sought and continue to seek to unlock the secrets of change. Among their primary interests are *causation* and *variation*. They want to understand what causes change, a quest that also necessitates accounting for stability (lack of change). They also desire to know why variations exist in the causes, processes, and consequences of change.

Scholars representing different perspectives may share a similar interest in change, but they frequently deviate when it comes to their particular focus or unit of analysis, the assumptions that guide their inquiry, their methods for collecting and interpreting data, and the concepts they use to account for their findings. It may be helpful to examine some examples of how educational change has been addressed by representatives of different perspectives.

Historical Perspectives.   Historians of education are intrigued by a variety of questions related to change. Do schools create or reflect social change? What were the origins of the forms of schooling that are so familiar to us—the way schools are organized and divided into age groups, the way classrooms are arranged and managed, the subjects studied in school? Why have so many aspects of our schools persisted for so long, despite periodic efforts to introduce change? Why are Americans so critical of their public schools, yet so reluctant to allow them to change?

Historians always consider their subject in context. Context encompasses location, culture, and temporality. To understand educational change, or the lack of it, therefore requires knowing what is going on outside of school as well as inside. In fact, if historians err, it tends to be on the side of external influences. They sometimes fail to appreciate the efforts of educators within schools to achieve change.

Katz (1975) adopted a historical perspective in order to explain why public schools in the United States came to be organized along bureaucratic lines. He noted that at least three options besides bureaucracy were available to reformers in the Boston school system between 1850 and 1884. The organizational options included paternalistic voluntarism, democratic localism, and corporate voluntarism. The victory of the bureaucratic option, according to Katz, was a reflection of (1) the need for an organizational model capable of handling the increasingly complex delivery of instruction and (2) the popularity of bureaucracy among civic leaders involved in organizing other municipal services. Katz cautioned, however, that the bureaucratization of Boston public schools did not occur overnight. The process was "piecemeal," or what some would call *incremental change* (Katz, 1975, p. 66).

When Katz shifted his attention to the *consequences* of school bureaucratization, he noted, with more than a hint of irony, that what the bureaucratic model was most successful at doing was resisting change (p. 57). That American schools in the 1970s, when Katz was writing, were essentially the same as schools a century earlier was attributed, in large measure, to their bureaucratic organization. Katz went on to point out that school bureaucratization was not particularly successful when it came to alleviating the social distress that public schools had been created to contain (p. 152).

Several decades after the publication of Katz's study, Tyack and Cuban (1995) revisited the issue of continuity in American public schools. Characterizing persistent features of schools as *the grammar of schooling,* the two educational historians accounted for these phenomena in terms of timing and the efforts of influential groups. "Reforms that enter on the ground floor of major institutional changes," they concluded, "have a good chance of becoming part of the standard institutional template"

(p. 86). Features of schooling, such as the graded school and the Carnegie unit, also persist because they are supported by powerful and prestigious groups.

Accounting for the origins of persistent aspects of public schools is one challenge; explaining why they endure is quite another. Tyack and Cuban, like Katz, credit the bureaucratization of schools for much of the grammar of schooling:

> Once established, the grammar of schooling persisted in part because it enabled teachers to discharge their duties in a predictable fashion and to cope with the everyday tasks that school boards, principals, and parents expected them to perform: controlling student behavior, instructing heterogeneous pupils, and sorting people for future roles in school and later life. Habitual institutional patterns can be labor-saving devices, ways to organize complex duties. Teachers and students socialized to such routines often find it difficult to adapt to different structures and rules. (1995, p. 86)

Psychological Perspectives.   If the historian's vantage point on change is a wide-angle lens, the psychologist's is a zoom lens. The former focuses on explaining broad social trends and major events, while the latter zeroes in on the behavior and beliefs of individuals. Interestingly, at the end of the above account of persistence in public education, Tyack and Cuban recognize the role of individual teachers and students in keeping change at bay. People are, for the most part, creatures of routine. Routines are a source of security and predictability. Once established, routines become addictive. That the professional routines of teachers can become impediments to educational change was acknowledged in Chapter 5's discussion of individuals' readiness for change.

Psychological perspectives on change are associated with concepts such as development, learning, motivation, readiness, efficacy, and expertise. These concepts are used to explain as well as describe how people experience change. People are regarded as more than mere pawns of social forces and institutions. They are capable, to use Mary Catherine Bateson's terminology, of *composing* their lives. They are endowed with abilities, understandings, sensitivities, memories, aspirations, and beliefs, all of which can play a role in determining how individuals respond to change.

Consider the concept of *expertise*. It is hard to imagine effective educational change without expertise. Until recently, however, relatively little was known about the nature of expertise and how it was acquired (Berliner, 1994). People frequently equated experience with expertise. As researchers began to probe the topic, they discovered that experience often was necessary, but insufficient alone to produce expertise. Expertise was found to develop in stages, each stage being distinguished by certain characteristics. According to one review of research, experts are characterized by superior memory, the ability to perceive large meaningful patterns, strong self-monitoring skills, and the capacity to spend large amounts of time analyzing problems (Tennant and Pogson, 1995, pp. 55–57). Of experts, Berliner (1994, p. 166) has written:

> If the novice is deliberate, the advanced beginner insightful, the competent performer rational, and the proficient performer intuitive, we might categorize the expert as often being arational. Experts have both an intuitive grasp of the situation and seem to sense in nonanalytic and nondeliberative ways the appropriate response to be made. They show

fluid performance, as we all do when we no longer have to choose our words when speaking or think about where to place our feet when walking.

Expertise can be a valuable asset during the change process, but it can also be an impediment. Not only do experts often find it difficult to pass on their knowledge, they may not be anxious to participate in the change process. After all, if they are experts, by definition they are high achievers at what they are doing. The motivation to move in a new direction understandably may be lacking.

One concept often leads to another when employing psychological perspectives on change. In an effort to explain why some educators achieve a high level of instructional expertise and others do not, researchers may consider such matters as motivation, personality, and self-efficacy. Variation in expertise may be a function, in other words, of desire, disposition, and belief. Consider self-efficacy, for example. According to Bandura (1989), self-efficacy is a belief regarding one's ability to achieve a desirable outcome. Trying to improve the teaching skills of teachers who do not believe they are capable of instructing struggling students can be frustrating for staff developers. If they understand self-efficacy theory, however, they realize that a prerequisite for instructional improvement may involve developing teachers' confidence that they can succeed with these students. Modeling has been found to be one effective mechanism for cultivating self-efficacy (Allen, 2000, pp. 303–305).

Group Dynamics Perspectives.   Individuals, for the most part, do not exist alone. They are members of various formal and informal groups—families, peer groups, departments, teams, and the like. A school actually is a collection of various groups, ranging from teaching teams and academic departments to social circles and ad hoc groups that rally around a particular issue. Those who adopt a group dynamics, or social psychological, perspective recognize that the behavior and beliefs of individuals are subject to the influence of groups. Whether people change or resist change, therefore, becomes a function of the groups in which they participate or with which they identify.

Cartwright (1951, p. 387) maintained that groups figure into the process of change in at least three different ways. The group can serve as the medium of change, the target of change, and the agent of change. Studies of educational change frequently trace unsuccessful reform to resistance by the faculty or some subset of the faculty. It is difficult to imagine an educational change that would not be subject to mediation by teachers.

Coburn (2001) conducted a study of a new reading initiative in a California elementary school that illustrated the influence of teacher groups on school change. Relying on institutional and sense-making theory, the researcher assumed that the "nature and structure of formal networks and informal alliances among teachers play a powerful role in shaping the sense-making process and ultimately the kind of sense that is made" (pp. 145–146). For a year, Coburn followed teachers as they engaged in efforts to improve reading instruction. Her analysis involved comparing the content and nature of teachers' conversations with observations of actual teaching practice.

Teachers at the elementary school tended to identify with colleagues who taught at the same grade level. These were the individuals most likely to meet and plan together when it came to responding to pressure for improvement in the reading program. The particular design for change at the school called for the development of standards and grade-level indicators for reading and the assessment of student progress toward meeting the reading standards. Coburn discovered that different grade-level groups of teachers interpreted their charge and how to respond to it in different ways. Rather than the design for reading improvement shaping teachers, teachers shaped the design. The researcher drew the following conclusion:

> What sense teachers ultimately made—the way in which they constructed understanding, made decisions to select some approaches and not others, and worked out technical and practical details necessary to enact the interpretation—was deeply shaped by whom teachers were working with and the conditions for conversation.

Adopting a group dynamics perspective in order to explain educational change requires identifying the formal and informal groups in which participants in the change process are involved. Investigators then must determine each group's position on proposed change. If a group is characterized by a strong position for or against change, it will be reflected in its norms governing participation in the change process. Group members who disregard these norms are likely to face sanctions and possible ostracism.

Like Coburn, Wideen (1994) conducted research that recognized the value of a group dynamics perspective. His study of school improvement efforts in an elementary school in British Columbia compelled him to acknowledge that the school was not always the most appropriate unit of analysis, at least when educational change was concerned. In recognizing the value of investigating the role of teacher groups in mediating reform, he also offered a reason why many researchers shy away from a focus on groups:

> Based on the experience of this case study, groups within the school appear to be a more appropriate unit upon which to focus. But, because of its unpredictability and unmanageability by outsiders, this approach has less appeal to researchers and policymakers than it does to those in schools. Group formation cannot be predicted in advance, nor can one always be assured that groups take on changes to their practice that meet the approval of outsiders.

Organizational Perspectives. Group dynamics perspectives assume that the behavior and beliefs of individuals are influenced by the groups in which they are involved. Organizational perspectives recognize the influence of organizational structure and culture on individuals and groups. Because of this concern, those adopting organizational perspectives take an interest when organizations such as schools and school systems attempt to change their structures and cultures. Like groups, organizations can be both targets of change and agents of change.

The structure of an organization has been characterized as "the relatively stable relationships among the positions, groups of positions (units), and work processes that make up the organization" (Shafritz and Ott, 2001, p. 197). In the discussion of historical perspectives, reference was made to Katz's work on the bureaucratization of

U.S. public schools. He argued that the development of this organizational structure helped explain the subsequent resistance of schools to substantive change.

Although many would accept Katz's conclusions, others might challenge them for being too highly generalized. It is not unusual for historians to lose resolution by opening the aperture wide enough to take in multiple settings and broad sweeps of time. Those who adopt organizational perspectives probably would urge Katz to recognize variations between and among schools. Although public schools are, indeed, bureaucratically organized, they vary in terms of their specific structural arrangements and responsiveness to reform. When historians paint all schools with the same broad brushstrokes, they gloss over details that often reveal important differences.

Students of organizations long have noted that all bureaucratic organizations do not function the same. Burns and Stalker (1961), for example, found that some companies were more innovative than others. These so-called *organic* systems were more likely than their *mechanistic* counterparts to deemphasize the hierarchical set of relationships around which work was organized and place greater importance on individual expertise and lateral connections among employees.

In a recent essay, Hanson (2001) has proposed that some educational organizations are smarter than others when it comes to solving problems and introducing change initiatives. Such variation illustrates the fact that educational organizations are capable of change and improvement. Hanson challenges conventional institutional theory that focuses primarily on the forces that constrain schools and prevent them from changing. He notes that schools and school systems frequently change in response to environmental shifts, regression, and shocks. That some respond more effectively than others can be traced, according to Hanson, to variations in organizational memory and information processing:

> Why would one school have a better memory than another? Returning to the chess analogy, if the player has recorded the strategies of few past matches, or gets them mixed up, or forgets the key strategic moves, his or her historic memory will provide little guidance. The same is true for the educational organization if records are not carefully kept and catalogued, if teachers and/or administrators with insightful experiences are routinely transferred, or if the value of consulting the historic memory is discounted.

Variations in how educational organizations deal with change have been linked to organizational culture as well as structure. Bolman and Deal (1997, p. 217) define organizational culture as "the interwoven pattern of beliefs, values, practices, and artifacts that define for members who they are and how they are to do things." The cultures of some schools and school systems encourage experimentation and the search for better ways to teach and learn. In other schools and school systems, however, continuity is preferred to change and those with new ideas are subject to criticism and isolation. Although organizational structure doubtless influences organizational culture, the relationship is likely to be reciprocal. Cultural factors, for example, may determine whether people take particular elements of organizational structure seriously.

Concluding Comments on Perspectives.   The four perspectives presented in this segment of the chapter represent only a sample of the possibilities. Educational change also can be explained using the concepts and methods of the anthropologist, the political scientist, the economist, and the philosopher. Each perspective promises to contribute insight and understanding to the investigation of the causes and consequences of change.

Two comments must be made in conclusion. First, each perspective encompasses a variety of interpretations of educational change. It would be a mistake to think that all historians rely on the same concepts, employ the same analytical tools, or arrive at the same explanations. Second, the conclusions regarding educational change that are drawn by representatives of different perspectives are not necessarily incompatible. The role of culture in accounting for change, for example, is acknowledged by those operating from various vantage points, including historical, organizational, and anthropological perspectives.

ACCOUNTING FOR SUCCESSFUL
EDUCATIONAL CHANGE

Educators may express interest in the root causes of educational change and the various ways in which the change process unfolds, but the topic for which they are likely to be most desirous of explanation is the consequences of educational change. Educators look to researchers to explain why some educational changes succeed while others fail. *Are there certain factors which consistently are associated with successful educational change?*

In order to address this question, it is helpful to refer back to the phases of the change process. A relationship exists between successful educational change and the actions taken by educators during each phase of the change process. Educators therefore are cautioned against assuming that the key to effective educational change resides in the successful execution of a particular phase. A wonderful design can fail because of a poor implementation plan. A well-thought-out implementation plan cannot save a design for which there is no compelling need. As a way of reviewing the keys to successful educational change, we shall revisit the four primary phases of the educational change process.

The Discovery Phase

First steps are always crucial. The first steps toward educational change typically involve discovering a need for change. This phase of the change process provides ample opportunity for mistakes to be made. Educators, for example, may overlook an important need, identify a need that threatens certain stakeholders, or fail to articulate a convincing rationale for change. Some mistakes during the Discovery Phase are sufficiently serious that the change process is brought to a grinding halt before it gains momentum. The impact of other mistakes may not be felt until educators are well down the road to reform.

Educational changes derive from various kinds of need. Some needs pertain to problems with the goals of education, including unclear goals, overly ambitious goals, incompatible goals, and outdated goals. Other needs relate to inadequate student achievement and ineffective professional practice. Needs are not always embedded in the current situation. In certain cases, a need for change may be based on anticipated developments, such as a projected increase in the number of non-English-speaking students or an expected rise in the demand for graduates with advanced technological skills.

The actions of educators during the Discovery Phase are most likely to contribute to successful educational change when they meet three requirements.

First, the need for educational change should be based on a thorough and careful examination of the current situation, emerging trends, and anticipated developments. Such an examination depends on systematic recordkeeping regarding student achievement, the effectiveness of existing programs, consumer satisfaction, and the performance of graduates in college and the workplace. Schools and school systems that do not have good information management systems have trouble accessing the data needed to determine whether change is called for. Hanson (2001, p. 659) observes that smart organizations evaluate new policies and programs and systematically store the findings so they will be available for analysis and planning.

Second, the need for educational change should be perceived as genuine and compelling by a large proportion of stakeholders. Meeting this requirement can present a challenge. At any given time, some individuals and groups are likely to be benefiting from the status quo. They are apt, therefore, to find change threatening. If improving achievement for at-risk students, for example, calls for reducing class size in basic courses and increasing the teacher–student ratio in advanced classes, parents of students enrolled in advanced classes are unlikely to welcome the move.

Whether stakeholders find the need for change compelling will depend, to a great extent, on the justification that educators offer. A convincing and credible justification requires honesty and a willingness to share all the data involved in identifying the need for change. When educators are afraid to reveal certain information because it may reflect negatively on their past efforts, they risk losing credibility in the eyes of those who are expected to support educational change.

Educational Change Benefits From—

- A thorough and careful examination of the current situation as well as emerging trends and developments
- A need for change that is perceived as genuine and compelling by a large proportion of stakeholders

---

The Design Phase

Determining how best to address a genuine and compelling need for educational change presents additional challenges. The likelihood of choosing a good design is increased when educators undertake a thorough and thoughtful design process. This means that time should be devoted to identifying and interrogating "sacred" assumptions about learning, teaching, and schooling. Failure to confront fundamental beliefs can result in designs that represent more of the same, not authentic reform. Good design also depends on exploring and assessing a wide range of design options. Devotion to a particular design and hasty selection of the first attractive design that is encountered are reasons why some design processes ultimately fall short of the mark. The third key to a productive Design Phase is systemic thinking. When educators think systemically, they recognize the interrelationships between and among particular design elements. They also are alert to the possible impact of a new design on existing features and functions of schools.

Good designs for educational change tend to share certain common characteristics. They address legitimate educational needs, not purely political purposes or the desires of leaders to further their chances for advancement. Good designs are supported by research and professional judgment and reflect a clear understanding of how people learn. The temptation to try anything when problems are truly daunting rarely results in meaningful educational change. No matter how bad the situation, it can always get worse when designs fail to draw on knowledge of good practice.

Since educational change does not take place in a vacuum, good designs take into account local conditions. Every setting is characterized by particular personnel, resources, policies, traditions, and beliefs. Disregarding these local characteristics risks undermining reform efforts. Educational change also can be subverted when designs threaten to affect some individuals adversely, despite the promise of improved conditions for others. Good designs do not provide help for some at the expense of educational opportunities for others. Good designs also recognize that educational resources are not abundant. Educational needs should be addressed as efficiently as possible without sacrificing effectiveness. Wasteful reforms not only tend to be short-lived, they cause policy makers and taxpayers to be skeptical about subsequent efforts to invest in improving schools.

The verdict is still out regarding the preferred magnitude of educational change. Although some experts advocate large-scale and comprehensive change, others make a brief for more modest and targeted reform. Examples of success and failure can be found for both options.

Educational Change Benefits From—

- A design process characterized by an examination of assumptions, consideration of various possibilities, and systemic thinking
- A design that addresses legitimate needs, reflects what is known about how people learn, and is consistent with research and professional judgment
- A design that takes into account local conditions
- A design that does not adversely affect any particular group of students in order to benefit other students
- A design that addresses needs efficiently without sacrificing effectiveness

The Development Phase

Once a need for change has been identified and a design selected to address the need, educators must decide how to implement the design. This process often entails the development of a formal implementation plan. The success of educational change can depend on the nature of the plan and the process by which it is developed.

A good implementation plan is based on a careful assessment of preparedness. This assessment, in turn, requires three separate but related analyses. First, the readiness of those who are expected to implement change must be determined. Readiness is a function of competence and commitment. Change can fail when only one of these is present. Second, the site of change—typically a school or school system—must have the capacity to support and sustain change. This capacity involves an organizational structure that facilitates change, an organizational culture that values change, and organizational resources sufficient to initiate and nurture change. The third element of preparedness concerns the willingness of the community to underwrite and embrace change. Indicators of community support include a clear understanding on the part of community members of the purpose and nature of proposed changes and a reasonably high level of community involvement in schools.

Plans for implementing change should take into account the results of these assessments of preparedness. The plan itself is a structured sequence of specific steps for achieving a design for change. A good implementation plan typically includes specific objectives, provisions for staff development, a timeline specifying when particular steps toward implementation should be completed, a list of necessary resources, and descriptions of the responsibilities of individuals involved in the implementation process. Additionally, the plan should provide for formative and summative evaluation and a means for keeping stakeholders informed of progress.

Educational Change Benefits From—

- An implementation plan based on a thorough assessment of individual readiness, organizational capacity, and community support
- An implementation plan that includes specific objectives, provisions for staff development, a timeline, a list of necessary resources, specific responsibilities for those expected to implement change, and provisions for formative and summative evaluation

---

The Implementation Phase

Implementation refers to the actual process of achieving intended change. This process can be characterized by accomplishment, disappointment, uncertainty, conflict, and surprise. Careful planning, although necessary, is insufficient alone to ensure successful educational change. Implementation can be adversely affected by problems inherited from prior phases of the change process as well as a host of new problems. The latter may include faculty divisiveness, overtaxed resources and personnel, and increased organizational complexity.

Research on successful educational change indicates that effective implementation often depends on continuing staff development. When the training necessary to support implementation stops at the onset of the Implementation Phase, staff members can find themselves inadequately equipped to initiate reforms. Implementation also benefits from a diverse pool of talent on staff and an organizational culture sufficiently collaborative to encourage people to use their talent in order to promote change. Flexibility is another key to implementation. Invariably circumstances shift between the identification of a need for change and the implementation of a design for change. Educators must be able to adapt themselves and their implementation plans to these changes. Ironically, successful change also requires a certain degree of organizational stability. When uncertainty prevails, resistance to change is frequently the reaction. People expect a measure of continuity in their lives. When they know that they can count on some aspects of their schools to remain unchanged, they are more likely to embrace specific reforms. The final ingredient of successful implementation is leadership. Leadership provides the direction and inspires the commitment necessary to cope with the challenges of change. Indications are that leadership is needed at all levels, not just at the top.

Successful implementation does not ensure that change will be sustained. Assuming that reforms are worth perpetuating, they will require the mobilization of broad-based support and secure funding. Leaders must maintain a focus on the realized as well as the potential benefits of change and make certain that a facilitative organization structure continues to be in place. This may involve incentives for those involved in reforms and a commitment to fill vacated positions with individuals willing to support reforms. Staff members must continue to monitor the progress of reforms on a regular basis so that problems can be addressed in a timely manner. In the final analysis, the fate of particular educational changes may depend on a little bit of luck, but luck has never complained about having hard work and intelligent planning for companions.

Educational Change Benefits From—

- Continuing staff development
- A diverse pool of talent
- An organizational culture that supports collaboration
- Flexibility and stability
- Capable leadership at all levels

TOWARD A COMPREHENSIVE THEORY OF EDUCATIONAL CHANGE

The social science literature is full of theories of change. Hatch (1997), for example, in her review of modern, symbolic, and postmodern perspectives on organization theory, identifies Lewin's theory of social change; Kanter, Stein, and Jick's "Big Three" theory of change; Hannan and Freeman's population ecology theory; and Greiner's organizational life cycle theory. In the field of political science, Kingdon (1995) spotlights Lindblom's theory of incrementalism and Baumgartner and Jones' adaptation of punctuated-equilibrium theory. These and other theories of change could be used, or have been used, to help explain educational change. Each, however, focuses on particular aspects of change. None could be regarded as truly comprehensive.

To be comprehensive, a theory of educational change should explain the causes of educational change, how educational change occurs under particular circumstances, and why specific educational change succeeds or fails. It also should account for variations in the process and outcomes of change within and across different sites. This is a tall order, and some experts are pessimistic regarding the prospects of ever developing a comprehensive theory of change. Fullan (1999, p. 21), for instance, is unequivocal when he states that "there never will be a definitive theory of change." He goes on to point out, "It is a theoretical and empirical impossibility to generate a theory that applies to all situations." Hatch (2002, p. 631) is more optimistic. He argues that we already have implicit theories of educational change embedded in most school improvement initiatives. These theories represent "the beliefs and assumptions about how innovation and improvement can take place" (p. 631). If a comprehensive theory of educational change is ever developed, it may derive, at least in part, from a compilation and analysis of these implicit theories of change.

One step toward a comprehensive theory involves creating a descriptive model of educational change. Based on the research covered in this book, five central elements of educational change have been identified. Educational change involves a need (or needs) for change, a process for determining how to address the need, a process for implementing change, a result of the implementation process, and consequences of this result. These basic elements of educational change are shown in Figure 9.1.

Educational change is triggered by a need (1), which may take the form of an unresolved problem (1.1), an unmet goal (1.2), or a newly identified possibility (1.3). A need, however, is not a change. Change refers to what must be done that is not currently being done, what must be undone, what must exist that does not currently exist or what must be eliminated, in order to address the need. Identifying what to change requires a process of some kind. In this book, the process of determining how to address an educational need (2) is represented by three phases—Discovery (2.1), Design (2.2), and Development (2.3). Once a change (or changes) has been identified, a second process—one for implementing the change (3)—is needed. This process culminates in a result (4) of some kind. The result may be the achievement of the intended

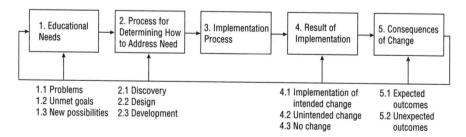

FIGURE 9.1 Model of Educational Change

change (4.1), unintended changes (4.2), or no change at all (4.3). Whatever the result, consequences (5) are likely to follow. The consequences of change may or may not reflect original expectations for improved performance (5.1; 5.2).

The systemic nature of educational change is captured in Figure 9.1's feedback loop linking the consequences of change (5) with the other elements of the model. In other words, the outcomes of the change process are likely to influence subsequent educational needs (1), the process for determining how to address these needs (2), the implementation process (3), the result of this process (4), and the consequences of this new round of change (5).

A model of educational change, such as that portrayed in Figure 9.1, identifies the elements and potential sources of variation that should be explained by a comprehensive theory of educational change. Such a theory will have to account for the origins of educational needs, the nature of the processes for determining how to address needs and implement changes, and the results and consequences of implementation. To assist in thinking about a comprehensive theory of educational change, several propositions have been extracted from discussions in preceding chapters.

> **PROPOSITION 1:**   Educational change tends to occur over time and involve predictable activities.

Experts prefer to think of change as a process rather than an event. In this book, the process of change has been characterized by four distinct phases in order to facilitate discussion and analysis. Although these phases may blur and overlap in reality, the change process typically entails a predictable set of activities, including the determination of a need for change, the selection of a change to address the need, and so on. The nature of these activities and the circumstances under which they are conducted can vary greatly within and across sites. Such variation probably helps to account for different outcomes of the change process. Accounting for variations in the change process and its consequences is a primary obligation of a comprehensive theory of educational change.

> **PROPOSITION 2:**   Opportunities to influence and shape educational change arise throughout the change process.

By recognizing that educational change occurs over time, we also raise the possibility that influence may be exerted at various points during the process of change. Efforts to influence change, for example, may take place relatively early in the process, when educators are determining whether or not a need for change exists. The possibility of influence does not end with implementation. Even after a reform is in place, attempts to modify it may still go on. Variations in the nature, results, and consequences of educational change can be explained, therefore, in terms of the kinds of influence being exerted and when in the change process they occur.

> **PROPOSITION 3:**   Efforts to influence educational change derive from internal and external sources.

The source of efforts to influence educational change also may help account for variations in the nature, results, and consequences of educational change. Two general sources of influence exist—those within schools and school systems (internal sources) and those outside of these entities (external sources). Internal sources include individual educators, groups of staff members, school and district leaders, and official bodies such as school boards. External sources include individuals and groups representing political parties, legislative bodies, government agencies, special interest groups, business interests, and philanthropic foundations.

PROPOSITION 4: At any given time, particular sources of influence are likely to play a greater role in the change process than other sources of influence.

Not all sources of influence carry the same weight. Certain individuals and groups enjoy greater influence at a given point in time than other individuals and groups. A particular principal, for instance, may have held unusual sway over a faculty, whereas her successor's influence is minimal. The influence of particular special interest groups ebbs and flows, depending on circumstances. Variations in the nature and outcomes of educational change may be traced to the particular individuals and groups that exercised influence at some point during the change process.

PROPOSITION 5: The influence of internal and external sources is mediated by economic, demographic, cultural, and organizational factors.

Influence over educational change is exerted by individuals and groups, but the nature of their influence and how they try to exert it are functions, to some extent, of the conditions in which they find themselves. These conditions involve available resources, present clientele, prevailing norms, and operative structures. How people behave and what they value are subject to the influence of economic conditions, the population to be served, local culture, and the kinds of organizations in which they participate. The mediating effects of these factors help to explain the nature and outcomes of educational change. Some of the specific variables associated with these mediating conditions include the time available to plan and implement change, the quantity and quality of staff development, and the processes by which formal decisions are made.

PROPOSITION 6: The results and consequences of particular educational changes help to determine the nature of subsequent educational changes.

In addition to the influence exercised by internal and external sources, educational change itself is a source of influence, albeit a derivative one. The results and consequences of a particular educational change help to determine whether identified needs are adequately addressed, thereby influencing the target for subsequent change initiatives. When a change results in a need being addressed effectively, time and resources can be liberated to address other needs. When educators succeed with one change, the likelihood of obtaining support for another reform may increase. Alternatively, a failed change often jeopardizes future efforts to implement change. In other words, the consequences of one change initiative are likely to exert an influence on subsequent change initiatives. It is this connection between past, present, and future change that leads many observers to think of educational change as a continuous process or system.

CLOSING THOUGHTS

We have traversed the territory of educational change and, in so doing, encountered a variety of obstacles. Most, it seems, are human-made. We have learned that men and women also are capable of avoiding or surmounting these obstacles. Is educational change today more challenging than it was in the past? Do today's educators confront more obstacles than did their predecessors?

There is no way to answer such an intriguing question definitively. Our society has been characterized by steadily rising expectations. What parents want less for their child than they had? A case can be made that rising expectations are directly related to pressure for change. As expectations climb, so, too, does the desire to alter the institutions, including schools, created to achieve these expectations. Consider the title of President George W. Bush's education bill—the No Child Left Behind Act. Could there be a clearer expression of our lofty education aims than "no child left behind"?

One reason educational change is so challenging is that it does not necessarily travel a path similar to individual change. Educational change, as represented by the No Child Left Behind Act, may charge ahead at warp speed, while individuals amble behind. As people grow older, their desire for change moderates and their skepticism regarding the possibilities of change grows. Reconciling our societal needs for substantial educational change to reduce disparities and expand opportunities with our individual desires for less change as we age may be the single greatest challenge of change.

Sometimes a metaphor can be helpful in capturing the essence of a phenomenon. When I think of educational change, I think of rainwater. In the proper amount, it is exceedingly beneficial. In fact, it is essential. Excessive amounts, however, can have devastating effects. Floods can carry away everything in their path.

The hope is that rainwater will fall to earth and be absorbed into the ground, giving life to plants and replenishing aquifers. When climatological conditions are not right, however, rainwater runs off or evaporates before it can be absorbed. Many educational changes likewise never reach the Implementation Phase where they can begin to do some good.

If rainwater does manage to be absorbed, it may travel to its destination by various routes. Depending on the geographical location, it may have to pass through soil and rock layers of different densities and composition. So, too, with educational change. Reforms are subject to a variety of influences. Just as the chemical make-up of rainwater may be altered as it is absorbed by different layers of the earth, the nature of educational reforms can change as they are exposed to various influences. Understanding educational change is a matter of appreciating how context shapes reform efforts and reform efforts shape context. Without such understanding, the achievement of educational change is unlikely.

> The art of progress is to preserve order amid change and to preserve change amid order.
>
> —Alfred North Whitehead

REFERENCES

Allen, Bem P. *Personality Theories,* 3rd edition. Boston: Allyn and Bacon, 2000.

Babbie, Earl. *The Practice of Social Research,* 9th edition. Belmont, CA: Wadsworth, 2001.

Bandura, Albert. "Human Agency in Social Cognitive Theory," *American Psychologist,* Vol. 44 (1989), pp. 1175–1184.

Barnes, Jonathan. *Aristotle: A Very Short Introduction.* Oxford: Oxford University Press, 2000.

Berliner, David C. "Expertise: The Wonder of Exemplary Performances." In John N. Mangieri and Cathy Collins Block (eds.), *Powerful Thinking in Teachers and Students.* Fort Worth, TX: Harcourt Brace, 1994, pp. 161–186.

Birkland, Thomas A. *An Introduction to the Policy Process.* Armonk, NY: M. E. Sharpe, 2001.

Bolman, Lee G. and Deal, Terrence, E. *Reframing Organizations,* 2nd edition. San Francisco: Jossey-Bass, 1997.

Burke, W. Warner. *Organization Change: Theory and Practice.* Thousand Oaks, CA: Sage, 2002.

Burns, Tom and Stalker, G. M. *The Management of Innovation.* Oxford: Oxford University Press, 1961.

Cartwright, Dorwin. "Achieving Change in People: Some Applications of Group Dynamics Theory," *Human Relations,* Vol. 4 (1951), pp. 381–392.

Coburn, Cynthia E. "Collective Sensemaking about Reading: How Teachers Mediate Reading Policy in Their Professional Communities." *Educational Evaluation and Policy Analysis,* Vol. 23, no. 2 (Summer 2001), pp. 145–170.

Cohen, David K. "Teaching Practice: Plus Que Ça Change . . ." In Phillip W. Jackson (ed.), *Contributing to Educational Change.* Berkeley: McCutchan, 1988, pp. 27–84.

Evans, Robert. *The Human Side of School Change.* San Francisco: Jossey-Bass, 1996.

Fullan, Michael. *Change Forces: The Sequel.* London: Falmer, 1999.

Hall, Gene E. and Hord, Shirley M. *Implementing Change.* Boston: Allyn and Bacon, 2001.

Hanson, Mark. "Institutional Theory and Educational Change," *Educational Administration Quarterly,* Vol. 37, no. 5 (December 2001), pp. 637–661.

Hatch, Mary Jo. *Organization Theory.* Oxford: Oxford University Press, 1997.

Hatch, Thomas. "When Improvement Programs Collide," *Phi Delta Kappan,* Vol. 83, no. 8 (April 2002), pp. 626–634, 639.

Katz, Michael B. *Class, Bureaucracy, and Schools,* Expanded edition. New York: Praeger, 1975.

Kingdon, John W. *Agendas, Alternatives, and Public Policies,* 2nd edition. New York: Longman, 1995.

Random House College Dictionary, Revised edition. New York: Random House, 1984.

Samuelson, Robert J. "Reform 'Hysteria'," *Washington Post* (July 17, 2002), p. A-23.

Sarason, Seymour B. *The Culture of the School and the Problem of Change.* Boston: Allyn and Bacon, 1971.

Shafritz, Jay M. and Ott, J. Steve. *Classics of Organization Theory,* 5th edition. Fort Worth, TX: Harcourt, 2001.

Strauss, Anselm and Corbin, Juliet. *Basics of Qualitative Research,* 2nd edition. Thousand Oaks, CA: Sage, 1998.

Tennant, Mark and Pogson, Philip. *Learning and Change in the Adult Years.* San Francisco: Jossey-Bass, 1995.

True, James L.; Jones, Bryan D.; and Baumgartner, Frank R. "Punctuated-Equilibrium Theory." In Paul A. Sabatier (ed.), *Theories of the Policy Process.* Boulder, CO: Westview, 1999, pp. 97–115.

Tyack, David and Cuban, Larry. *Tinkering toward Utopia.* Cambridge, MA: Harvard, 1995.

Wideen, M. F. *The Struggle for Change.* London, Falmer, 1994.